CONCORDIA UNIVERSITY
H62.J5835
READINGS IN AMERICAN

Y0-DLX-136

3 4211 000037036

WITHDRAWN

Readings in American Social Studies

Edited by
Roger E. Johnson
Milton Kleg
University of South Florida

MSS EDUCATIONAL PUBLISHING COMPANY, INC.
19 EAST 48th STREET, NEW YORK, N.Y. 10017

This is a custom-made book of readings prepared for the courses taught by the editors. For information about our program, please write to:

    MSS Educational Publishing Company, Inc.
               19 East 48th Street
             New York, New York 10017

MSS wishes to express its appreciation to the authors of the articles in this collection for their cooperation in making their work available in this format.

Copyright © 1971
By
MSS Educational Publishing Company, Inc.
All Rights Reserved.

Contents

Preface 5

What Is Social Studies? 7

    Assessing Recent Developments in the Social Studies
        JACK ALLEN 8
    The Social Uses of Social Science
        ROBERT REDFIELD 13

Values and Valuing Social Studies 21

    An Assessment: The Edge of the Future
        RALPH TYLER 22
    U.S. Ideals Cancel Out Each Other
        SIDNEY HARRIS 29

Learning Process and Inquiry 31

    The Act of Discovery
        JEROME S. BRUNER 32
    The Taxonomy: Guide to Differentiated Instruction
        JOHN JAROLIMEK 47
    Value Teaching in the Middle and Upper Grades: A
    Rationale for Teaching But Not Transmitting Values
        MELVIN EZER 50
    An Inquiry-Conceptual Theory of Social Studies Curriculum
    Planning
        JOHN U. MICHAELIS 53
    Why Inquiry Fails in the Classroom
        MARTIN LAFORSE 57
    Inquiry: Does It Teach How or What to Think?
        GARY A. MANSON and ELMER D. WILLIAMS 60

Social Studies and the Social Sciences 65

    The Interdisciplinary Approach to Teaching Social Studies
        STUART C. MILLER 66
    The Common Denominator of Cultures
        GEORGE PETER MURDOCK 70
    Organizing a Curriculum Around Social Science Concepts
        LAWRENCE SENESH 74
    A Case for Anthropology in Public School Curricula
        ROBERT A. HELLMANN 92
    Political Science in the Social Studies
        ROBERT E. CLEARY AND DONALD H. RIDDLE 94
    New Viewpoints in Sociology
        E. MERLE ADAMS, Jr 107

Content and Curriculum 115

    Fable of the Activity Curriculum
        Anonymous 116
    What Are We Teaching in Social Studies and Science?
        DONALD L. BARNES 117
    Elementary Social Studies: Content Plus!
        HUBER M. WALSH 120

Challenging the Expanding-Environment Theory
  RONALD O. SMITH and CHARLES F. CARDINELL.................123
Clarifying Social Studies Terms
  JOE PARK AND O. W. STEPHENSON............................126
A Problem in Deviation
  MILTON KLEG..132
Social Studies Curriculum Reform: An Appraisal
  EDWIN FENTON...133
Learning about Time Zones in Grades Four, Five, and Six
  O.L. DAVIS, Jr...146
What Social Studies Content for the Primary Grades?
  RALPH C. PRESTON...152
Trends in Social Studies
  ROGER E. JOHNSON...154

Methods and Materials......................................159

Adding Insult to Injury
  ART BUCHWALD...160
The First Supersonic Flight
  ART BUCHWALD...162
Yes, We Have Bananas
  ART BUCHWALD...164
The Proud Parents
  ART BUCHWALD...166
The Selection and Evaluation of Textual Material
  MILTON KLEG..168
Reading Skills in the Social Studies
  JOHN R. O'CONNOR...176
How Readable Are Our Elementary Social Studies Textbooks?
  ROGER E. JOHNSON...180
Docility, or Giving Teacher What She Wants
  JULES HENRY..190
The Teaching Unit: What Makes It Tick?
  WALTER E. McPHIE...199
Scheduling Problems: How Many? How Long?
  SIDNEY L. BESVINICK......................................203
Role-Playing and Social Studies
  ROGER E. JOHNSON...206
Take a Realistic Look at People and Cultures
  ROGER E. JOHNSON...211

Social Issues..215

One Hundred Per Cent American
  RALPH LINTON...216
The Nature of Human Relations Problems in the Classroom
  GERTRUDE NOAR..219
The Importance of Attitudes in Social Studies
  MILTON KLEG..223
Contributions of History and Geography to Education Designed
to Combat Racial Prejudice
  LOUIS FRANCOIS...232
Recommendations Concerning Terminology in Education on
Race Questions
  A. BABS FAFUNWA..237
A Profession without Professionals?
  MILTON KLEG..242

Preface

To most people social studies simply refers to history, geography, and citizenship. But for the trained educator, social studies education is exceedingly more complex. Indeed, so complex is the nature of social studies education there is no standard textual treatment of the social studies which meets the expectation of all those faced with the task of training teachers.

There are a number of reasons for the apparent lack of agreement among those of us in social studies education and it seems only fair to cite a few. First of all, the term social studies has undergone a number of changes in meaning over the past decades, and though one or two definitions have come close to general acceptance, no one definition has ever been universally accepted. Secondly, the content of social studies education seems to change drastically as social and cultural changes occur throughout the world. Thirdly, a review of the history of social studies education will reveal that the objectives or goals of social studies education has been continually revised.

In consideration of these aforementioned reasons and the lack of a basic comprehensive text, it is apparent that the training of teachers in social studies is probably as diverse as the number of professors and instructors in the social studies. As a result each of us is forced to develop our training programs in a rather cut and paste manner. In such a process we are usually forced to dig out those sources which seem most valuable in teacher training. It often becomes necessary to spend additional hours of investigating topics not covered in a specific text.

As an alternative approach to filling in gaps by lecturing, it seems most reasonable to compile a book of readings which although far from comprehensive, would relate major topics in social studies to the student and a act as a springboard for discussion and *inquiry*. It is with this intention in mind that *Readings in the American Social Studies* has been published.

R.E. Johnson
M. Kleg
June 1971

WHAT IS SOCIAL STUDIES?

Assessing Recent Developments In the Social Studies

by Jack Allen

OF ONE THING, we can be sure. There is enough going on in the social studies (the magic word today is "ferment") to elicit complaints from some quarters, in the manner of the inimitable Jimmy Durante, that everybody wants to get into the act. Or, to use a more current idiom, if one wants to go where the action is, he needs only to peer around the nearest corner.

Consider the situation generally. First, at the local level. In the fall of 1965 the National Council for the Social Studies addressed an inquiry to almost 500 school systems. Virtually all indicated that they had some type of curriculum revision under way. Or, take many of the states. Here we find not only a sizable number of respectable state-wide curriculum projects, but a mushrooming within the past two or three years of social studies coordinator positions in the state departments. Finally, at the national level, we see some half a hundred projects, mainly in universities, supported by funds from the federal government and foundations.

And this by no means completes the list. One could cite a number of local social studies projects, many supported in part by outside funds, as yet largely unreported in the literature. Illustrative from my own experience would be the program at the Nova Schools in Broward County, Florida; a new elementary curriculum in Brentwood, Long Island; and innovative teaching with an inductive approach by the Christian Brothers in parochial high schools, mainly in the Middle West. Again, there is the broad movement in teacher education where one finds developing alliances, both formal and informal, between academic specialists and professional educators in colleges and universities, as well as the NDEA Title XI institutes and other federally-sponsored programs.

When we examine these many movements and fit them into the context of other developments currently influencing the program of the nation's schools, it seems reasonably apparent that the educational historian of, say, the 1990's, reflecting on the present decade, will report it as one of the most productive periods of change in the chronicles of American education. But how much of this change will represent genuine progress must still remain an open question. This brings us to the pesky question of significance.

Some insight into the present may be gained by recalling certain reasonably modern periods of change in the social studies. We might begin with a brief look at the 1890's.

Early in this educationally significant decade, important social studies developments began to emerge. They culminated, in a sense, in 1899, with the influential report of the famed Committee of Seven of the American Historical Association. A body of specific recommendations for curriculum content, the report had the effect of firmly establishing the dominant position of history in the social studies curriculum of the secondary school. Less noted, but an important feature of the report, was a wise statement on prevailing needs in the area of teacher education.

A second major curriculum thrust came in 1916 in the form of a report from the Committee on Social Studies, one of ten subject area subcommittees of the NEA's Commission on the Reorganization of Secondary Education. Challenging the exclusiveness of the Committee of Seven's secondary school history program, the 1916 committee directed its attention to the role of the social studies in the development of effective citizens. To implement this broad purpose, a course in civics was recommended for grade 9 and problems of democracy for grade 12, with the consequent replacement of history at these levels.

By combining the 1899 and 1916 recommendations, we find much that has remained influential in the secondary school social studies program throughout this century. Some have gone so far as to claim that nothing has substantially changed since these early pronouncements. This is a questionable judgment, however, in view of the many influential curriculum movements that have appeared in the intervening years.

Early developments and influences in elementary school social studies are more difficult to pinpoint. It perhaps suffices to note that elementary programs

---

Jack Allen *is Chairman of the Division of Social Science at George Peabody College for Teachers. This article is based on a speech he gave at the annual meeting of the National Education Association in Miami Beach in late June, 1966.*

Social Education, 1967, Vol.31, pp. 91-103.

were recommended by the NEA as early as 1892 and 1895, by the American Historical Association's Committee of Seven in 1899, by another committee of the Association in 1908, and by Yearbooks of the National Society for the Study of Education in 1902 and 1903.

Much optimism about a bold new national effort in the social studies arose in the early 1930's with the establishment of the American Historical Association's Commission on Social Studies in the Schools. But, though the Commission succeeded in producing reports that ultimately ran to 16 volumes, many of lasting educational value, its curriculum pronouncements were confined to such generalities as "the development of rich and many-sided personalities" and the building of American society "in accordance with American ideals of popular democracy, personal liberty, and dignity."

Despite the inability of the Commission on the Social Studies to produce identifiable changes in the grade placement of subject matter, it doubtless had more subtle influences. In addition, the period of the Great Depression brought its weight to bear upon the social studies program by directing the bright light of inquiry on a host of social and economic problems. From it emerged such curriculum movements as intercultural education and such teaching strategies as the use of problem-solving techniques.

In the immediate aftermath of World War II came vigorous attention to the movement for international education, a movement that by the middle and latter 1950's was directing a considerable portion of its energy toward the study of the non-Western world. In the late 1940's the economic education movement emerged in much more explicit form and has continued vigorously without a break to the present. A citizenship education movement, heavily political in orientation, flowered in the early fifties, and, though it lost some of its force after a time, shows evidence of resurgence.

Now to our own decade. Here, in the America of the 1960's, we see a society of wealth and influence committed to the pursuit of excellence in its economic, social, and civic endeavors. Coincidentally, it is a society that may well be involved in the most revolutionary age in human history, a time when man's most fundamental values are being challenged and restructured. For us Americans, the unrelenting forces of history are being brought inexorably to bear on the most cherished of our institutions and ways—on the principles of individual freedom and the processes of constitutional government; on the functioning of a capitalist-oriented economy; on the nature of the family as a social system; even, as blaring headlines remind us almost daily, on the tenets of traditional religion. What is happening in the social studies today must be viewed within this context, for inevitably the various activities in the areas both of curriculum and learning are either explicitly or implicitly a response to such developments.

In our assessment of current developments in social studies, certain considerations should be kept in mind.

First, although some energetic school systems can justly claim to have been continuously in the process of curriculum revision, and a few movements, such as economic education, have been in progress for many years, most of the current major national efforts have come into being within the past three or four years. Thus, in a very real sense, we are only in the early phases of a movement. In any kind of historical perspective, the clock has but recently been wound.

A second consideration relates to the nature of the projects themselves. Unlike the specific curriculum recommendations handed down in *a priori* fashion by national commissions in 1899 and 1916, the present movement is proceeding along a broken front, hoping in the process to fashion fresh points of view and build empirical bases for judgment. Thus we find work on individual units, as in the high school anthropology project; single courses, as in the high school geography project; limited studies of sequence, as with Northwestern's American history project; the preparation of specialized learning resources, as with Berkeley's Asia project; distinct student populations, as in Carnegie Tech's program for able students; particular teaching strategies, as with the Western Behavioral Sciences Institute's simulation studies. Interestingly enough, except for the work of some state and local school systems, very few studies are, like the Minnesota project, concerned with the total scope and sequence of the social studies curriculum.

No less important in its implications is a third consideration. Unlike the relative simplicity of the widely publicized recommendations for a new high school physics, or even a new elementary and secondary school mathematics curriculum, the social studies program is fashioned from a loose federation of social sciences, each discipline seeking what it regards as its proper role. To rationalize the conflicting claims of history, geography, political science, economics, anthropology, sociology, and social psychology into a balanced curriculum for children and youth has never been, nor will it ever be, easy. Some may well be led to the conclusion that it is virtually impossible.

Finally, even if some reasonable allocation of content could be made from among the various social sciences, there would still remain a whole complex of questions as to how it should be organized for instructional purposes. To illustrate this dilemma we need do no more than pose a pair of familiar issues: (1) Should the integrity of the disciplines be maintained, or should the approach be interdisciplinary? (2) Should specific subject areas be identified at separate grade levels, or should there be a sequential arrangement of non-graded units extending through the curriculum?

Within the context of the foregoing considerations, what are the current social studies curriculum developments seeking to achieve? Some commonality may be observed through an examination of their objectives. These might be categorized under three headings: (1) the mode or process of inquiry, (2) knowledge of content, and (3) attitudes and values in the so-called affective domain. Here we find little that is distinctly new. Only in refinements and points of emphasis is there potential significance.

A mode of inquiry based on the process of induction appears to be a goal of paramount concern for a considerable number of projects. Illustrative of its philosophic justification was an observation by Alfred North Whitehead, many years prior to the current movement, that "our rate of progress is such that an individual human being, of ordinary length of life, will be called upon to face novel situations which find no parallel in his past. The fixed person, for the fixed duties, who, in older societies, was such a godsend, in the future, will be a public danger." Its psychological rationale has perhaps been suggested with greatest effect by Bruner in his *Process of Education* and other writings. In more explicit terms the goal has been amplified by Bloom and Krathwohl in their *Taxonomy of Educational Objectives: Handbook I, the Cognitive Domain*.

Content knowledge, likewise categorized in the cognitive domain by the Bloom-Krathwohl *Taxonomy*, is recognized as an objective of fundamental importance, but the tendency of the projects is to conceive it more as a means than as an end. In pragmatic terms this represents a contrast to traditional instruction both in schools and colleges where, in practice if not in theory, the tendency has been to regard acquisition of information as an end in itself. Current curricular efforts seem much less certain as to what knowledge is most important. What is more, they find their problems greatly complicated by the immense volume of data pouring from social science research, not to mention the inroads of other social science disciplines into the domain traditionally dominated by history and geography.

Less needs to be said at the moment about attitudes and values. A widely recognized body of goals, it is as yet a relatively unexplored dimension of current social studies activity.

As we examine curriculum developments in relation to objectives, certain emphases emerge and some deficiencies become apparent. From virtually every source, whether national project or local school system, attention is being directed in some manner to the basic concepts and structures of the various social sciences. The efforts range from the elements of a single discipline, functioning at a particular grade level, to a conceptual framework for a total k-12 program. In the process of development, a number of ideas and procedures are emerging that can be regarded as potentially significant for the future of the social studies.

For one thing, statements about concepts and structures are being formulated for each of the social sciences in such a manner as to make them available for curriculum purposes. Particularly notable in this activity is the fact that social science scholars are being drawn directly into the work, a function that is tending to bring many academic specialists and curriculum workers into closer alliance and understanding. If the school person regards this as a means of bringing the university professor out of his ivory tower, the academic specialist thinks of it as a way of building more integrity into the program. A detached observer can only be inclined to regard it as a victory for both.

In the conceptualization process some other interesting things are occurring. Being challenged by other social sciences is the traditional dominance of history and geography in the upper elementary grades and junior high school, and history in the senior high school. As a concomitant, there is a growing emphasis upon a study of the contemporary world and current issues, for these things, after all, are the very stuff of political science, economics, sociology, social psychology—the broad realm of the behavioral sciences. Indeed, the behavioral movement is having its influence, both as regards scholarly research and curriculum development, in such areas as history, geography, and anthropology as well.

Finally, the conceptual framework is becoming increasingly global. More than such a comparatively simple process as making a world history course truly "world" oriented, it is the bringing of a global view into the social processes of the young kindergarten child a questioning of the traditional perception of expanding environments in the early elementary years, and the permeation of other subject areas in a variety of ways, cutting across the whole spectrum of the school curriculum.

The search for a conceptual framework would seem to suggest a direct and immediate concern for curriculum scope and sequence. Often this is the case with the state programs and with many local efforts. School systems, after all, are confronted with the stark reality of dealing with a fresh collection of minds and bodies each fall. For good or ill, some kind of program has to be in operation. The national projects can afford to be more cavalier. They, as a consequence, have been included, as we noted earlier, to ride off in many different directions. The hope is that their efforts ultimately will react in some manner to the common good. In such a situation there may be some comfort for those who harbor fear of a superimposed national curriculum. If, in the past, there has existed some semblance of national consensus about the framework for a social studies curriculum—and I think there has—certainly one cannot detect a new one emerging from the various national endeavors currently under way.

Closely allied with the idea of concept and structure is a growing interest in what might be broadly labeled as skills development. Here we find new dimensions characterized by such terms as "discovery approach," "the method of induction," "simulation," "game theory," and the like. Integrated with newly developed course materials, they are leading to the development of interesting teaching strategies. In some learning situations, to paraphrase Carl Becker, they seek to make every man his own historian, or geographer, or sociologist, or archeologist, or economist. Often, the aim is to develop habits of self-direction on the part of the students. Again, the goal may be establishment of group initiative. Whatever the direction, there remains much to be learned in this crucial area of teaching strategy and skills development. Hard data on comparative performance in relationship to more traditional procedures is still in short supply.

Closely associated with the seemingly more sophisticated perceptions of skills development is an explosion in the area of learning resources. In many modern schools, the traditional single-purpose library is being replaced with exciting, attractive learning resources laboratories. And a few schools are moving closer to the limits of current educational technology through the development of information retrieval centers. To provide appropriate learning materials for these laboratories and centers is one of the responsibilities being undertaken by some of the national projects. A number, in response to an emphasis on inductive learning, are producing printed materials—document collections, case studies, selected reading to illustrate different interpretations of conflicting points of view, etc. One also finds such items as tape recordings, film-strips, transparencies, artifacts, and the like. Unquestionably, this multimedia approach to learning, old though it is in theory, is beginning to have a new kind of impact.

There is, of course, more to the enrichment of resources than the growing acceptance of new learning theory, important as this may be. For one thing, potentialities are being expanded by constant advances in technology. For another, our growing affluence is making it increasingly realistic to consider the use of these instructional tools. Not only is local support increasing, it is being enhanced by the benevolent arm of the federal government.

The expansion of conceptual frameworks to encompass all the social sciences, the enrichment of learning theory to provide, among other things, for more adequate development of skills, and the potentialities existent in a mounting volume of learning resources are placing heavy responsibilities on teachers in service and on teacher education institutions. Relatively little attention has been devoted to this problem by the national curriculum projects. Fortunately, however, one does find a growing recognition of the need at the local level, with school systems reacting in a variety of ways to in-service needs. Institutional pre-service programs are also being modified in an effort to adapt to new curriculum trends. Recently the federal government has moved into this area in ways that seem potentially promising. One example is the new Experienced Teacher Fellowship Program; another is the Prospective Teacher Fellowship Program.

But perhaps the strongest emotional shot in the arm for the social studies profession came in the summer of 1965 with the initiation of NDEA Title XI institutes in history and geography, a program now being expanded into other social science areas. It was my good fortune to serve as one of the evaluators for the first group of Title XI history institutes. To visit with institute participants and staff and, subsequently, to compare experiences with fellow evaluators, was something of an inspiration. Clearly, as with any beginning endeavor, there were glaring weaknesses in a number of institute programs; but one could not gainsay the professional attitudes of the great majority of teacher participants and the missionary zeal of institute directors and their staff. We evaluators were left with an abiding impression that the American social studies teacher was earnestly committed to the improvement of his professional competence in the light of new developments that were impinging upon him.

In the flush of renewed recognition, it is perhaps inevitable that the social studies movement in the United States should number in its camp a body of vocal new converts possessing all the zealousness that comes with the emotionalism of fresh conversion, as well as a staunch body of traditionalists who, by nature, tend to regard virtually anything different as threatening. From the former the claims are often excessive, from the latter the doubts unreasonable. Without endeavoring to find some rational resolution of these extremes, there are a number of deficiencies in the current efforts that seem clearly apparent.

There is, for instance, this fundamental question of teacher education. At the preservice level, both the academic community and professional educators have a lot of work before them. While one can develop considerable optimism about the sympathetic understandings emanating from both groups, the cooperation needs to move much further to be truly effective for purposes of effective preservice education.

Another facet of the preservice problem can be illustrated by the situation inherent in two such relatively unrelated goals as inductive learning and the development of global viewpoints. To assist students with the process of induction, teachers themselves need experiences with this teaching strategy. For prospective teachers, these should come from their own college classrooms. Similarly, if teachers are to be global in orientation, their college training should bring them into contact with content knowledge appropriate for this purpose.

The inservice teacher education problem is equally complicated—much more, it would seem, than the experience we have witnessed in recent years with the new mathematics. Here, as with the preservice problem, the situation will demand a high order of cooperation between the academic community and the profession.

The remaining unfinished business which I would like to mention relates more directly to current curriculum developments. As noted earlier, one of the strong motivating forces stimulating current curriculum change is the revolutionary character of our age. This is a circumstance that has special relevance to the affective domain. Yet, to date, we find very little work in this crucial values area. One of the national projects, that at Harvard, seems directly concerned with this objective. Also worthy of mention is the Good American Program, an elementary-school project in Ossining, New York, conducted under the auspices of the Council for Citizenship Education.

Some of the soundest thinking in the values area is currently emanating from the Social Science Education Consortium in West LaFayette, Indiana, which is approaching the study of values by drawing a distinction between those that are personal, in the sense of tastes and basic needs, and those that are judgments or conclusions about the relative superiority of different procedures or entities based on the use of empirical data. One may hope, and reasonably expect, that a major thrust in the social studies in the immediate future will be work on the treatment of values in the curriculum.

Another relative deficiency of the current curriculum efforts relates to the social studies program in the elementary school, particularly at the earliest levels. There is, of course, some notable activity here that should be applauded. On any comparative basis, however, the elementary school is not receiving its just dues. Particularly in projects where university social scientists are intimately involved, the tendency has been to direct curriculum activity toward the secondary school. Perhaps, among other reasons, it is because the specialist feels more comfortable, as well as knowledgeable, at the more advanced levels, since they are closer to his own experiences in higher education. In this connection, it is interesting to note that of the 84 Title XI history institutes in the summer of 1965, 76 were devoted in some manner to the secondary school. In the geography institutes the elementary school fared somewhat better. Effective as these secondary school efforts may be, one is forced to observe that, if current curriculum efforts in the social studies are to make anything close to a maximum impact on the schools, much more attention will have to be directed to the education of young children.

Closely associated with the elementary school question is the need to establish better relationships between curriculum building and child development research. It is not enough for those responsible for current curriculum development to rely on experience and intuition in deciding how and what should be taught about the social sciences to children. To deal with this deficiency, it is just as important for child development psychologists to be brought into close alliance with curriculum workers as it is to involve social science specialists in this activity. By the same token, it is essential that available data on children's learning be inextricably interwoven into the preservice education of social studies teachers.

The final need I would mention is in the area of evaluation. We all recognize that curriculum is a terribly difficult thing to research. And yet we must surely develop better techniques and instruments for this purpose than we have had in the past. Many of the national projects speak confidently of evaluation as an essential dimension of their activity. But I am not yet persuaded that much really significant work in this area is emerging. There is no question about innovation. The woods are full of it. We must, however, distinguish between innovation and experimentation. Much of the innovative activity in social studies today is exciting, different, and interesting. It will have much more appeal for purposes of curriculum change when supported by experimental designs and results that are persuasive. Until this is accomplished, social studies curriculum development will move, as it has in the past, in response to prestigious voices, enactments of legislative councils, reactions to sources of money, and even sheer inertia. Should current curriculum activity degenerate into a movement influenced by those who can speak the loudest and most persuasively in the right places, then it would lose much of its significance, and negate the high level of expectation that we may have for it. The activity might bring substantial change, but there would be no assurance that it would also be progress.

Our faith today is that, at least haltingly, we are making some progress. Our sincere hope is that in the years to come we will find that it has been truly significant progress.

ROBERT REDFIELD

The late Robert Redfield was a Professor of Anthropology at the University of Chicago

The Social Uses of Social Science

The subject of my remarks ... might be expressed as a question for which three different forms of words suggest themselves: What beneficial functions may social science hope to perform in our society? What is the task of social science? Why have a social science?

Institutions are good not only for what they are but also by reason of what we strive to make them. I think, then, not only of what social science is, but also of what it might be. I think of social science as one of many institutions that contribute toward the making of the life we want and that could do it better than they do. I would review the functions and the goals of social science as I would review the functions and goals of medicine, the fine arts, or the press.

The social uses of medicine are to reduce human suffering and to prolong life; this is well understood, and it is clear that to great degree medicine performs these functions. The social uses of the press are to tell people, truthfully and comprehensively, what happens around them, to provide forums for public discussion, and to reflect and clarify the ideals of our society. It is more or less well known that this is what our press is expected to do, whether or not it does it as well as it should. But the social uses of social science are not, I think, so generally recognized. People do not know, at once, why there should be social science or even what social science, ... to make clear its nature and its usefulness.

It will not be necessary for me to say much about the nature of social science. It is a group of disciplines that provide descriptions of human nature, human activity and human institutions. These disciplines are scientific, first in that they are concerned with telling us What Is, not What Ought to Be; and second, in that they exercise objectivity, pursue special knowledge and move toward systematic formulation of this knowledge. So they strive for descriptions that are more illuminating, valid and comprehensive than are the corresponding descriptions of common sense.

You will readily understand that I have in mind the social sciences that one meets in the catalogues of graduate schools and in the membership of the Social Science Research Council. Just which of them are to be included

University of Colorado Bulletin, May, 1947, Vol.24, pp. 19-26.

in any roster of the social sciences does not concern us here; the existing division of labor as among the special social sciences is not wholly defensible and may not endure. I am not thinking of ethics, which is the criticism and organization of principles of right conduct. I am not thinking of the social arts and professions, such as law or social service administration, which are ways of acting on people to get certain results. I am thinking of the application of the scientific spirit toward the description and explanation of man in society. I am asking how its application there serves the common good.

A further limitation of my subject is required. History is not in my mind today. The social uses of history have a special and important character which I shall not discuss. History, being a content of preserved and considered experience, has those social uses which memory and tradition have. From history, as from memory, we expect "a knowledge of our own identities," "orientation in our environment, a knowledge of its usual uniformities, including . . . some knowledge of the characters with whom we must deal, their strengths and weaknesses, and what they are likely to do under given circumstances." Further, " . . . we all hope to draw from past experience help in choosing successfully between the alternatives offered by present events." These social uses of history have been recently summarized by Garrett Mattingly,[1] from whom I quote these phrases. Today I am thinking of that social science which is analytical rather than historical, which seeks to understand a social problem or which describes the general characteristics of some class of social phenomena. How does such social science serve the common good?

The familiar answer is that social science tells us how to do what we want to do. The reply is that the understanding that social science gives can be applied to the purposes of society. The descriptions of social science lead to more effective practical action than would be possible without social science. Social science, is, from this point of view, like physics or biology. Just as those sciences reach understanding and explanation of the physical and the organic worlds which lead to practical applications in engineering and in medicine, so social science reaches understanding of man in society which leads to practical applications in social action.

Surely it is true that social science does this. It does tell us how to do what we want to do. It tells us some things that common sense does not tell us or does not tell us nearly so well about how to select people to pilot airplanes or to perform other special tasks, how to predict the consequences of a given tax policy, or how quickly to discover fluctuations in the opinions of over a hundred million people on current issues. The competence of social science to guide useful social action has grown greatly in a few

[1] "A Sample Discipline—The Teaching of History" (address delivered at the Princeton University Bicentennial Conference, February 20, 1947).

years. The contributions of social science to the national effort at the time of World War I were almost limited to certain studies of prices, to the work of historians in war information, and to developments in mental testing. The contributions of social science in connection with World War II were so numerous and varied that a mere list of them would fill many pages. In the army and in the navy, and in scores of civilian agencies, social scientists were employed for the reason that their efforts as social scientists were recognized as helping to win the war or the peace. This direct service to the community, through the application of their special knowledge, continues in the efforts of social scientists after the war. Of the many fields of research which have already found practical justification I mention three: the understanding of problems of morale and of human relations in industry; the prediction of human behavior in regard to the stability of marriage, criminal recidivism, and certain other kinds of behavior where dependable prediction is useful; and the analysis and control of communication made to mass audiences through print, radio or screen. Social science had indeed so well established its usefulness in certain fields that specialized technicians are recognized in those fields—professional appliers of social science knowledge. I mention clinical psychiatrists and city planners.

The question I asked appears at once to be answered. Why have a social science? Have it because it is useful. Have a social science because it gets things done that society wants done. According to this answer social science has the same nature and the same justification that physics and chemistry have. It is supported by society as physics and chemistry are supported by society: because what is learned can be directly applied to the service of mankind. Society less and less can take care of itself; more and more is it true that conscious decisions are required in the management of human affairs, and social science provides guidance in the making of these decisions, just as biological science provides guidance for decisions as to health and hygiene. This is the simple answer that is often made.

I will state my own position at once. I think that this is a true answer but that it is far from a complete answer. I think social science is notably different from physics and chemistry, and that its social uses are not exhausted when one has recognized the practical applications of social science. I think that social science has other important social uses in the testing and in the development of social values.

What has social science to do with the proving and making of values? What is its role in regard not merely to the valuation of a means to reach an end sought, but also to the more ultimate values of society?

The plainest values with which social science is concerned are those necessary to science: objectivity, honesty, accuracy and humility before the facts. To the preservation and cultivation of these the social sciences are devoted. In the course of carrying out research the social scientists invent and promote means to realize them. In doing so the social scientist shares with the physicist and the biologist the effort to maintain and extend the common morality of the scientific mind. It is, moreover, a morality quite consistent with the morality which the citizen who is not a scientist, may embrace. Honesty, accuracy, humility before the facts, and faith in the power of truth to prevail in Milton's free encounter are virtues in their own right. Science is one of the institutions that contribute to the cultivation of these virtues.

In the work of cultivation of these values the position of social science is critical because it is by no means sure that even our free and liberal society will allow the extension of the scientific spirit to the study of social problems. Many people do not understand that it is useful to society to extend it there. While the usefulness of physics and biology is generally acknowledged, the scientific study of many social problems is popularly regarded as either futile or dangerous. This is because many of the subjects studied by the social sciences are protected from rational examination, for the general population, by tradition, sentiment and inviolable attitude.

In short, the subject matter of social science is not morally indifferent. It is morally significant. The social scientist himself, and his neighbors and fellow citizens, are also concerned with that subject matter. They have convictions, prejudices, sentiments and judgments about the tariff, party politics, relation between the sexes, and race relations. All of these things the social scientist studies, and what he has to say about them in the course of his trying to improve our understanding of them encounters these convictions, prejudices, sentiments and judgments. They are all "tender" subjects. People feel a sense of distress if their convictions or assumptions on these matters are challenged or controverted. Often they are distressed at the mere looking at these subjects objectively. Some social scientists study such subjects as the relations between husband and wife or the attitudes people have toward racial or religious minorities or the profit motive in economic activity. It makes some people uncomfortable to hear that these subjects are being studied with critical impersonality. The social scientist is then resented or distrusted. If, furthermore, his descriptions or conclusions appear inconsistent with the more sacred values of the community, a cry may go up that the social scientist be restrained or that his publication be suppressed or that he lose his job.

Therefore social science is the test case of the vitality of those ideals I have mentioned which are common to all science and which play so large a part in the freedom of the modern mind. The scientists as a whole understand this. In discussions which are now going on as to the drafting of a bill for a national science foundation, it appears that almost all the scientists, natural scientists as well as social scientists, think that if government money is to be provided for the support of science, social science should be included. On the other hand, with similar unanimity the scientist understands that Congressmen are much less likely to provide such support for social science than for natural science. The scientists see that science is one way of looking at the world around us, a way applicable to men and society as it is applicable to molecules and cells. They feel this common morality of the scientific mind, and respect the usefulness of social science in not only making useful social inventions but also in developing this morality throughout society. But they also know that people who are not scientists do not see it that way, and imagine social science to be political propaganda or doctrine, or speculative futility. These scientists perhaps realize what I believe to be true: that that freedom of the mind to enquire, propose, test and create which is so central and precious a part of the more ultimate values of our manner of life may, in a military or reactionary trend of events, be first tested and won or lost in our country in the freedom of social science.

In effect social science is a new instrument, not only for the getting of certain specific things done in the management of society, but for the clarification and development of our more ultimate values. The social uses of social science are not exhausted when we have said that social science can improve the efficiency of industrial production or test the aptitudes of young people for one kind of occupation rather than another. Social science is one of the ways to form our convictions as to the good life. This it does not as preaching does it, by telling us what the good is and what our duty is. It does not do it as ethics does it, by examining central questions as to the nature of conduct and by criticizing and formulating systematic rules of conduct. It does it by remaining science. It does it by making clear to us where our choices lead us and what means must be employed to reach what ends. It does it by extending our understanding of where our ideals are in conflict with each other. And it does this through those intensive studies of particular societies and particular men which are not ordinarily carried on in ethics and which are outside the powers and the responsibilities of the preacher.

An example may make this clear. Recently a study of the Negro in the United States was made by Gunnar Myrdal, a Swedish social scientist. The resulting books are not sermons nor are they analyses of the principles of conduct. They are descriptions of the Negro in American business, government and social life. They are also descriptions of the white man in his positions toward the Negro in American life. These books do not tell us didactically what we ought to do. The propositions that make up the books are Is-propositions not Ought-propositions. Nevertheless the book can hardly be read carefully by anyone without some effect upon the reader's system of values, his conceptions of duty, justice and the good life. The effect is enhanced, in this particular case of social science research, because the authors took for their problem the relation of the Negro's place in our society to the ideals of freedom, liberty and democracy which are genuinely held in our nation. They were interested in finding out what effect, on the white man especially, results from the presence of practices and institutions inconsistent with these ideals. The book does not argue for any norm of conduct. It just tells about norms in relation to customs and institutions But any American reader, at all thoughtful, finds himself understanding better than he did the choices that are open to him: less democracy, liberty and equality, and race relations as they are; or more democracy, liberty and equality, and a change in race relations. Or, as a third possibility, he learns something of the effects on his state of mind if the inconsistency persists. And this increased understanding is a leaven in those workings of the spirit which lead to the remaking of our system of ideals.

I think it is self-delusion for a social scientist to say that what he does has no concern with social values. I think that people are right when they express their feelings that social science does something to the values they hold with regard to such particular institutions as restrictive covenants or the tariff. For one thing social science tests those special values, by showing what they cost. It hears the people say, We want freedom. Social science listens, studies our society and replies, Very well, if you want freedom, this is what you will pay in one kind of freedom for enjoying so much of another. To every partisan the social scientist appears an enemy. The social scientist addresses himself to the question, How much security from idleness and want is compatible with developed capitalism? and equally to the question, How much political and civil freedom is compatible with socialism? To partisans on both sides he appears unsympathetic and dangerous.

For social science, along with other science, philosophy and the general spirit of intellectual liberty, is asserting the more general and comprehensive values of our society against the more limited and special interests and values. It hears society say, We believe in the right of the human mind to examine freely, to criticize openly, to reach conclusions from tested evidence.

Very well, replies social science, if this is your desire then you must endure pain of the examination and the testing of the particular customs and institutions which you hold dear. Social science says to all of us: Except where your special interests are involved, you recognize that mankind has passed the period in which he took his ethical convictions from his grandfathers without doubt and reflection. Now we have to think, investigate and consider about both the means and the ends of life. Social science is that science, which in other fields you so readily admire, directed to human nature and the ways of living of man in society. By your own more general convictions you have authorized and validated its development.

It follows that the successful functioning of social science is peculiarly dependent upon education. The realization of the social uses of social science depends closely upon the dissemination of the findings of social science and of the understanding of the very nature of social science among all the people. So a responsibility falls upon you and me who have thought something of the matter to make social science known to all. It is for us to make it clear to our fellow citizens what social science is and why its development is so needed today.

Social science does not need to be sold to the people. It needs only to be explained. There never was a time when social science was more needed than it is today. The extreme peril in which we live arises from the small political and social wisdom we have in the face of our immensely dangerous material strength. We should have more control over the physical world, yes, surely; but it is far more necessary that we learn to control the relations among men. We know now that we can destroy one another and the fruits of civilization, and we are far from sure that we can prevent ourselves from doing so. If social science could effect an improvement of our chances of preventing it of no more than one percent, a great expenditure in social science would be justified.

In explaining social science it needs to be said that social science is not only a box of tools. It is also a light. The social scientist is not only a sort of plumber to the circulatory and other ills of society; he is also, at his best, a source of understanding and enrichment. It should be pointed out that the test of good social science is not only: Will it work? There is another test: Does it make sense? For social science also justifies itself to the extent to which it makes life comprehensible and significant. That social science, also, has worth which, though it solves no problem of unemployment or of selection of competent administrators, shows men the order and the pattern of their own lives. Good social science provides categories in terms of which we come to understand ourselves. Our buying and selling, our praying, our hopes, prejudices and fears, as well as the institutions which embody all these, turn out, under the light of sound social science to have form, perspective, rule. Shown the general, we are liberated from the tyranny of the particular. I am not merely I; I am an instance of a natural law.

To say this is not to say that social science should be speculative or philosophical. The significant generalization may first appear in a flash of insight. Or illuminating generalizations may be built up out of many detailed observations. Out of the innumerable painstaking studies of particular facts, in biology, anthropology and sociology, emerges now a broad conception of society, inclusive of ants, apes and men, and the notion that the mechanisms of evolution operate through, not merely individuals, but the social groups themselves. This but illustrates the fact that comprehensive general understanding of society is often the work of many men over much time.

So we will praise social science both as a practical servant of mankind, useful as biology and physics are made useful, and also as a handmaiden of the spirit. It has on the other side some of the social uses of the humanities. It makes a knowledge which helps to define the world of human relations in which we live, which makes clear to ourselves our place in a social cosmos. Social science is not essentially a series of inventions to be applied. The inventions come, and they are useful. But primarily social science is a chain of understandings to be communicated.

And we will make it clear that in this work of increasing understanding, there is a moral commitment and a moral purpose. Social science is objective in that it cultivates deliberate consideration of alternative explanations, demands proof, and submits to the conviction which facts compel. But it is not indifferent. It will not tolerate cynicism. It expects responsibility from its followers, responsibility to use special knowledge for the common good and to act on convictions reached by reason and through special knowledge. It demands that the values that are implied in the conduct of its work be declared. It commits itself to the use of man's rational nature and the methods of modern empirical investigation to the service of society. The service is one not only to the strength of the social body. It is also a contribution to its soul. Social science is a proving ground of values. It is a means to wisdom. Let us, who are social scientists, so conduct our work as to make it yield more of the wisdom the world so sorely needs. Let all of us, who know something of social science, explain that this is its purpose, its highest ideal.

VALUES AND VALUING SOCIAL STUDIES

An assessment: the edge of the future

Ralph Tyler

During the progress of this conference, the present status of the social sciences has been clarified and the opportunities for further development have been explored. Professor Odegard pointed out the critical nature of the social problems which face us, and the importance of developing much more adequate knowledge in the social sciences. He also described the substantial improvements which have taken place in recent years in both the methods of inquiry and the substance of these disciplines. However, his caveat against the tendency for each of the social sciences to isolate itself from the other branches of knowledge is a significant caution for the future. Finally, he forcibly emphasized the need to study policy questions rather than to deal only with neutral matters.

Professor Hanna reminded us of the great progress made in the period from 1920 to 1940 in the development of social studies programs in American schools. During this time, we have learned how to work with children when the learning activities involve their natural interests. We have also identified a variety of units of instruction in the social studies field which children can carry on successfully. Now, he stated, the time is ripe to develop an ordered and comprehensive curriculum, in which the scope and the sequence of the social studies are clearly outlined.

Dean Quillen gave us a brief history of the efforts to build the curriculum of the American secondary school from the work of the Committee of Ten in 1892 to the recent formulations of the National Council for the Social Studies. His presentation gave us grounds for optimism. He showed the real progress which has been made in selecting relevant materials for the curriculum, and the improvement which has taken place in the conditions of teaching and learning in the schools.

Professor Bellack defined the basic elements of the social studies as concepts and methods. His illustrations of the possibilities for a more unified social studies curriculum gave support for a sustained effort to develop such an educational program even though it is difficult.

The earlier papers have provided an accurate and helpful summary of the development of the social sciences and of the social studies curriculum. I do not challenge the points that have been made, but I do not think sufficient emphasis has been given to the need for rebuilding the present educational program in the social studies. Our audience may have gained the impression that things are going well and all that is required is the time to continue the present slow evolution. Such a view, I believe, to be completely wrong.

Although there are some notable exceptions, on the whole, the social studies are the least effective educationally of any of the basic areas taught in the American public schools. This sweeping generalization is supported by a variety of evidence, the most recent of which is the report by Martin Mayer[1] of his visits to the classrooms of teachers in various parts of the country. The instruction given in these classrooms had been identified by teachers and administrators as superior illustrations of social studies teaching. The data from standardized-interest inventories place the social studies in the lowest quarter of school subjects in terms of the interest pupils express in courses they are taking in this field. High-school alumni questionnaires

---
[1] Martin Mayer, *Where, When, and Why* (New York: Harper & Row, 1963).

The Social Studies Curriculum Proposals for the Future, 1963, pp. 121-132.

indicate a similar low rating by high-school graduates of the courses they took in the social studies. My own observations over the years in many schools found some excellent courses and excellent teaching in this field, but these cases were in the distinct minority. Commonly the classes were dull, spiritless, and lacking in clearly defined content or method.

There are several reasons for the current inadequacy of the social studies. In the first place, the American public and school people are both confused about the educational purposes for teaching the social studies. For example, history is often confused with the communication of myths or the indoctrination of students in the prejudices of their communities. Thus, the state histories in many Southern schools teach children things which are directly in conflict with what children in Northern states are taught. History is sometimes regarded and taught as a body of proved facts, rather than an account of developments, an account which is a subject of continuing inquiry and reinterpretation in the light of new information and knowledge.

As another example, geography is sometimes considered to be a listing of places on a map, sometimes a subject for explaining the location of peoples and industries in terms of climate and other physical features. Sometimes it, too, is treated as a description of foreign people and places which emphasizes the esoteric features. Wonder and surprise are likely to be overplayed at the expense of accuracy and understanding. Economics is often treated as a set of doctrines explaining the superiority of American life, sometimes as a set of exercises in calculating rent, interest, insurance costs, and the like, and rarely as a science for studying the allocation of resources. Civics, too, presents confusion, sometimes treated as a detailed description of the American political structure, sometimes as a subject for debating current political issues, without benefit of necessary knowledge and tools of analysis, and sometimes as a means of understanding aspects of the political process. The confusion seen in psychology arises from courses which try to be a sophisticated Dorothy Dix in providing advice on personal problems, while other courses impress one as a kind of distorted or "fractured Freud." Still other courses appear to be a pseudo-psychometrics, with students taking a variety of cognitive and personality tests, and thus getting a "scientific" description of themselves. The subjects of sociology and anthropology rarely appear in the social studies curriculum.

The state of confusion regarding the educational objectives of the social studies is widespread throughout the country. Popular magazines and newspaper editorials reflect deep misunderstanding of the educational potential of these subjects. Discussions with parents reveal a similar misapprehension. This confusion is not limited to laymen. Teachers and administrators also share the uncertainty about the functions of this field.

A second reason for the current inadequacy of the social studies is the fact that the schools have had inadequate intellectual resources upon which to draw in developing the educational program in this field. This lack of resources is understandable. Several of the social sciences have come of age only recently and, until now, they had very little to offer of solid content or effective methods of inquiry. Heretofore, there have been few efforts made to involve highly competent social scientists in curriculum work with teachers in the schools. During the depression of the 1930's particularly in connection with the Eight-Year Study, the Commission on the Secondary School Curriculum of the Progressive Education Association had been able to interest a few recognized scholars in the social sciences who worked effectively with high-school teachers in beginning the development of a social studies curriculum. Dean Quillen was a leading participant in this project. However, the Second World War brought this endeavor to a halt. Since that time, the schools have not had these intellectual resources to draw upon.

The social studies curricula have been poorly planned. This is a third reason for their current inadequacy. Because the educational purposes have not been clear, there has been no well-defined aim to guide us in deciding on the emphasis to be given, the kind of materials to be used, the sequence to follow, and the way in which social studies should relate to other school subjects. As a result, most courses lack unity and emphasis. The materials used are often ineffective in stimulating and maintaining active student learning. Students complain both of repetition in content from grade to grade, and of the lack of depth possible through sequential treatment. They see few connections between their work in this field and the other subjects which they study.

A fourth reason for the inadequacy of social studies is the fact that the social studies are very frequently assigned to teachers whose major field of interest lies elsewhere. In the social studies, more than in any other basic subject, teachers are likely to be assigned in terms of their having an extra period or two during the day when they are not working in their major field of interest and preparation. This curious method of assigning teachers arises, at least partly, from the fact that not many social studies teachers have been well educated in fields other than history. At the high-school level, history is the only subject in the social studies which is commonly offered for more than one year. Most colleges do not provide a major sequence to prepare teachers for courses involving anthropology, economics, political science, psychology, and sociology.

Another factor in the assignment of teachers may be the common attitude on the part of school people as well as the public, that the social studies have no important content which is not part of the common-sense experience and knowledge of every college graduate. With such a view, special preparation in the social sciences is not deemed essential.

This pictures the present sorry condition of the social studies, but it should not cause us to conclude that the social studies field is hopeless. What Professor Odegard has so well presented regarding the importance of education in this field is true. Furthermore, the time has come when the state of the social studies can be greatly improved.

Now that we are conscious of our confusion in aims, we can select consistent, central purposes. In doing so, however, we must keep in mind that the role of the subject fields in education is not as ends in themselves, but as resources which can be used to equip the student with ways of thinking, feeling, and acting which can help him to live more effectively and with greater dignity and satisfaction. For us to use each subject in this way, we need to understand what the subject really is, at its best, so that we can avoid prostituting it in a caricature for school children. This kind of understanding can be obtained only from serious scholars and scientists who are actively involved in the subject.

Competent historians, for example, do not find history primarily a list of items for memorization, but, to them, history is a study of developments taking place over time. History offers us a way of looking at questions in terms of the time dimension; it offers us methods of inquiry for studying development; it enables us to work out explanations which are always subject to reinterpretation in the light of new knowledge; and it also offers us a way of gaining appreciation for contributions of man's past experiences. Similarly, serious anthropologists, economists, geographers, political scientists, psychologists, and social scientists can help us see potential intellectual and emotional contributions which the study of their subjects can give. None of these subjects give immediate or final answers to important questions, but rather they can contribute to understanding through inquiry, and to appreciation through understanding and the emotional concomitants of active efforts to learn.

In emphasizing the importance of involving scholars and scientists with school people in the task of selecting consistent, central educational purposes for the social studies, I do not mean to imply that the potential contributions of each subject are to be considered in a vacuum. Since we have so little time for school learning, not everything of value can be taught there. A careful selection of those things most important to learn must be made. In judging importance, we need to consider the demands and opportunities of contemporary life. What students learn should assist them in meeting the demands of life, or enable them to take advantage of the opportunities available to them for self-realization. We need also to assess the extent to which what is proposed can be effectively learned in the school by the students in question. Finally, our selection of what is to be taught in the social studies, as well as in other fields, must take into account the extent to which it makes a contribution to the human values cherished by the school, such as helping to develop in each student a concern for others, respect for the dignity and worth of every human being, independence, and the ability to use intelligence in solving human problems. But the point I am stressing here is that the social studies cannot really aim at what the disciplines are not honestly able to contribute.

We have reached the time when we cannot only select consistent central purposes, but we can now draw upon more adequate intellectual resources. The social sciences have much more to provide than was true even a decade ago. Serious and competent social scientists have become interested in helping. Last December, a conference was held here with three representatives of each of six of the social science disciplines. The purpose of the conference was to explain the need for moving ahead with rebuilding the social studies in a fashion somewhat similar to that currently under way in mathematics and the natural sciences. Representatives from all of the disciplines present expressed the view that this was of such importance that leading social scientists would be willing to cooperate fully in such an endeavor. Since that time, nearly a score of them have actually begun work.

Furthermore, funds are increasingly available to support work on the social studies curriculum. The United States Office of Education is putting funds into Project Social Studies. The National Science Foundation has begun to support course content improvement studies in the social sciences, and several of the private foundations are furnishing financial assistance. Finally, a number of colleges and universities are providing more adequate opportunities for educating teachers in this area. Although the extent of these resources would not permit every school district to embark upon a comprehensive program of curriculum reconstruction, there are now available what is required for ten or a dozen major projects.

A concerted effort can now be made to develop intelligent and feasible plans for the curriculum plans which provide for carefully designed sequences of social studies instruction in both elementary and secondary schools, and which afford relevant and helpful integration with other fields in the curriculum. It is not necessary here to illustrate the kinds of plans I have in mind since Professor Hanna's paper was largely devoted to one possible plan. It is important, at this stage, to develop several possible plans since it is likely that there is no one best design for an effective curriculum.

With carefully planned curricula and more well-prepared teachers, it will not be many years before it is possible to assign most social studies classes to persons who have interest and competence in this area. Now is the time for a thorough-going rebuilding of the curriculum in the social studies because the factors which have largely accounted for the present inadequacies are no longer controlling. We can be clear about purposes. We have the resources. We can make better plans and we can develop better-prepared teachers.

That there is increasing recognition of the possibility now of making great changes in the social studies curriculum is indicated by the number of efforts already under way. Professor John Michaelis, of the University of California, Berkeley, prepared a report for the Association for Supervision and Curriculum Development[2] on twenty-four current projects in the social studies, either planned or under way. Some of these appear to be promising initial steps in more comprehensive efforts. Others are inadequate in conception or implementation. From the experience with mathematics and science, I believe we can undertake the task of improving the social studies in a way that has high probability of success.

A promising method of attack will involve several centers of development, experimentation, and appraisal. The National Science Foundation supported only one center for development of a high-school physics course, the Physical Science Study Committee, centered at the Massachusetts Institute of Technology. Although this one center produced a successful course, it had to select from among several promising lines of development, and it is quite possible that some of the lines which were not followed by PSSC would have produced a better course for certain purposes or certain groups of students, or a course which would have been more compatible with the background and teaching abilities of some high-school teachers. At the Conference on Policies and Strategy for Strengthening the Curriculum of the American Public Schools, which convened at Stanford University, January 24-27, 1959, the first recommendation which was unanimously adopted included not only the establishment of centers for curriculum development, but also emphasized the importance of more than one in each field. The recommendation read:

There should be established immediately study groups for the redefinition of objectives, content, and organization, of the public school curriculum,

---

[2] Published March, 1963.

and for the development of, and experimentation with, instructional materials for the courses thus designed. There should be at least two study groups in each subject so as to encourage original thinking and efforts rather than to restrict exploration and experimentation to a single plan.

Each study group should be composed of schoolteachers and college and university professors. The study groups might also include supervisors, administrators, and persons from schools of education who could bring particular kinds of competence, experience, or ideas helpful to the study undertaken. The probable priority in the establishment of study groups is:
   A. social studies
   B. English
   C. biology
   D. others
Where possible, each study group should work on the curriculum from the earliest introduction of the subject on through high school.

A second unanimous recommendation of the conference was closely related to the first:

There should be established one or more study groups on problems of organization of the curriculum as a whole, its sequence, and grade placement, the relations among the several subjects, and the conditions required for stimulating and guiding effective learning. Whereas the primary concerns of study groups recommended in No. 1 are the development of course objectives, outlines of content, and instructional materials for a separate strand of the school curriculum, the primary tasks of the study groups recommended in No. 2 are to work on ways of relating effectively the several subjects, and ways of achieving a truly sequential organization. Since these questions would involve both subject experts and psychologists, it seemed appropriate also to ask these groups to investigate conditions for effective learning of curriculum tasks.

The purposes of these two recommendations are (a) to bring together again scholars and scientists and school people to make use of their special knowledge and experience in curriculum planning; (b) to establish a means for investigation, experimentation, and evaluation of curriculum ideas, materials, and practices, so that they can be tried out in schools and revised and improved on the basis of the results from trials; (c) to establish multiple centers so as to prevent any monopoly of curriculum thinking, and to encourage several independent lines of thought and effort whose relative values can be discovered by experimentation and appraisal.[3]

These recommendations, which were made four years ago, are still the best suggestions that I know. Since the time they were made, the experience with the development of science and mathematics curricula has served to demonstrate the value of the procedure outlined. One additional task for these centers was not mentioned in the 1959 conference, but has been found important in the implementation of the new courses in science and mathematics. Opportunities must be provided to enable teachers who have not been involved in the development of a course to become familiar with its purposes and its content, and to learn how to use the instructional materials relevant to the course. In the case of science and mathematics, summer institutes, academic year institutes, and in-service courses of various types have proved invaluable in providing for the dissemination and utilization of the new courses.

These course content improvement projects have been successful in getting cooperation among the scientists and mathematicians and school people. They reflect much more adequately than earlier courses

---

3 Ralph W. Tyler, "Do We Need a 'National Curriculum'? A Conference Report," *The Clearing House*, Vol. 34, No. 3, (November 1959), pp. 144-145.

the nature of these subjects as intellectual disciplines. Furthermore, the instructional materials and devices developed are proving effective in aiding student learning. These projects have not, however, involved a comprehensive selection of educational purposes, nor have they given much consideration to the sequence of the total curriculum, nor to the relation of each of the subjects to the rest of the educational program. The attack upon the social studies curriculum can benefit from the successful experience in science and mathematics. It can also give more comprehensive consideration in selecting objectives and in giving explicit attention to curriculum sequence and integration.

The foregoing review of the current status of the social studies, and the suggestions for improvement, are not made as an academic exercise with indifferent consequences. Young people growing up today need the understanding, the appreciation of the values, and the skills which history, geography, political science, economics, anthropology, psychology, and sociology can help provide. But, to make this needed educational contribution, new social studies curricula need to be developed. We are ready for it. Now is the time to do it.

Sidney Harris
U.S. ideals cancel out each other

WANT TO KNOW what America believes?

It believes that all people are basically the same everywhere — but that you can't really trust foreigners.

It believes that private enterprise is a fine idea — but that your own special interest should try to get as much from the government as it can.

It believes that the Latin people know how to relax and enjoy life better than we do — but that they're lazy and will never get anywhere.

It believes that everybody should have as much education as possible — but that people who talk and act as if they were educated are untrustworthy intellectuals.

It believes that Russia is a Godless, materialistic state — but that it's good for us to acquire as many material possessions as we can get our hands on.

It believes that environment creates most criminals — but it spends billions to lock up criminals, and virtually nothing to change their environment.

It believes that every man is entitled to his opinion — but that it doesn't take any effort or knowledge or careful reasoning to distinguish an opinion from a mere prejudice.

It believes that children should get pretty nearly everything they ask for — but that parents are to blame if their children become spoiled and willful from this indulgence.

It believes that the caste system has no place in a democratic society — but that the size and price of the car you drive is a mark of your relative social position.

It believes that you can't fool all the people all the time — but that you have to respect the politicians and promoters who manage to do so most of the time.

It believes that Jesus' advice to turn the other cheek is the only Christian way to behave — but that we have to build up our military strength so that we will be in no danger of losing the next war.

It believes, in short, a mass of contradictory statements, half of which cancel out the other half, and all of which add up to the most confused set of ideals that any mighty nation has fallen heir to in the history of the world.

Majority of One, Houghton Mifflin, 1957.

LEARNING PROCESS AND INQUIRY

JEROME S. BRUNER
Harvard University

The Act of Discovery[*]

Maimonides, in his *Guide for the Perplexed*,[1] speaks of four forms of perfection that men might seek. The first and lowest form is perfection in the acquisition of worldly goods. The great philosopher dismisses such perfection on the ground that the possessions one acquires bear no meaningful relation to the possessor: "A great king may one morning find that there is no difference between him and the lowest person." A second perfection is of the body, its conformation and skills. Its failing is that it does not reflect on what is uniquely human about man: "he could [in any case] not be as

---

[1] Maimonides, *Guide for the Perplexed* (New York: Dover Publications, 1956).

---

[*] Reprinted with the permission of the author and the publisher from the article of the same title, *Harvard Educational Review*, 31 (1961), 21-32.

Harvard Educational Review, 1961, No.31, pp. 21-32.

strong as a mule." Moral perfection is the third, "the highest degree of excellency in man's character." Of this perfection Maimonides says: "Imagine a person being alone, and having no connection whatever with any other person; all his good moral principles are at rest, they are not required and give man no perfection whatever. These principles are only necessary and useful when man comes in contact with others." "The fourth kind of perfection is the true perfection of man; the possession of the highest intellectual faculties. . . ." In justification of his assertion, this extraordinary Spanish-Judaic philosopher urges: "Examine the first three kinds of perfection; you will find that if you possess them, they are not your property, but the property of others. . . . But the last kind of perfection is exclusively yours; no one else owns any part of it."

It is a conjecture much like that of Maimonides that leads me to examine the act of discovery in man's intellectual life. For if man's intellectual excellence is the most his own among his perfections, it is also the case that the most uniquely personal of all that he knows is that which he has discovered for himself. What difference does it make, then, that we encourage discovery in the learning of the young? Does it, as Maimonides would say, create a special and unique relation between knowledge possessed and the possessor? And what may such a unique relation do for a man—or for a child, if you will, for our concern is with the education of the young?

The immediate occasion for my concern with discovery—and I do not restrict discovery to the act of finding out something that before was unknown to mankind, but rather include all forms of obtaining knowledge for oneself by the use of one's own mind—the immediate occasion is the work of the various new curriculum projects that have grown up in America during the last six or seven years. For whether one speaks to mathematicians or physicists or historians, one encounters repeatedly an expression of faith in the powerful effects that come from permitting the student to put things together for himself, to be his own discoverer.

First, let it be clear what the act of discovery entails. It is rarely, on the frontier of knowledge or elsewhere, that new facts are "discovered" in the sense of being encountered as Newton suggested in the form of islands of truth in an uncharted sea of ignorance. Or if they appear to be discovered in this way, it is almost always thanks to some happy hypotheses about where to navigate. Discovery, like surprise, favors the well prepared mind. In playing bridge, one is surprised by a hand with no honors in it at all and also by hands that are all in one suit. Yet all hands in bridge are equiprobable: one must know to be surprised. So too in discovery. The history of science is studded with examples of men "finding out" something and not knowing it. I shall operate on the assumption that discovery, whether by a schoolboy going it on his own or by a scientist cultivating the growing edge of his field, is in its essence a matter of rearranging or transforming evidence in such a way that one is enabled to go beyond the evidence so reassembled to additional new insights. It may well be that an additional fact or shred of evidence makes this larger transformation of evidence possible. But it is often not even dependent on new information.

It goes without saying that, left to himself, the child will go about discovering things for himself within limits. It also goes without saying that there are certain forms of child rearing, certain home atmospheres that lead some children to be their own discoverers more than other children. These are both topics of great interest, but I shall not be discussing them. Rather, I should like to confine myself to the consideration of discovery and "finding-out-for-oneself" within an educational setting—specifically the school. Our aim as teachers is to give our student as firm a grasp of a subject as we can, and to make him as autonomous and self-propelled a thinker as we can—one who will go along on his own after formal schooling has ended. I shall return in the end to the question of the kind of classroom and the style of teaching that encourages an attitude of wanting to discover. For purposes of orienting the discussion, however, I would like to make an overly simplified distinction between teaching that takes place in the *expository mode* and teaching that utilizes the *hypothetical mode*. In the former, the decisions concerning the mode and pace and style of exposition are principally determined by the teacher as expositor; the student is the listener. If I can put the matter in terms of structural linguistics, the speaker has a quite different set of decisions to make than the listener: the former has a wide choice of alternatives for structuring, he is anticipating paragraph content while the listener is still intent on the words, he is manipulating the content of the material by various transformations, while the listener is quite unaware of these internal manipulations. In the hypothetical mode, the teacher and the student are in a more cooperative position with respect to what in linguistics would be called "speaker's decisions." The student is not a bench-bound listener, but is taking a part in the formulation and at times may play the principal role in it. He will be aware of alternatives and may even have an "as if" attitude toward these and, as he receives information he may evaluate it as it comes. One cannot describe the process in either mode with great precision as to detail, but I think the foregoing may serve to illustrate what is meant.

Consider now what benefit might be derived from the experience of learning through discoveries that one makes for oneself. I should like to discuss these under four headings: (1) The increase in intellectual potency, (2) the shift from extrinsic to intrinsic rewards, (3) learning the heuristics of discovering, and (4) the aid to memory processing.

1. *Intellectual potency.* If you will permit me, I would like to consider the difference between subjects in a highly constrained psychological experiment involving a two-choice apparatus. In order to win chips, they must depress a key either on the right or the left side of the machine. A pattern of payoff is designed such that, say, they will be paid off on the right side 70 per cent of the time, on the left 30 per cent, although this detail is not important. What is important is that the payoff sequence is arranged at random, and there is no pattern. I should like to contrast the behavior of subjects who think that there *is* some pattern to be found in the sequence—who think that regularities are discoverable—in contrast to subjects who think that things are happening quite by *chance*. The former group adopts what is called an "event-matching" strategy in which the number of responses given to each side is roughly equal to the proportion of times it pays off: in the present case R70 : L30. The group that believes there is no pattern very soon reverts to a much more primitive strategy wherein *all* responses are allocated to the side that has the greater payoff. A little arithmetic will show you that the lazy all-and-none strategy pays off more if indeed the environment is random: namely, they win seventy per cent of the time. The event-matching subjects win about 70% on the 70% payoff side

(or 49% of the time there) and 30% of the time on the side that pays off 30% of the time (another 9% for a total take-home wage of 58% in return for their labors of decision). But the world is not always or not even frequently random, and if one analyzes carefully what the event-matchers are doing, it turns out that they are trying out hypotheses one after the other, all of them containing a term such that they distribute bets on the two sides with a frequency to match the actual occurrence of events. If it should turn out that there is a pattern to be discovered, their payoff would become 100%. The other group would go on at the middling rate of 70%.

What has this to do with the subject at hand? For the person to search out and find regularities and relationships in his environment, he must be armed with an expectancy that there will be something to find and, once aroused by expectancy, he must devise ways of searching and finding. One of the chief enemies of such expectancy is the assumption that there is nothing one can find in the environment by way of regularity or relationship. In the experiment just cited, subjects often fall into a habitual attitude that there is either nothing to be found or that they can find a pattern by looking. There is an important sequel in behavior to the two attitudes, and to this I should like to turn now.

We have been conducting a series of experimental studies on a group of some seventy school children over the last four years. The studies have led us to distinguish an interesting dimension of cognitive activity that can be described as ranging from *episodic empiricism* at one end to *cumulative constructionism* at the other. The two attitudes in the choice experiments just cited are illustrative of the extremes of the dimension. I might mention some other illustrations. One of the experiments employs the game of Twenty Questions. A child—in this case he is between 10 and 12—is told that a car has gone off the road and hit a tree. He is to ask questions that can be answered by "yes" or "no" to discover the cause of the accident. After completing the problem, the same task is given him again, though he is told that the accident had a different cause this time. In all, the procedure is repeated four times. Children enjoy playing the game. They also differ quite markedly in the approach or strategy they bring to the task. There are various elements in the strategies employed. In the first place, one may distinguish clearly between two types of questions asked: the one is designed for locating constraints in the problem, constraints that will eventually give shape to an hypothesis; the other is the hypothesis as question. It is the difference between, "Was there anything wrong with the driver?" and "Was the driver rushing to the doctor's office for an appointment and the car got out of control?" There are children who precede hypotheses with efforts to locate constraint and there are those who, to use our local slang, are "pot-shotters," who string out hypotheses non-cumulatively one after the other. A second element of strategy is its connectivity of information gathering: the extent to which questions asked utilize or ignore or violate information previously obtained. The questions asked by children tend to be organized in cycles, each cycle of questions usually being given over to the pursuit of some particular notion. Both within cycles and between cycles one can discern a marked difference on the connectivity of the child's performance. Needless to say, children who employ constraint location as a technique preliminary to the formulation of hypotheses tend to be far more connected in their harvesting of information. Persistence is another feature of strategy, a characteristic compounded of what appear to be two components: a sheer doggedness component, and a persistence that stems from the sequential organization that a child brings to the task. Doggedness is probably just animal spirits or the need for achievement—what has come to be called *n-ach*. Organized persistence is a maneuver for protecting our fragile cognitive apparatus from overload. The child who has flooded himself with disorganized information from unconnected hypotheses will become discouraged and confused sooner than the child who has shown a certain cunning in his strategy of getting information—a cunning whose principal component is the recognition that the value of information is not simply in getting it but in being able to carry it. The persistence of the organized child stems from his knowledge of how to organize questions in cycles, how to summarize things to himself, and the like.

Episodic empiricism is illustrated by information gathering that is unbound by prior constraints, that lacks connectivity, and that is deficient in organizational persistence. The opposite extreme is illustrated by an approach that is characterized by constraint sensitivity, by connective maneuvers, and by organized persistence. Brute persistence seems to be one of those gifts from the gods that make people more exaggeratedly what they are.[2]

Before returning to the issue of discovery and its role in the development of thinking, let me say a word more about the ways in which information may get transformed when the problem solver has actively processed it. There is first of all a pragmatic question: what does it take to get information processed into a form best designed to fit some future use? Take an experiment by Zajonc[3] as a case in point. He gives groups of subjects information of a controlled kind, some groups being told that their task is to transmit the information to others, others that it is merely to be kept in mind. In general, he finds more differentiation and organization of the information received with the intention of being transmitted than there is for information received passively. An active set leads to a transformation related to a task to be performed. The risk, to be sure, is in possible overspecialization of information processing that may lead to such a high degree of specific organization that information is lost for general use.

I would urge now in the spirit of an hypothesis that emphasis upon discovery in learning has precisely the effect upon the learner of leading him to be a constructionist, to organize what he is encountering in a manner not only designed to discover regularity and relatedness, but also to avoid the kind of information drift that fails to keep account of the uses to which information might have to be put. It is, if you will, a necessary condition for learning the variety of techniques of problem solving, of transforming information for better use, indeed for learning how to go about the very task of learning. Practice in discovering for oneself teaches one to acquire information in a way that makes that information more readily viable in problem solving. So goes the hypothesis. It is still in need of testing. But it is an hypothesis of such important human impli-

---

[2] I should also remark in passing that the two extremes also characterize concept attainment strategies as reported in *A Study of Thinking* by J. S. Bruner et al. (New York: J. Wiley, 1956). Successive scanning illustrates well what is meant here by episodic empiricism; conservative focussing is an example of cumulative constructionism.

[3] R. B. Zajonc (Personal communication, 1957).

cations that we cannot afford not to test it—and testing will have to be in the schools.

2. *Intrinsic and extrinsic motives.* Much of the problem in leading a child to effective cognitive activity is to free him from the immediate control of environmental rewards and punishments. That is to say, learning that starts in response to the rewards of parental or teacher approval or the avoidance of failure can too readily develop a pattern in which the child is seeking cues as to how to conform to what is expected of him. We know from studies of children who tend to be early over-achievers in school that they are likely to be seekers after the "right way to do it" and that their capacity for transforming their learning into viable thought structures tends to be lower than children merely achieving at levels predicted by intelligence tests. Our tests on such children show them to be lower in analytic ability than those who are not conspicuous in overachievement. As we shall see later, they develop rote abilities and depend upon being able to "give back" what is expected rather than to make it into something that relates to the rest of their cognitive life. As Maimonides would say, their learning is not their own.

The hypothesis that I would propose here is that to the degree that one is able to approach learning as a task of discovering something rather than "learning about" it, to that degree will there be a tendency for the child to carry out his learning activities with the autonomy of self-reward or, more properly by reward that is discovery itself.

To those of you familiar with the battles of the last half-century in the field of motivation, the above hypothesis will be recognized as controversial. For the classic view of motivation in learning has been, until very recently, couched in terms of a theory of drives and reinforcement: that learning occurred by virtue of the fact that a response produced by a stimulus was followed by the reduction in a primary drive state. The doctrine is greatly extended by the idea of secondary reinforcement: any state associated even remotely with the reduction of a primary drive could also have the effect of producing learning. There has recently appeared a most searching and important criticism of this position, written by Professor Robert

White,[4] reviewing the evidence of recently published animal studies, of work in the field of psychoanalysis, and of research on the development of cognitive processes in children. Professor White comes to the conclusion, quite rightly I think, that the drive-reduction model of learning runs counter to too many important phenomena of learning and development to be either regarded as general in its applicability or even correct in its general approach. Let me summarize some of his principal conclusions and explore their applicability to the hypothesis stated above.

> I now propose that we gather the various kinds of behavior just mentioned, all of which have to do with effective interaction with the environment, under the general heading of competence. According to Webster, competence means fitness or ability, and the suggested synonyms include capability, capacity, efficiency, proficiency, and skill. It is therefore a suitable word to describe such things as grasping and exploring, crawling and walking, attention and perception, language and thinking, manipulating and changing the surroundings, all of which promote an effective—a competent—interaction with the environment. It is true of course, that maturation plays a part in all these developments, but this part is heavily overshadowed by learning in all the more complex accomplishments like speech or skilled manipulation. I shall argue that it is necessary to make competence a motivational concept; there is *competence motivation* as well as competence in its more familiar sense of achieved capacity. The behavior that leads to the building up of effective grasping, handling, and letting go of objects, to take one example, is not random behavior that is produced by an overflow of energy. It is directed, selective, and persistent, and it continues not because it serves primary drives, which indeed it cannot serve until it is almost perfected, but because it satisfies an intrinsic need to deal with the environment.[5]

I am suggesting that there are forms of activity that serve to enlist and develop the competence motive, that serve to make it the driving force behind behavior. I should like to add to White's general premise that the *exercise* of competence motives has the effect of strengthening the degree to which they gain control over behavior and thereby reduce the effects of extrinsic rewards or drive gratification.

---

[4] R. W. White, "Motivation Reconsidered: The Concept of Competence," *Psychological Review*, LXVI (1959), 297–333.
[5] *Ibid.*, pp. 317–18.

The brilliant Russian psychologist Vigotsky[6] characterizes the growth of thought processes as starting with a dialogue of speech and gesture between child and parent; autonomous thinking begins at the stage when the child is first able to internalize these conversations and "run them off" himself. This is a typical sequence in the development of competence. So too in instruction. The narrative of teaching is of the order of the conversation. The next move in the development of competence is the internalization of the narrative and its "rules of generation" so that the child is now capable of running off the narrative on his own. The hypothetical mode in teaching by encouraging the child to participate in "speaker's decisions" speeds this process along. Once internalization has occurred, the child is in a vastly improved position from several obvious points of view—notably that he is able to go beyond the information he has been given to generate additional ideas that can either be checked immediately from experience or can, at least, be used as a basis for formulating reasonable hypotheses. But over and beyond that, the child is now in a position to experience success and failure not as reward and punishment, but as information. For when the task is his own rather than a matter of matching environmental demands, he becomes his own paymaster in a certain measure. Seeking to gain control over his environment, he can now treat success as indicating that he is on the right track, failure as indicating he is on the wrong one.

In the end, this development has the effect of freeing learning from immediate stimulus control. When learning in the short run leads only to pellets of this or that rather than to mastery in the long run, then behavior can be readily "shaped" by extrinsic rewards. When behavior becomes more long-range and competence-oriented, it comes under the control of more complex cognitive structures, plans and the like, and operates more from the inside out. It is interesting that even Pavlov, whose early account of the learning process was based entirely on a notion of stimulus control of behavior through the conditioning mechanism in which, through contiguity a new conditioned stimulus was substituted for an old unconditioned stimulus by the mechanism of stimulus substitution,

---

[6] L. S. Vigotsky, *Thinking and Speech* (Moscow, 1934).

that even Pavlov recognized his account as insufficient to deal with higher forms of learning. To supplement the account, he introduced the idea of the "second signalling system," with central importance placed on symbolic systems such as language in mediating and giving shape to mental life. Or as Luria[7] has put it, "the first signal system [is] concerned with directly perceived stimuli, the second with systems of verbal elaboration." Luria, commenting on the importance of the transition from first to second signal system, says: "It would be mistaken to suppose that verbal intercourse with adults merely changes the contents of the child's conscious activity without changing its form. . . . The word has a basic function not only because it indicates a corresponding object in the external world, but also because it abstracts, isolates the necessary signal, generalizes perceived signals and relates them to certain categories; it is this systematization of direct experience that makes the role of the word in the formation of mental processes so exceptionally important."[8]

It is interesting that the final rejection of the universality of the doctrine of reinforcement in direct conditioning came from some of Pavlov's own students. Ivanov-Smolensky[9] and Krasnogorsky[10] published papers showing the manner in which symbolized linguistic messages could take over the place of the unconditioned stimulus and of the unconditioned response (gratification of hunger) in children. In all instances, they speak of these as *replacements* of lower, first-system mental or neural processes by higher order or second-system controls. A strange irony, then, that Russian psychology that gave us the notion of the conditioned response and the assumption that higher order activities are built up out of colligations or structurings of such primitive units, rejected this notion while much of American learning psychology has stayed until quite recently within the early Pavlovian fold (see, for example, a recent

---

[7] A. L. Luria, "The Directive Function of Speech in Development and Dissolution," *Word*, XV (1959), 341–464.

[8] *Ibid.*, p. 12.

[9] A. G. Ivanov-Smolensky, "Concerning the Study of the Joint Activity of the First and Second Signal Systems," *Journal of Higher Nervous Activity*, I (1951), 1.

[10] N. D. Krasnogorsky, *Studies of Higher Nervous Activity in Animals and in Man*, Vol. I (Moscow, 1954).

article by Spence[11] in the *Harvard Educational Review* or Skinner's treatment of language[12] and the attacks that have been made upon it by linguists such as Chomsky[13] who have become concerned with the relation of language and cognitive activity). What is the more interesting is that Russian pedagogical theory has become deeply influenced by this new trend and is now placing much stress upon the importance of building up a more active symbolical approach to problem solving among children.

To sum up the matter of the control of learning, then, I am proposing that the degree to which competence or mastery motives come to control behavior, to that degree the role of reinforcement or "extrinsic pleasure" wanes in shaping behavior. The child comes to manipulate his environment more actively and achieves his gratification from coping with problems. Symbolic modes of representing and transforming the environment arise and the importance of stimulus-response-reward sequences declines. To use the metaphor that David Riesman developed in a quite different context, mental life moves from a state of outer-directedness in which the fortuity of stimuli and reinforcement are crucial to a state of innerdirectedness in which the growth and maintenance of mastery become central and dominant.

3. *Learning the heuristics of discovery.* Lincoln Steffens,[14] reflecting in his *Autobiography* on his under graduate education at Berkeley, comments that his schooling was overly specialized on learning about the known and that too little attention was given to the task of finding out about what was not known. But how does one train a student in the techniques of discovery? Again I would like to offer some hypotheses. There are many ways of coming to the arts of inquiry. One of them is by careful study of its formalization in logic, statistics, mathematics, and the like. If a person is going to pursue inquiry as a way of life, particularly in the sciences, certainly such study is essential. Yet, whoever has taught kindergarten

---

[11] K. W. Spence, "The Relation of Learning Theory to the Technique of Education," *Harvard Educational Review*, XXIX (1959), 84–95.
[12] B. F. Skinner, *Verbal Behavior* (New York: Appleton-Century-Crofts, 1957).
[13] N. Chomsky, *Syntactic Structure* (The Hague, The Netherlands: Mouton & Co., 1957).
[14] L. Steffens, *Autobiography of Lincoln Steffens* (New York: Harcourt, Brace & World, 1931).

and the early primary grades or has had graduate students working with him on their theses—I choose the two extremes for they are both periods of intense inquiry—knows that an understanding of the formal aspect of inquiry is not sufficient. There appear to be, rather, a series of activities and attitudes, some directly related to a particular subject and some of them fairly generalized, that go with inquiry and research. These have to do with the *process* of trying to find out something and while they provide no guarantee that the *product* will be any *great* discovery, their absence is likely to lead to awkwardness or aridity or confusion. How difficult it is to describe these matters—the heuristics of inquiry. There is one set of attitudes or ways of doing that has to do with sensing the relevance of variables—how to avoid getting stuck with edge effects and getting instead to the big sources of variance. Partly this gift comes from intuitive familiarity with a range of phenomena, sheer "knowing the stuff." But it also comes out of a sense of what things among an ensemble of things "smell right" in the sense of being of the right order of magnitude or scope or severity.

The English philosopher Weldon describes problem solving in an interesting and picturesque way. He distinguishes between difficulties, puzzles, and problems. We solve a problem or make a discovery when we impose a puzzle form on to a difficulty that converts it into a problem that can be solved in such a way that it gets us where we want to be. That is to say, we recast the difficulty into a form that we know how to work with, then work it. Much of what we speak of as discovery consists of knowing how to impose what kind of form on various kinds of difficulties. A small part but a crucial part of discovery of the highest order is to invent and develop models or "puzzle forms" that can be imposed on difficulties with good effect. It is in this area that the truly powerful mind shines. But it is interesting to what degree perfectly ordinary people can, given the benefit of instruction, construct quite interesting and what, a century ago, would have been considered greatly original models.

Now to the hypothesis. It is my hunch that it is only through the exercise of problem solving and the effort of discovery that one learns the working heuristic of discovery, and the more one has practice, the more likely is one to generalize what one has learned into a style of problem solving or inquiry that serves for any kind of task one may encounter—or almost any kind of task. I think the matter is self-evident, but what is unclear is what kinds of training and teaching produce the best effects. How do we teach a child to, say, cut his losses but at the same time be persistent in trying out an idea; to risk forming an early hunch without at the same time formulating one *so* early and with so little evidence as to be stuck with it waiting for appropriate evidence to materialize; to pose good testable guesses that are neither too brittle nor too sinuously incorrigible; etc., etc. Practice in inquiry, in trying to figure out things for oneself is indeed what is needed, but in what form? Of only one thing I am convinced. I have never seen anybody improve in the art and technique of inquiry by any means other than engaging in inquiry.

4. *Conservation of memory*. I should like to take what some psychologists might consider a rather drastic view of the memory process. It is a view that in large measure derives from the work of my colleague, Professor George Miller.[15] Its first premise is that the principal problem of human memory is not storage, but retrieval. In spite of the biological unlikeliness of it, we seem to be able to store a huge quantity of information—perhaps not a full tape recording, though at times it seems we even do that, but a great sufficiency of impressions. We may infer this from the fact that recognition (i.e., recall with the aid of maximum prompts) is so extraordinarily good in human beings—particularly in comparison with spontaneous recall where, so to speak, we must get out stored information without external aids or prompts. The key to retrieval is organization or, in even simpler terms, knowing where to find information and how to get there.

Let me illustrate the point with a simple experiment. We present pairs of words to twelve-year-old children. One group is simply told to remember the pairs, that they will be asked to repeat them later. Another is told to remember them by producing a word or idea that will tie the pair together in a way that will make sense to them. A third group is given the mediators used by the second group

---

[15] G. A. Miller, "The Magical Number Seven, Plus or Minus Two," *Psychological Review*, LXIII (1956), 81–97.

when presented with the pairs to aid them in tying the pairs into working units. The word pairs include such juxtapositions as "chair-forest," "sidewalk-square," and the like. One can distinguish three styles of mediators and children can be scaled in terms of their relative preference for each: *generic mediation* in which a pair is tied together by a superordinate idea: "chair and forest are both made of wood"; *thematic mediation* in which the two terms are imbedded in a theme or little story: "the lost child sat on a chair in the middle of the forest"; and *part-whole mediation* where "chairs are made from trees in the forest" is typical. Now, the chief result, as you would all predict, is that children who provide their own mediators do best—indeed, one time through a set of thirty pairs, they recover up to 95% of the second words when presented with the first ones of the pairs, whereas the uninstructed children reach a maximum of less than 50% recovered. Interestingly enough, children do best in recovering materials tied together by the form of mediator they most often use.

One can cite a myriad of findings to indicate that any organization of information that reduces the aggregate complexity of material by imbedding it into a cognitive structure a person has constructed will make that material more accessible for retrieval. In short, we may say that the process of memory, looked at from the retrieval side, is also a process of problem solving: how can material be "placed" in memory so that it can be got on demand?

We can take as a point of departure the example of the children who developed their own technique for relating the members of each word pair. You will recall that they did better than the children who were given by exposition the mediators they had developed. Let me suggest that in general, material that is organized in terms of a person's own interests and cognitive structures is material that has the best chance of being accessible in memory. That is to say, it is more likely to be placed along routes that are connected to one's own ways of intellectual travel.

In sum, the very attitudes and activities that characterize "figuring out" or "discovering" things for oneself also seems to have the effect of making material more readily accessible in memory.

The Taxonomy: Guide to Differentiated Instruction

John Jarolimek

DISCUSSIONS of differentiated instruction in the social studies ordinarily focus upon variations to be made in learning activities which the pupil is expected to perform. Most frequently the recommendations have to do with variations in reading requirements or variations in work-study activities. The teacher is advised to use more difficult reading material with the more capable pupil than with the less able one. Similarly in the case of work-study activities, the suggestion is made that the able pupil be directed toward activities which involve more independent research, more reading and elaborative thinking than his slower-learning classmate. In general, these recommendations are sound ones; but they are apt to be something less than adequate unless, in addition, careful consideration is given to the complexity of the intellectual tasks with which each of the pupils is going to concern himself.

Varying the difficulty of intellectual tasks relating to a social studies unit is a procedure which seems to have received less attention from teachers than it deserves. The hope is that if pupils are placed in reading materials of varying difficulty and are involved in varying types of instructional activities, this will, in itself, result in some differentiation of instruction with respect to complexity of learnings. No doubt this occurs to some extent. However, variations in complexity should be a deliberate and planned part of the teaching plan rather than be allowed to come about by a happy accident. In order to build such diversity in conceptual complexity into the program, one needs to begin with instructional objectives. The procedure under consideration here would hold general objectives constant, but would vary specific objectives in terms of the capabilities of individual pupils.

In an effort to plan deliberately for differentiated instruction in terms of the complexity of intellectual operations, the teacher may find Bloom's *Taxonomy of Educational Objectives, Handbook I: Cognitive Domain*[1] to be a helpful model. The *Taxonomy* classifies various types of educational objectives into six groups or categories as follows:

1. Knowledge
2. Comprehension
3. Application
4. Analysis
5. Synthesis
6. Evaluation

These are ordered in terms of an hierarchy representing an increasingly complex set of cognitive relationships as one moves from category one to category six. Behaviors in each succeeding category are to some extent dependent upon an understanding of related objectives in a prior category. Sub-heads of each of the six categories indicate that they, too, are ordered from simple relationships to complex ones. Hence, children in the primary grades need not concern themselves solely with objectives in the *Knowledge* category but may make applications, analyses, and evaluations providing these are kept simple and clearly within the realm of direct experience.

It is perhaps true that the bulk of elementary social studies instruction concerns itself with objectives represented in category one—*Knowledge*. This includes knowledge of specifics, facts, terminology, events, etc. To a degree, an emphasis on knowledge is inevitable at early levels since pupils are rapidly building their cognitive structure. However, the *Knowledge* category is

---

John Jarolimek, a member of the Board of Directors of the National Council for the Social Studies, is an Associate Professor of Education at the University of Washington in Seattle.

[1] Benjamin S. Bloom *et al. Taxonomy of Educational Objectives, Handbook I: Cognitive Domain.* New York: Longmans, Green and Company, 1956.

Social Education, 1962, Vol.26, pp. 445-447.

itself spread along a continuum ranging from a knowledge of specifics to a knowledge of universals and abstractions in a field. Pupils of varying abilities might be expected to deal with different specific objectives in the *Knowledge* category. Instruction is limiting and narrow when all pupils deal with *Knowledge* objectives pertaining only to specifics, facts, terminology, and events.

The teacher must, of course, be concerned with objectives in category one—*Knowledge*—because it is fundamental to all of the others. Particularly important would be the development of a knowledge of the terminology of the social studies. Without a grasp of the vocabulary, the pupil is unable to consider problems in the social studies thoughtfully. Knowledge of specific facts is important, too, not as an end in itself but because such specifics are prerequisite to the achievement of more complex intellectual objectives. Objectives in this category are relatively easy to teach and evaluate because they depend almost entirely upon recall of information. They have traditionally been a part of the social studies curriculum in most schools and consequently are familiar to teachers. While they are important, at the same time this does not give the teacher license to teach them in ways which are educationally and psychologically unsound.

In addition to knowledge of specifics, one finds in this category two other types of knowledge objectives. The first of these—"knowledge of ways and means of dealing with specifics"—would seem to have especial significance for the social studies. Included would be such knowledge of conventions as might be called for in the understanding of procedures in various affairs of citizenship—how a bill becomes a law, how government officials are elected, how laws are enforced, and so on. It deals, too, with trends and sequences such as knowledge of events which led up to more important events, steps in the production of goods, or the chronology associated with historical developments. The third large subhead entitled "knowledge of the universals and abstractions in a field" constitutes the highest order of the *Knowledge* category. In the social studies it would call for a knowledge of major generalizations relating to the social sciences as these are forged out of the varied experiences of pupils. An example of such a generalization would be "Man's utilization of natural resources is related to his desires and his level of technology."

The second large category—*Comprehension*—requires somewhat more complex intellectual activity than recall, as is the case in the *Knowledge* category. "Translation" and "Interpretation" are the two facets of *Comprehension* most appropriate for elementary social studies. Data gathering brings the pupil into contact with a great variety of source materials. He uses maps, charts, graphs, encyclopedias, atlases, and others. Data so abstracted must be translated into usable form for the purpose of problem solving. Literary material, when used, requires both translation and interpretation. Much of the social studies reading material is presented in highly condensed form and has within it many possibilities for interpretation and extrapolation. If pupils are to avoid making "bookish" reports, for example, they need to be able to make a translation of the material into their own everyday language. Social studies programs could be greatly enriched, especially for the capable pupil, by directing greater attention to objectives which fall into this category—translation, interpretation, and extrapolation.

The third category is called *Application*. It means essentially that the pupil is able to use what he learns; that he can bring his knowledge to bear upon the solution of problems. Numerous authors have called attention to the need for pupils to apply what they learn. Many interesting and stimulating experiences for children have resulted in situations where imaginative teachers have provided opportunities for children to apply what they have learned to life about them. Applications of learning may be represented by some classroom activity such as dramatic play, a construction, or a report given to the class; or they may include a service project in conservation, school government, or community service. Applications need not manifest themselves in overt behavior; applications may be made wholly at the intellectual level. The pupil may, for example, apply and use knowledge previously gained in thinking creatively about new problems or situations. Perhaps most of the applications which are made are of the intellectual type.

Categories four and five—*Analysis* and *Synthesis*—represent high-order intellectual processes. In the case of *Analysis*, the pupil must delve into the subject to a sufficient depth to perceive its component elements, relationships, or organizational principles. Such procedure enhances the development of concepts in depth, for the pupil is led to ever finer discriminations in what is relevant and what is irrelevant with reference to topics under study. Problems in the social studies oftentimes seem deceptively simple because an inadequate analysis is made of factors relating to them. It is only when one explores a problem in depth and makes a careful analysis of fundamental elements, relationships, or organizational principles that he appreciates the complexity of it. Many elementary pupils are ready for the stimulation which such analyses could provide.

While *Analysis* calls for the isolation of relevant data, *Synthesis* requires the bringing together of related elements and reorganizing them into new cognitive structures. In the *Taxonomy*, *Synthesis* is further described as "the production of a plan or proposed set of operations," or the "derivation of a set of abstract relations." For elementary social studies, *Synthesis* can be represented by the reporting of research which a pupil has conducted over a period of time. The reporting of work done on "Pupil Specialties" would be a case in point. Bright pupils find this to be an especially challenging and interesting learning experience. A capable fifth- or sixth-grade child can, through accumulated research, present an amazingly well prepared synthesis if he has proper guidance from his teacher.

The final category—*Evaluation*—concerns itself with judgments. It assumes a considerable knowledge of the topic on the part of the pupil in order to make such judgments. To some extent it demands the use of learnings which are represented in all of the other categories. Judgments, according to the *Taxonomy*, are of two types—those based on internal evidence and those based on external criteria. Internal evidence would constitute evaluation made on the basis of clearly recognized standards with respect to internal consistency, organization, or structure. For example, a pupil looks at a map and must decide whether or not it is a correct and honest representation—rivers cannot be shown to run toward higher elevations; cities cannot be placed across rivers; colors used on the map must be consistent with those in the key, and so on. Charts, graphic material, or written reports should not contain conflicting data. A mural showing the life of the Woodland Indians should not show an Indian weaving a Navajo blanket. Judgments of this type are not especially difficult to make when one is thoroughly familiar with the material and knows what standards to apply. Judgments in terms of external criteria probably involve a level of criticism too complex and much too involved to be handled by elementary-school-age children.

It is apparent that the *Taxonomy* has much to recommend its use as a model in planning for differentiated instruction in elementary social studies. The teacher would have to become thoroughly familiar with it and with the types of objectives which might be placed in each of the categories. Perhaps the teacher would find it helpful to prepare the various categories in chart form, and in planning a unit, list possible objectives in the various categories. Use of the *Taxonomy* may also result in objectives stated more clearly in behavioral terms, as has been suggested by some authors.[2] Thus, with a knowledge of the capabilities of individual members of his class, the teacher could move pupils in the direction of those objectives which are best suited to their abilities. This would insure that all categories had been considered and that ideas would be dealt with at varying levels of difficulty.

Thus as the teacher plans his unit, he makes a careful analysis of the topic to be studied. Then he identifies specific, attainable objectives which could be classified in several categories included in the *Taxonomy*. In accordance with this knowledge and a knowledge of the pupil he teaches, he plans appropriate learning activities which make the attainment of those objectives possible. Combining this procedure with other generally accepted practices for individualizing instruction, the teacher would present his class with a highly diversified and stimulating attack on the study of problems in the elementary social studies. Certainly the *Taxonomy* deserves further investigation not only in terms of its usefulness in curriculum improvement but also as a guide to the teacher in differentiating instruction.

---

[2] Dale P. Scannell and Walter R. Stellwagen. "Teaching and Testing for Degrees of Understanding." *California Journal for Instructional Improvement* 3:1; 13. March 1960.

Value Teaching in the Middle and Upper Grades: A Rationale for Teaching But Not Transmitting Values

by MELVIN EZER

Professor and Chairman of Elementary Education
University of Bridgeport

"ALL EDUCATION, we may assume, is aimed at the transmission of values of our culture, and the development of socially acceptable attitudes [and behavior] towards problems and conflicts."[1]

"Rubbish! Not only rubbish, but . . . repulsive," exclaims Michael Scriven.[2] The reason for Scriven's rejection of this educational objective is that in the name of morality, immoral behavior is advocated. The author of this paper is in agreement with Scriven's position as it relates to value teaching in the middle and upper grades of the elementary school, and an alternative proposal for teaching values in these grades will be presented.

If there is concern with ethics, as expressed in the opening quote, then a fundamental proposition in ethics asserts that the individual has the right to determine for himself what is right or wrong concerning the basic issues of conduct. It then becomes the responsibility if not the duty of the public schools in a democratic society to inform the pupil of the alternatives available to him, to describe the modes and consequences of his behavior, and to teach him the skills that are necessary to evaluate these alternatives. The teaching of values does not give the teacher the right to force his solutions on the children he teaches, except in so far as the information given to the children persuades them to accept his views. Underlying this position of value teaching are the assumptions that value disputes can be settled by rational means and that children in the middle and upper grades of the elementary school are capable of making their own value judgments by use of the intellect.[3]

It thus becomes obvious that it is not the teacher's responsibility to tell children what is right or wrong, but rather it is the responsibility of the teacher to raise value questions and to discuss these within the restrictions of evidence, the rules of logic, and the use of reason. The children should be given opportunities to investigate and discuss value questions under the teacher's guidance, and then the children should be allowed to make up their own minds about these vital matters without being unduly influenced by their teachers.[4]

It is at this point that the question of teacher bias is usually raised; that is, if a teacher is already committed to a value position (much in the way this author has particular enthusiasm for his view regarding the teaching of values to children), is it then possible for him to present other points of view in an objective and effective manner? The answer to this query is that children can and perhaps should be taught values by teachers who have taken a position on a particular problem or issue, because it is not only possible but quite probable that many teachers who hold particular views can present other views fully and fairly. In addition, there should be the opportunity for pupils, and supporters of other views, to make their presentations with equal zeal.[5]

Concomitant with the responsibility of presenting various points of view on value questions is the responsibility of the middle and upper grade teacher to teach children to become proficient in such skills as clarifying issues, verifying information on which values are based, and analyzing the logic inherent in the solution of problems. The teaching and attainment of these skills is crucial to the method of presenting values proposed herein.

Let us now take a value question and illustrate the manner in which it can be presented to children utilizing the format that has been suggested. Let us examine the problem presented when a decision regarding the abrogation of free speech is in question,

---

[1] Preston E. James. "Geography." *The Social Studies and the Social Sciences.* Sponsored by the American Council of Learned Societies and the National Council for the Social Studies. New York: Harcourt, Brace & World, Inc., 1962, p. 42.
[2] Michael Scriven. "The Structure of the Social Studies." In G. W. Ford and Lawrence Pugno, editors. *The Structure of Knowledge and the Curriculum.* Chicago: Rand McNally & Company, 1964, p. 101.
[3] *Ibid.*

[4] Nancy W. Bauer, editor. *Revolution and Reaction: The Impact of the New Social Studies.* Bloomfield Hills, Michigan: Cranbrook Press, pp. 75-76.
[5] Scriven, *op. cit.*, p. 102.

Social Education, 1967, Vol.31, pp. 39-41.

a value that is jealously guarded. The problem had arisen in the midst of an explosive situation that occurred in a suburb of Chicago in August, 1966, when tensions resulting from Civil Rights demonstrations were at their highest. George Rockwell, the self-proclaimed leader of the American Nazi movement, applied for permission to schedule a rally and speech in this community. These events could have led to rioting, destruction of property, and even the loss of life. The problem that faced the authorities and that could have been presented to an elementary school class was whether Rockwell should have been prevented from speaking.

An approach that is commonly utilized in this type of problem situation, if it is discussed at all, is for the teacher to ask the children what decision they would make if they were the authorities. In many classrooms the teachers would inform the children what the correct or right decision is or ought to be. Parenthetically, it is highly questionable whether the teacher's solution is more valid than the children's since his view may have no better factual or analytic basis than the children he is teaching. In most instances it is at these junctures that the discussion of the value question ends.

The author has stated previously that all possible solutions should be presented; in this instance, the children's, the teacher's, that of newspaper editorials, radio and television commentators, civic authorities, and so forth. These viewpoints must be examined using the skills and criteria described earlier. Additional questions must be raised and discussed—such questions as the importance of the value of free speech as compared with the value of life and property. What would the consequences be to our society if we abandoned one or both? What would be the logical consequences for other values in our society if we abandoned the right to speak when speaking threatens life or property? Who is to decide and upon what basis when speech threatens life and property? What relief for wrong decisions is available?[6]

Only after these discussions and explorations have taken place should the decisions be made, and then the children should be allowed to provide their own answers and solutions to the problem as individuals. The goal of educational process described above is to have children arrive at value decisions through rational means. It is also the attempt to develop the cognitive skills that are essential in the study of value problems.

Moral reasoning and the moral behavior it indicates should be taught and taught about, if for no other reason than that it is immoral to keep children ignorant of the empirical and logical bases behind the law and institutions which incorporate this country's virtues and permit its vices. But in addition to this intellectual payoff is the practical benefit to a society whose members are skilled in making value judgments. Such a society becomes a moral community offering important benefits to all its members.[7]

Another question that has not yet been answered but that is most important to this discussion is the place and treatment of "basic," "ultimate," or "absolute" values. As teachers and their classes engage in the analysis of values, the problem of "ultimate" values will certainly arise. The argument about the existence of "ultimate" values is not the concern of this paper. It is of little import here, also, because the author has been attempting to demonstrate that the majority of value problems that children will confront in their public school classes can be settled by empirical investigation and logical analysis. The school's responsibility is fairly clear on this issue. It is to have the children use the processes already described to push the value "frontier" as far as possible without worrying about the last "frontier."[8]

Any discussion of value teaching must consider the affective as well as the cognitive realm, because discussions of value questions that only employ the cognitive processes for their solution may become academic exercises for the children, devoid of meaning for their own lives. In the treatment of a value question there should be emotional involvement by the child as well as insight. While as full and complete an understanding as possible of the value problem should be the first order of business and is necessary, it is, however, not sufficient. The discussion of value questions requires that the child see himself in another's position whenever possible. In short, it requires empathy and sympathy on the part of the pupil. All forms of ego-involving activities are most relevant and appropriate in teaching values.

Here again an example that actually occurred will be given in order to portray the interdependence of intellect and emotion in value teaching.

In a fifth grade class discussion concerning equality of rights (a value, by the way, to which this nation is fully committed), the various means of attaining this value by political, religious, ethnic and/or racial groups were considered. Revolution was suggested as a way of achieving equality of rights, thus raising the moral question of the "means-end" relationship. The concept of revolution was examined using Brinton's *Anatomy of Revolution* as the authority.[9] Three revolutions, the American, Cuban, and Orwell's *Animal*

---

[6] Michael Scriven. "Values in the Curriculum." *Social Science Education Consortium Newsletter*, II, No. 1, April 1966, p. 1.

[7] *Ibid.* p. 2.

[8] *Ibid.*, p. 1.

[9] Crane Brinton. *The Anatomy of Revolution*, rev. and exp. New York: Vintage Press, 1965.

Farm[10] were studied in light of the Brinton thesis. At the termination of the study, the children understood the causes of revolution and some might have even resolved the value question regarding the justification if not of revolution, *per se*, then of a particular revolution. However, it is very doubtful if the children had any empathy for revolutionaries attempting to achieve equality of rights. The problem became one of attempting to have the children feel as nearly as possible how people can be moved to revolt. To this end the following situation evolved.

One day shortly following their discussions on revolution, a "new" teacher who was to replace the "regular" teacher was introduced to the class. The "new" teacher then changed existing classroom procedures. The children who had been seated in a semicircular grouping were separated by the "new" teacher into two groups on the basis of eye color. One group was composed of only blue-eyed children, the other group contained other-color-eyed children. Any contact between the two groups was forbidden. Two separate doors for entrance to and exit from the classroom were used, one by the blue-eyed group and one by the other-colored-eye group. Separate toilet facilities, water fountains and lunchroom tables were assigned to the two groups. The "new" teacher informed the blue-eyed children that they were to sit only in the seats at the rear of the school bus when coming to or returning from school. The blue-eyed children were made to feel inferior in other ways because their toilets and drinking fountains were located at a greater distance from the classroom and because their table in the lunchroom was in a less desirable location. Separation of the two groups was reinforced by taking the children to the playground and lunchroom using different doors for both groups and by having children use the different tables while eating their lunches. Complete and total segregation of the blue-eyed group from the rest of the class was accomplished approximately one hour after the "new" teacher had entered the classroom. It was at this point that the "new" teacher left the classroom intimating that he would return again the following day and that the "old" or "regular" teacher would now resume her role. The children reacted immediately after the "new" teacher left the classroom. They demanded that they be allowed to resume their former semi-circular seating arrangement in spite of the warnings that the "new" teacher would return. Several children suggested that they act as a delegation

---

[10] George Orwell. *Animal Farm.* New York: The New American Library Inc., 1946.

An Inquiry-Conceptual Theory of Social Studies Curriculum Planning

by JOHN U. MICHAELIS

IN MOST of the new curriculum projects, steps have been taken to move beyond the mere outlining of a set of topics to be studied. Attention has been given to both conceptual and inquiry approaches to the teaching of significant topics. In some curriculum centers, emphasis has been given to a conceptual approach; others have emphasized an inquiry approach.

What is needed is an inquiry-conceptual approach to the study of significant topics. The best of both inquiry and conceptual approaches should be combined in a program which develops modes and processes of inquiry along with the concepts that are most fruitful in studying dynamic aspects of man's cultural heritage. The modes and processes should be those that may be used in daily life, are useful in social studies instruction, and are consistent with ways of inquiry in the supporting disciplines. The concepts should be those that are most useful as tools in putting modes and processes to work in the study of important settings or topics. Modes and processes should be linked with concepts as students investigate human activities in a variety of settings.

A Model for Interrelating Major Components of the Social Studies Program

The model presented in Chart 1 is designed to show how modes and processes, concepts, and significant settings may be interrelated. This model was developed by a statewide social sciences education committee that believed an inquiry-conceptual approach would be more productive of effective teaching and learning than approaches which had been tried in the past.[1] To the writer's knowledge this is the first program in which the inquiry, conceptual, and topical components have been explicitly interrelated. The guiding principle is to interlink the inquiry and conceptual components and to put them to use in studying selected settings.

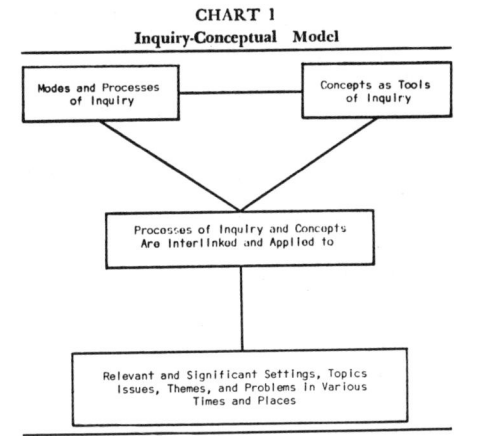

CHART 1
Inquiry-Conceptual Model

```
┌─────────────────────┐         ┌─────────────────────┐
│ Modes and Processes │         │  Concepts as Tools  │
│     of Inquiry      │         │     of Inquiry      │
└──────────┬──────────┘         └──────────┬──────────┘
           └──────────────┬────────────────┘
                          │
           ┌──────────────┴──────────────┐
           │ Processes of Inquiry and    │
           │ Concepts Are Interlinked    │
           │         and Applied to      │
           └──────────────┬──────────────┘
                          │
           ┌──────────────┴──────────────────┐
           │ Relevant and Significant        │
           │ Settings, Topics Issues,        │
           │ Themes, and Problems in Various │
           │ Times and Places                │
           └─────────────────────────────────┘
```

Modes and Processes of Inquiry

A single mode is inadequate for studying the variety of topics and problems included in the social studies. Three highly interrelated modes are needed to deal with the scientific, humanistic, and policy-making (decision-making) sides of the social studies, as shown in Chart 2. First, an *analytic mode* is needed to engage in economic, political, spatial, and social analysis—the scientific and generalizing side of the social studies. Second, an *integrative mode* is needed to bring together the unique and particular aspects of the events, individuals, groups, countries, regions, and other special topics—the humanistic and particularizing side of the social studies. Third, a *policy mode* is needed to make decisions or judgments related to urban, minority, economic, political, and other issues and problems—the decision-making and evaluative side of the social studies.

Processes of inquiry that are used in the various modes include defining, observing, classifying, interpreting, comparing, contrasting, hypothesizing, generalizing, predicting, analyzing, synthesizing, evaluat-

---

[1] John U. Michaelis. *An Overview of the Report of the Statewide Social Sciences Study Committee, K-12 Social Sciences Education Framework.* Sacramento: State Department of Education, 1968.

JOHN U. MICHAELIS *is a Professor in the Department of Education, University of California, Berkeley, California.*

Social Education, January, 1970, Vol.34, pp. 68-71.

ing, inferring, and communicating. The policy mode typically involves defining the problem, identifying relevant values, gathering data, proposing and testing alternatives, and making decisions.

These three modes are widely used in daily life in an untutored and implicit manner. For example, the analytic mode is used to make generalizations about vacations, shopping, clubs, voting, recreation, and other activities as we examine various factors in detail such as cost, value received, procedures, and the like. By examining several cases we can arrive at generalizations of fairly broad applicability. On the other hand, the integrative mode is used when we wish to reconstruct or recreate a particular vacation, shopping trip, club activity, or recreational event. For example, we might bring together (synthesize or integrate) the details that portray the unique and special aspects of the best vacation we ever had. Here the emphasis is on a particular event or set of events rather than on an analytic study that will lead to a broad generalization. We use the policy mode when we want to make a decision or judgment about vacations, shopping, voting, and other activities. For example, we draw ideas from the best and worst vacations (integrative mode) and ponder generalizations about cost and other factors (analytic mode) as we consider alternative plans for a vacation. We assess the alternatives in light of values and try to pick the one that is best.

The three modes may be used in the social studies as attempts are made to promote balanced instruction that will enable students to develop basic inquiry skills. Ideally, a well-designed program should provide opportunities for students to master each mode and to learn the strengths and limitations of each. For example, instructional materials can be selected and teaching strategies can be devised to promote students' competence in using each mode. Units of instruction can be planned and sequenced to provide for cumulative growth. Both disciplinary and interdisciplinary patterns of organization may be used as needed. Evaluation may be planned to assess growth in the three modes that are useful in daily life as well as in disciplined planning.

Scholars on the committee noted above and others consulted by the committee state that these three basic modes are cross-disciplinary, and that they are consistent with modes of inquiry which they use. For example, geographers for years have carried on systematic or topical studies (analytic mode), area or regional studies (integrative mode), and urban planning (policy mode). Similarly, sociological or anthropological analysis may be used to arrive at generalizations about the role of leaders, social interaction, impact of technology, and other factors in group activities (analytic mode). Or, a study may be made of a particular group (minority, tribal, etc.) in order to identify the special characteristics that make the group unique (integrative mode). At other times the policy mode may be used in making plans or decisions related to the resolution of minority problems, community development programs, and the like. Economists and political scientists use the analytic mode as they build models and generalizations related to political and economic systems, the integrative mode as they study a particular system, and the policy mode as they help to set policies related to various public issues and problems.

CHART 2

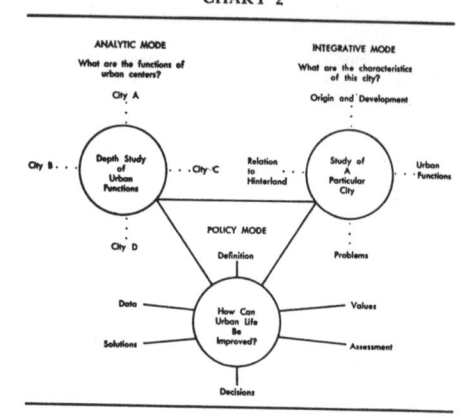

Concepts as Tools of Inquiry

Concepts must not only be learned in an inquiry-conceptual program, they also must be put to use in observing, classifying, generalizing, and other processes. Both analytic (general) and integrative (particular) concepts should be used as needed in a given study or inquiry. General concepts such as role, division of labor, economic systems, processes of social interaction, and methods of social change are illustrative of analytic concepts. Special or particular concepts such as the Loop in Chicago, the Fertile Crescent, Spoils System, Muckrackers, Jacksonian Democracy, and Manifest Destiny are illustrative of integrative concepts. A guiding principle is to select and use those concepts that are most useful in applying processes of inquiry. Concepts should be viewed as tools that guide the use of observation, classification, and other processes.

An Inquiry-Conceptual Curriculum Design

The two examples presented in Charts 3 and 4 are illustrative of one way in which the inquiry, conceptual, and topical components may be brought together. Each is headed by an inquiry question that gives a focus for study. Inquiry processes are identified in each mode so that attention may be given to them as needed. Related concepts that are useful in pursuing the inquiry question are noted. The settings are suggested as good possibilities but may be changed to meet local conditions.

CHART 3
Why Are There Rules for Everyone?

INQUIRY PROCESSES	CONCEPTS
Analytic	Rules, roles
Observation: selective	Family, community, social group
Objects and behavioral patterns	Needs, material wants, scarcity
Direct and mediated	Age and sex statuses, infant
Classification: constructed classes	dependency
In terms of physical properties	Division of labor and of authority
In terms of patterns of behavior	by age and sex statuses
Integrative	Work, Play
Comparison	Need for rules
Similarities of observed events	
with one's own experience	
Policy	
Valuing	

SETTINGS

Our Class   Our Families   Our Neighborhood   Our Community   Community Workers
Other Families   Other Communities

CHART 4
How Do Societies Decide What Is To Be Done and Who Is To Do It?

INQUIRY PROCESSES	CONCEPTS
Analytic	Types of societies: tribal
Observation: selective	Political system
Classification: constructed classes	Political culture
Definition: behavioral	Authority, legitimacy
Contrastive analysis	Political socialization
Communication	Constitution
Generalization	Decision-making
Policy Mode	Interest articulation
Valuing	Interest aggregation
	Rule-making
Others As Needed	Rule application
	Rule adjudication
	Social values

SETTINGS

A Tribal Society   Our School   Peer Groups   Our City   Our State   Other States
          Our Country   Other Countries

A Design for Planning at the Classroom Level

The example which follows is illustrative of how the various components may be brought together in daily instruction planning. A statement of specific objectives is followed by inquiry processes, concepts, and a teaching strategy that brings the inquiry and conceptual components together.

WHERE IS OUR COUNTRY?

Major Understandings

Location of the United States. We live on a certain part of the earth. The name of our part of the earth is the United States.

Objectives

The children should develop the ability to:

Recognize the name "United States of America," and state that it is the name of our country.

Point to the location of the United States, including Alaska, Hawaii and Puerto Rico, on pictures of the earth and on the classroom globe.

State the colors used to show land and water in textbook pictures and on the classroom globe.

Teaching Strategy

Inquiry Processes	Questions and Activities	Data, Concepts Generalizations
	Introduction:	
Observing	Look at the large picture on the bottom of page 5. What does this picture show?	
Interpreting	What does the blue color show? What colors show land? Point to a part that shows water; that shows land.	COLOR SYMBOLS: Blue is used for water, various naturalistic colors for land.
	Development:	
Observing	Something special is marked on this drawing of the earth. What is it?	LINE SYMBOLS: Lines are used on globes to show the borders between countries.
Interpreting	Point to the two white lines that go across part of the land. What is shown between the two white lines? What is the name of our country? Point to this part of our country.	BOUNDARY LINES: The area between the white lines is the largest part of the United States.
Observing, Interpreting	Other places on the earth are part of our country too. What can you see on this picture that marks off another part of our country? Point to that part. What is that part called?	LINE SYMBOL: The white line in the north area marks off the state of Alaska.
Observing, Interpreting	Look at the part that shows an ocean. What do you see there that shows another part of our country? What is that part called?	LINE SYMBOL: Arrows are used to point out specific, small areas. The state of Hawaii is shown in the Pacific Ocean.
	Conclusion:	
Synthesizing	Our country, the United States, is shown in different places. Who can point to all of them to show us our whole country?	LOCATION: States and communities in the United States can be located on the globe.
Classifying	Which part of our country is the largest? Which part has water all around it? Which part is closer to the North Pole? Which parts are away from the largest part of our country?	PARTS OF THE UNITED STATES: Hawaii is surrounded by water, Alaska is to the north. Both of these states are away from the largest part of our country.

This model can be generalized to other topics, processes, and concepts. A guiding principle is to identify processes and concepts that are relevant in each phase of the teaching strategy.

Summing Up:

The preceding discussion describes a way in which the conceptual and inquiry approaches can be unified into a useful instructional model. Such models can make significant contributions to social studies instruction.

Why Inquiry Fails in the Classroom

by MARTIN LAFORSE

MODESTY, common sense and a "decent respect to the opinions of mankind" compel even the marginally reasonable writer on education to shrink from confidently asserting why inquiry fails in the classroom. The over-inflated rhetoric characteristic of many of our contemporary social critics has been commonplace among educational commentators for generations. A sense of our own limitations, therefore, seems to be the best frame of mind in which to approach this topic. Since this article is not founded upon exhaustive scientific research studies based on matched random behavior samples, its main thrust will be historical and philosophical. This writer is convinced that a historic and social sense and a philosophic understanding of inquiry are most pertinent to a clarification of the issues. Accordingly, the question of why inquiry may fail in the classroom is viewed here not so much as a problem of how to improve teaching technique—although that, to be sure, is important—but, rather, as an attempt to clarify our use of words and concepts and identify those forces which make an impact on educational policy and, ultimately, teacher behavior.

The new emphasis on "inquiry" or "discovery" or "inductive" teaching—not so new an idea really—has manifested itself in the midst of the crystallization of powerful historical forces which combine to make ours one of the great watershed periods in the history of this species. We may be in the midst of the transition from civilization to post-civilization as Kenneth Boulding has persuasively argued. In view of this kind of transcendent outlook, the inquiry approach as presently advocated seems to lack a sense of change being undergone and of the fix in which the species finds itself. Judging by the kinds of concerns deemed worthy of the discovery efforts of children, the new advocates are at some remove from where the children are and have a paucity of imagination in forecasting where they might have to go. Their underlying world view is static, still evoking success and achievement in the manner of our Protestant heritage. Not considered is the possible dysfunctionality of the anxiety achievement mode not only for the future but the immediate present.

MARTIN LAFORSE *is an Associate Professor of Education at Ithaca College, Ithaca, New York.*

A Look at the Past

Unfortunately, there is nothing new about this kind of unreflectiveness, and the history of education in America may be viewed, after all, as a series of missed opportunities. The record of educators and social scientists as forecasters and relevant policy planners is not encouraging. What, for example, were our young students "discovering" about the Black experience in America in our schools in 1954? Our traditional school history, for example, not only seems to have left the ideas out, it also omitted phenomena which later, ironically, surprised us by the suddenness of their importance.

An assessment of the outcome of past educational reform movements is small comfort to those of us pondering the impact of the present inquiry mania on the classroom. That Herbart's proposals in American hands hardened into the rigid five step pattern of instruction ought to give us pause. No less relevant is the transformation of John Dewey's formulations by those who romanticized the raw impulse of the child. These dogmatic progressives so sentimentalized the child that Boyd Bode was moved to warn them that progressive education would come to little unless its proponents got their minds off the child long enough to work out a thorough democratic philosophy. Well might we now ponder how absurd became the attempts of some progressives to act on their own slogans. In the pages of the house organ of the Progressive Education Society, for example, children never seemed to "listen" to music or "read" books or "draw" graphs; they were always "experiencing" them.

The glorious and evocative word was "experience," even as the words "inductive" and "discovery" and "inquiry" seem now to adorn all new textbook materials, program packages and pronouncements of state education departments. Despite the shift in language, the beholder sometimes gets the feeling that little of fundamental importance has changed.

If the fate of the so-called "life adjustment" movement is yet another unpromising example from the past, there is a parallel movement to the inquiry enthusiasm that might well require scrutiny. One cannot help suspecting a certain element of dysfunctionality in the current interest in the non-graded elementary school. Advocates of this type of organization tend to exhibit a zeal to fix each child at just the right level of achievement in each and every aspect of his school experience. As a result, they may be engaging in a flurry of measuring which could yet make the non-graded school the most graded educational institution yet conceived.

The saddest aspect of these examples is that they contained much that was sound and held out great promise when first proposed. As a matter of fact, the contemporary discovery approach seems to embody an elaboration of John Dewey's original notions, which tends to slight his great concern for the vital facts of child development. It is as if process has now overwhelmed person. It is sad to note that a rereading of Dewey's writings of fifty years ago and more moves the reader to the rather puzzling conclusion that little of what he advocated has as yet been tried out in our schools. In the rush to obtain certainty, the discovery advocates may have neglected some essential elements of discovery—suspended judgment, an attitude of searching and a spirit of excitement.

The cultural phenomenon which originally leads us astray and then provokes a defensive attitude which can preclude reassessment may be the peculiarly American necessity for obtaining premature closure and hard feedback. Inside the classroom and out we Americans have not been noted for tolerance of ambiguity. This characteristic may help to explain the fads which periodically sweep our educational establishment in response to environmental pressures. Our high demand for answers is reinforced by the efforts of vested interests which present certain commercial programs to teachers and administrators as the answer to their social and political needs to appear innovative.

It sometimes seems that it is almost a sin in our culture to suspend judgment, to admit that we are not really sure in any given instance. Teaching is particularly prone to ambiguities. Moreover, it may well be that we are only in the very early stages of attaining some reliable understandings of the outcomes of the teaching act. For many years to come adequate feedback may be difficult to come by and it is this kind of indeterminacy, particularly in a product-oriented society, that frustrates the human being.

It is in this context that the impact of the work of people like Skinner and Bruner on the education of teachers becomes understandable. Rather than promoting a devotion to open-mindedness, the work of these behavioral scientists and others often has been seized upon in an effort to obtain positive classroom procedural justification. The hard science emphasis in social and behavioral science tends to dominate at this juncture, aided by hard research dollars from the United States Office of Education. No one would deny that the work of these men has a place in the preparation of teachers. Perhaps, we ought to approach their findings, however, in a spirit of inquiry rather than as dissemination of a gospel. Catching the tides in the affairs of men can be dangerous for the work of seminal thinkers as the fate of the ideas of Dewey and Herbart attests. Well might the original thinker exclaim, "God save me from my disciples!" And well might the teacher-in-training or in service agree as he faces the disciples. The current proliferation rate of ideas makes it imperative that we adopt an attitude of sensible skepticism before we find ourselves overwhelmed by fixed dogmas.

The Values of Freedom of Inquiry

The vision of the teacher as heroic figure may be relevant to genuine inquiry. For to take inquiry seriously, he and his pupils must examine ideas in the classroom including the teacher's and those of his pupils and their parents. Even in elementary grades this can raise the issue of academic freedom. Examining issues that people may care something about is, like democracy itself, a risky business. Yet, teachers on the firing line probably will have to face the consequences. For inquiry must have the freedom to move explorations in directions which may produce unpredictable outcomes. Can teachers construct a hospitable environment in which to function? They may be the only ones who can, and in so doing they have to instruct a reluctant community in the values of free inquiry, if that is demanded. However, they cannot do this unless they themselves understand these values and internalize them. Moreover, the young people with whom the teacher interacts probably have to share in these decisions increasingly as they progress through school. As if this were not enough, there is still that uncertainty of outcome to contend with, an uncertainty which an inquiry approach will probably only exacerbate. Consequently, the teacher may have to learn to live without the kinds of visible returns on efforts which lend meaning to the lives of salesmen, engineers, electricians, micro-biologists, and the stray published poet.

However, rather than viewing this as a lamentable situation, we could see unusual opportunity in it. We might even decide to depart from the humorless and pedestrian discovery materials now flooding the education market. For example, we could put affect first, deciding that pupil self-involvement and excitement ought to be our chief concern. We might even start by admitting that what we mainly know about the teaching act itself is that it can be enjoyable, exciting and compelling and that discovery may be relevant to this. However, the old social studies dominated so long by narrative history seems now about to be replaced by a concept of discovery which almost by design kills off pupil initiatives which generate excitement. Well might we recall how John Dewey, years ago, wondered why children were so full of questions outside of school and so silent within. The problem with many pre-packaged materials is that they abstract out the burning cares of youth while failing to generate new concerns. While they may simplify the task of the teacher, these materials and an excessively mechanical conception of inquiry can reduce the whole procedure to a ritual.

In summary, what I am suggesting is that we teachers ought to view the programs of the exponents of inquiry as a fit subject for discovery. We need to understand the social, historical and economic movements which propel us toward discovery methodology. We ought to be self-aware and socially aware. Teachers must have a philosophy of society, a sense of where the action and the concerns are, a chance to prepare carefully and back off, a sensitivity to where the children are burning and a cautious effort to help them find the flame, a due regard to the growing processes in the child, a perception of the values which have propelled us in the past and an assessment of their appropriateness in the future life of our children. This list is not exhaustive, but its realization may be exhausting. Perhaps, what we can best do is to resist the tide—as tide, and skepticism and a touch of irony might help. After all the fuss and fume, the notion of induction is not new. After all there once was a fellow named Francis Bacon, and it was he who formulated four reasons for human error. The last of these he called the "Idols of the theater," which, he noted, were those fads and fashions of the time which can lead us into error.

Inquiry:
Does It Teach How or What to Think?

by GARY A. MANSON AND ELMER D. WILLIAMS

NUMBERS of social studies educators, including classroom teachers, curriculum developers and teacher educators, have come to regard inquiry as both a powerful means of instruction and an important competency to be learned by pupils.[1] Such acceptance of inquiry has been a reaction to the tremendous proliferation of knowledge—its sheer quantity rendering transmission to children virtually impossible—and a conviction that investigation-oriented learning is more durable. The advocates of inquiry maintain that existing curricula and instructional practices have overemphasized information, lecture, and memory while neglecting the key ideas, investigative methodologies, and thinking skills requisite to understanding the social sciences and resolving social problems. Although such views are neither wholly accurate reflections of the current status of knowledge nor the events occurring in many social studies classrooms, it is fair to say that much social studies instruction does not adequately prepare students to cope with knowledge explosions, to direct technological revolutions, and to participate in cultural transformations. It is out of this context that a strong case for inquiry has been constructed.

The search for a capsule definition of inquiry is, and will continue to be, futile; the nature of the word itself suggests continual redefining. Some evidence for this proposition was provided at a recent conference of social studies educators[2] at which a group of inquiry's most responsible proponents was unable to establish a mutually acceptable meaning for the term. There is, nevertheless, widespread consensus that if inquiry were placed on a continuum of teaching methods ranging from expository-didactic to hypothetical-heuristic, it would certainly approximate the latter. If, on the other hand, inquiry is taken to imply intellectual activity by learners, then seeking and transforming knowledge is certainly more appropriate than accepting and reproducing it.

Instruction based on the pupil as a knowledge seeker is generally posed as the antithesis of expository teaching in which the learner is to be a knowledge recipient. Learning may occur in either situation, but proponents of inquiry maintain that the nature of the learning is likely to differ. This is to be expected since the purposes for which the methods were designed are quite different. Exposition may be better suited to transmitting knowledge while investigation may be more effective in developing thinking; however, the paucity of research does not permit a final conclusion about such a claim. What can be asserted is that learning resulting from expository teaching need not be meaningless, and that learning resulting from inquiry teaching need not be meaningful. Lecture is not inherently bad nor is inquiry necessarily good. "Problem solving can be just as deadening, just as formalistic, just as mechanical, just as passive, and just as rote as the worst form of exposition."[3] The instructional format should not be mistaken as adequate assurance of desirable learning.

Unfortunately, basic points of agreement concerning what inquiry is and is not are often obscured by the use of terms such as problem solving, the scientific method, techniques of the scholar, reflective thinking and discovery in a manner suggesting they are synonymous. These are not completely interchangeable concepts; some refer to teaching methods while others relate to intellectual processes. In fact, a problem central to the issues surrounding the meaning and implications of inquiry lies in a failure to distinguish ways in which a person learns from ways in which one individual causes another to learn. It is

---

[1] Bernice Goldmark, *Social Studies: A Method of Inquiry.* Belmont, California: Wadsworth Publishing Company, Inc., 1968; H. Millard Clements, William R. Fielder, and B. Robert Tabachnick, *Social Study: Inquiry in Elementary Classrooms.* Indianapolis: The Bobbs-Merrill Company, 1966; Byron Massialas and Benjamin Cox, *Inquiry in Social Studies.* New York: McGraw-Hill, Book Company, 1966.

[2] The 48th Annual Convention of the National Council for the Social Studies at Washington, D.C., November 25 to 30, 1968.

GARY A. MANSON *and* ELMER D. WILLIAMS *are Predoctoral Lecturers in the College of Education, University of Washington, Seattle.*

[3] J. P. Guilford, *The Nature of Intelligence.* New York: McGraw-Hill Book Company, 1967.

Social Education, January, 1970, Vol.34, pp. 78-81.

this distinction between inquiry as intellectual activity of the pupil, as it is inferred from what the pupil does, and inquiry as instructional conditions created by the teacher that provides the basis for the remainder of this article.

Inquiry and Student Responses

To investigate, to analyze, to validate, to reflect and to solve requires the generation of additional information beyond that which is given. During an inquiry session, for instance, a class may be confronted with situations incongruent with their previous experiences, e.g. agriculture without machines; eras without wars; families without fathers. In resolving such incongruities, the student is expected to ask questions, to formulate hypotheses, to search for additional data, to draw inferences and to reach tentative conclusions. But the amount and kind of responses produced by the student involves more than sheer ability to go beyond what is given. His statements and queries are also influenced by an interpretation of the learning task and a perception of the teacher's purposes, two critical variables often overlooked in the design and conduct of inquiry.

From the teacher's point of view, confrontations with problematic situations entail one of two basic instructional designs: *convergent* or *divergent*. A convergent model prevails when the quantity, kind and structure of information given the pupil are sufficient to determine his response. In other words, there is only one legitimate answer to the problem, and the relevant data is organized to guide the learner to the answer, the procedure to be used is clearly implied or even stated, and the task of the learner is to arrive at that answer. Programmed learning and the game "Twenty Questions" usually follow convergent formats. A divergent model prevails when information content and organization, while influencing student responses, permit and indeed encourage a range of legitimate alternatives. Multiple-answer questions, remote association tasks, and problem finding are usually of divergent quality. The differences between divergent and convergent tasks may be summarized thusly: "In the former case, restrictions are few; in the latter there are many. In the former, the search is broad; in the latter, it is narrow. In the former, output is in quantity; in the latter, it is limited. In the former, criteria for success are vague and somewhat lax and may, indeed, stress variety and quantity; in the latter, criteria are sharper, more rigorous

---

[4] *Ibid.*, pages 214-215.

and demanding.... The information produced (by the student) is more or less fitting in light of the search model."[4]

From the student's point of view, an inquiry task can be perceived as applying a known procedure in order to resolve an imposed problem with the objective of arriving at an answer already known to the teacher. Such a perception, while it may be quite accurate, should not be expected to contribute to intellectual flexibility, fluency, and originality, characteristics of much scholarly investigation. Inquiry, however, may also be perceived by the student as devising a means to resolve a discovered problem with the objective of arriving at one of several "correct" answers. In such a situation, a student is more willing to utilize hypotheses that deviate from the norm, information that initially appears to others as irrelevant, and solutions that are innovative, or at least so they seem to him.

It should not be assumed that the divergent model is to be preferred in all cases, since competency in convergent problem solving is also a legitimate instructional objective. While it is probably true that convergency pervades most learning, and therefore may suggest greater efforts in direction of divergency, it is more important that the teacher first become aware of the differences between the two and then select the model suitable to his objective.

Inquiry Teaching in the Convergent Model

The instructional conditions contributing to learning are largely determined by the classroom teacher. In the process of inquiry he may select and present the problems, provide the bulk of the resources utilized during the investigation, and respond to the ideas and questions of the pupils. During the process of pupil-teacher interaction, the instructor influences the kind and amount of thinking that his pupils display; that is, the instruction may lead to few or many ideas being forwarded and, in turn, may develop either convergent or divergent thinking strategies.

In the convergent model, the inquiry task is chosen and organized by the teacher. Pupils are expected to recall information or to seek additional data before posing answers or hypotheses. In all likelihood, the teacher has thought through the problem and anticipated possible student responses. He also knows which one of these responses is conventionally accepted, either by the populace at large or by social scientists. This becomes the answer that he tends to accept even though pupils may be able to substantiate, at least partially, other alternatives. Unanticipated or unusual pupil responses are usually acknowledged but quickly dismissed.

To illustrate use of a convergent inquiry model, consider the case of an elementary school class involved in a study of today's modern shopping centers. Derived from his own observations and reading, the teacher designs an inquiry task requiring pupils to determine the shopping center plan that will create maximum customer flow throughout the center. Perhaps this teacher's experience is limited to those shopping centers having the major department stores located in the center of the development acting as "traffic generators." Centralized placement of large stores, in this case, is the principal variable in customer movement. Should additional investigation suggest this same spatial arrangement, he may believe that it constitutes "the best solution," and that his pupils, through investigation and careful thinking, should arrive at this solution and only this solution.

Having been presented with the task, the pupils call upon their previous experiences with shopping centers and seek further information through observation, reading, or questioning. This data serves to direct student responses to the problem and to filter out inappropriate or unrealistic proposals. For example, if a pupil knows that a large number of customers frequent a center during peak hours, that centers are intended to concentrate business activity, or that the construction of a center requires huge outlays of capital, then he is less likely to propose moving the buildings to the people as a means of maximizing customer flow. While it may represent a creative effort, such a proposal is neither logical nor supported by the data. Legitimate criteria for a problem's solution is required in both the convergent and divergent models.

During the period of student inquiry the teacher interacts with the pupils by organizing research activities, providing information and focusing individual efforts on the task. If the convergent model prevails, the teacher's verbal as well as nonverbal behavior, deliberately or not, are employed to guide pupil efforts toward "the best answer." Reinforcement strategies are used by the teacher to support desired responses and to eliminate the undesired. The student soon perceives this intention and will structure his thinking to "match" that of the teacher or refrain from responding. This perception leads the student to believe that there is one correct answer; thus "reasonable" alternatives may not be pursued. In effect, the teacher serves as a filter or criterion for the student's proposed solution(s) in a manner similar to reason and information. While the pupil can accept reason and data as appropriate tests for his ideas, he may find it difficult to understand the teacher's seemingly arbitrary rejection of an answer he believes to be fairly well substantiated.

Inquiry Teaching in the Divergent Model

Inquiry as an instructional process may also facilitate the generation of divergent thinking, the situation where the desired behavior of pupils is production of a number of verifiable and defensible alternatives rather than one "best" answer. Although the criteria of knowledge and reason must still be fulfilled, the approach now is one of allowing for pupil responses that might be regarded as deviant or irrelevant in the convergent model.

How does the divergent model differ from that previously presented? The teacher's personal experience with shopping centers could point out layouts that do not place the traffic generators in the center of the complex. He may have seen successful shopping centers that positioned the large department stores at opposite ends of the center, and as customers walked from end to end for comparative shopping purposes they would be passing the multitude of establishments situated between these large business "magnets." Or, while preparing the unit of study, the teacher may encounter similar information leading him to the realization that various spatial arrangements exist and persist. The implication of these statements is clear; if the teacher does not have experience with numerous alternatives, and if his resource material does not adequately represent the range of reasonable choices, distortion, error and unwarranted convergent-type answers are equally likely outcomes.

As the teacher employs the divergent form of inquiry, his objective is neither arriving at "one" answer agreed upon by all nor the mastery of a prescribed procedure for investigating and solving. Instead, he is more concerned with the process of delineating an entire range of proposals meeting the criteria established for legitimate responses: "Does the data warrant the proposal?" and "Is the proposal reasonable?". He anticipates, desires, and supports a variety of viewpoints. His behavior, both verbal and nonverbal, communicates his wish to engage them in the process of determining and justifying a variety of alternatives. Although the teacher may have anticipated a number of pupil responses, he recognizes the possibility of more than one being correct. He is receptive to those answers that he did not anticipate and provides pupils with the opportunity to explain the reasoning that led to them. While the criteria of knowledge and reason continue, the preferences and preconceptions of the teacher no longer serve as a barrier or filter for pupil thinking.

Experience with divergent inquiry may be expected to influence the pupil's perception of his responsibility as a learner and reinforces those types of cognitive behavior that result in multiple and less conventional responses. The learner understands that his task is not the reproduction of known information but rather is the generation and verification of propositions. The teacher becomes less concerned with correctness and more concerned with the degree of appropriateness; in divergent inquiry truth is relative. If, on the other hand, the goal of the teacher is transmission of knowledge that the students are to accept whether that knowledge be factual or conceptual, then divergent inquiry may not be the most efficient or the most effective mode of instruction.

Summary. Perhaps the most fitting way to summarize is to pose some questions suggested by this discussion:

1. Is inquiry the appropriate term when the person structuring the learning task knows the answer and delineates the procedure in such a way so that only this answer can be "discovered" by the learner?
2. Can the teacher provide for divergent inquiry and at the same time insure the mastery of facts, concepts, and generalizations?
3. Does training in the convergent model of inquiry have a deleterious effect on subsequent tasks requiring divergent responses?
4. Is inquiry simply a new means of teaching students "what to think"?

SOCIAL STUDIES AND THE SOCIAL SCIENCES

The Interdisciplinary Approach to Teaching Social Studies

by STUART C. MILLER

THE central position of history in the high school social studies curriculum is now being seriously challenged by the historian's academic cousins in the social sciences. Their silence, or relative silence, until recently has been due, in part, to the theory that history offered the best synthesis for all of the social sciences. The very nature of history makes it easier to fuse useful concepts and theories from many fields as the story of the development of man and society is unfolded. Since all of the social sciences could not be taught in the high school, this seemed to be the best compromise. Today, few social scientists believe that any real fusion takes place in the geography and history courses which make up the bulk of the curriculum. Unlike many of the popular critics of this curriculum, they refuse to take the title of a course at face value. They know that upon closer examination a course entitled "Understanding Current Problems in Our Country" is apt to be a standard course in American history. My own experience indicates that Arthur Bestor's "social stew" exists more often in curriculum theory than in the classroom.

But the rebellion has gone far beyond this. These social scientists no longer want any fusion, but separate courses in their own disciplines. Too often the fusion of economics, the economist argues, is at best superficial, and taught by someone illiterate in this discipline. More often than not it is economic history and not economics. Inflation, for example, may be dutifully mentioned at the appropriate time in the history of the Western world, but rarely is any attempt made to conceptualize it from the point of view of the economist, illustrating the relationship between the economic variables involved. It is no wonder that "inflation" has been used so effectively to frighten voters into supporting a program that virtually starves the public sector. Generations of Americans have been taught that inflation is an unmitigated evil instead of understanding that a certain amount of it is probably a necessary evil in an expanding economy. There are many such examples in economics. The Federal Reserve System is taught frequently by having the students memorize districts and how many directors there are for each Federal Reserve Bank, etc., without once mentioning its relationship to the need for an elastic supply of money. When the latter is pointed out, too often the mechanics of controlling bank credit and the amount of money in circulation is erroneously presented, attributing control to its discount rate rather than its open market operations. Budgets may be mentioned when the history teacher gets to the New Deal, or in discussing current events, but rarely is fiscal policy discussed as a possible stimulant for economic growth. As a result, the economist is demanding, and getting, a separate course on the high school level, and a greater share in the training of high school teachers.

The behaviorists, anthropologists, sociologists, and social psychologists have even gone beyond simply a demand for a separate course. They often argue that history is not a social science at all and does not offer the best possible synthesis for these disciplines. Professor Chilcott has put in a bid for anthropology, and Professor Donald Oliver for social psychology to displace history in this role. Their disciplines, it is argued, would not ignore history but would focus on contemporary society, and more efficiently achieve that often stated goal in teaching social studies: to develop an understanding of the political, economic, and social world in which we live.[1]

The fears and complaints of these social scientists are not without justification. The teacher of social studies receives the bulk of his training from historians who frequently manifest a kind of siege mentality in rejecting any kind of influence from the behavioral sciences. Thus it is not simply ignorance of these disciplines when a teacher refuses the aid of any of their analytical tools, but a strong bias against such "sociological jargon." If the curriculum for training teachers requires some exposure to them, the historian tells the student to equate it with their education courses as utter nonsense, and certainly to leave it outside of their history classrooms. Per-

---

STUART C. MILLER, *an assistant professor of Social Science at San Francisco State College, delivered this address at the 43rd Annual Meeting of the National Council for the Social Studies held in Los Angeles last November.*

[1] J. H. Chilcott. "A Proposal for the Unification of Secondary School Courses Through Anthropology." *Clearing House* 36:391; 1962; Donald Oliver. "The Selection of Content in the Social Studies." *Harvard Educational Review* 27:294-301; 1957.

Social Education, April, 1964, vol.28, pp. 195-198.

naps, some of the very exciting history being written using behavioral concepts by such traditionally trained historians as David Potter and Lee Benson will alter this in the future.

The teacher of social studies should take a second look at the possibilities of an interdisciplinary approach to history. Actually he fuses concepts given to him by the geographer and political scientist all the time. He would consider this a legitimate part of history. But it might be that the behavioral sciences can offer him concepts and theories which will enable him to organize and explain historical data more efficiently. History courses in grades 10 and 11 already encompass more material than can possibly be covered with any meaning in a single year. The teacher frequently presents huge doses of factual and descriptive material, more closely resembling antiquarianism than history, simply because he does not know how to conceptualize the material. A model like W. W. Rostow's stages of economic growth could provide him with a useful conceptual scheme upon which to hang his facts and show important relationships between political, economic, and social variables. Or the theory of "status politics" may be worth the time needed to develop it in class if it affords a clearer explanation of the behavior of the abolitionists, progressives, and McCarthyites. Historians such as David Donald and Richard Hofstadter have, in fact, used this last concept to interpret these movements.

In teaching a high school history course it behooves the teacher to examine the different ways in which anthropologists and sociologists have conceptualized social change. As an example, let us look at one possibility. We often hear of the dichotomy between "heroes" and "social forces" in explaining change. But these social forces are rarely spelled out in the classroom. They remain vague and almost mystic to the student. Max Rafferty's recent lamentation over the disappearance of the hero from the classroom has little relationship to reality.[2] True, Nathan Hale and John Paul Jones may be missing, but that is only because we have so much more history to cover; and other types of heroes—industrial, technical, and political ones—are deemed more important. It is not unusual for even bright students to arrive at college under the impression that Andrew Jackson brought about mass democracy, T. R. broke the trusts, and F.D.R. was the cause of the New Deal.

How can the behaviorists help us to get across a more realistic view of social change? For one thing, they are more interested in social forces than individuals and spell out the important sources of change. Generally they are divided into six categories: Technological change, population change (size, migration, and distribution), changes in natural resources, changes in neighboring communities, natural occurrences, and lastly, ideas. The last category is seriously debated by some who view ideas more as a rationale for change already occurring than as a source of change. These forces first affect our value system which leads to institutional change, the behaviorist contends. The teacher might justifiably ask which of the myriad definitions of social values and social institutions he should use. Certainly a study of these definitions leads to a good deal of semantic confusion. My advice would be to use the one best understood by himself, and best suited for classroom use. I would define social values as an emotionally charged preferential list of cultural products, standards or ideas which the people of a society prize not only for themselves, but for the group and the descendants of that group. These products and patterns of behavior and belief have importance in themselves over and beyond their practical utility; e.g., Christianity, individualism, democracy, Shakespeare, the automobile. Social institutions I would define as formal groups engaged in behavior directed at meeting the basic needs of man or society. Putting across these concepts requires illustration by the teacher, but their utility in a history course may be worth the time invested.

Armed with such a conceptual model of social change, the teacher can efficiently explain a good deal about both the past and the present. It can be introduced at almost any point and used again in later units. The two broad areas through which it cuts most efficiently in American history are Westward expansion and industrialization. The student can more readily visualize how values would undergo change as a result of migration, rapidly expanding economic opportunity, and adaptation to new conditions. For example, the values associated with egalitarianism, individualism, mass democracy and social mobility can be explained in terms of people migrating ahead of many of their social institutions. The lack of occupational specialization, one of the key determinants of social stratification, made equality a reality to begin with along the frontier. Since these pioneers had to serve as lawyers, judges, doctors, and preachers at one time or another, they were less in awe of the authentic professional with traditional training once he did arrive. The potential abundance and wealth of the West enhanced the value placed upon the self-made man and again lessened the esteem of those upper classes of inherited wealth. There is no end to the available travel books and diaries to illustrate this in the classroom. Reverend Bayard Rush Hall, a Union and Princeton graduate who went out to the Iowa territory, quoted one Westerner who paused outside of his house to

---

[2] Max Rafferty. "What's Happened to Patriotism?" *Readers Digest*. October 1961.

exclaim to a friend: "Well thats whar thet grammur man lives that larns 'em latin and grandlike things. Allow we'll oust him yet." Hall also quoted a circuit rider's sermon to illustrate his resentment of the presence of a formally trained minister in the territory:

> Yes, bless the Lord, I am a poor humble man—and I don't know a single letter in the ABC's, and couldn't read a chapter in the Bible no how you could fix it, bless the Lord! I jest preach like old Peter and Pall by the Speret. Yes, we don't ax pay in cash nor trade neither for the Gospel, and aren't no hirelings like them high-flowered college larned sheepskins.

De Tocqueville said a good deal about the American's predilection for equality, even at the expense of freedom if necessary.[3] This insight can help to explain both the populists and the McCarthyites. What better way to explain the Wisconsin Senator's reckless attacks upon the very pillars of our society, such symbols of authority and inequality as *The New York Times*, Harvard, Yale, and Princeton, the National Council of Churches, and the State Department, or his preoccupation with traitors who were born with a silver spoon in their mouths?[4] There was more to McCarthyism than this, to be sure. "Status politics," ethnic considerations (German and Irish) and isolationism all help to explain this phenomenon, but the strong egalitarian motive in our society can also help to account for it.

What institutional change resulted from this alteration in values associated with the frontier? Well, the more democratic manner in which presidential candidates were nominated and elected, the spoils system and log cabin campaigns all reflect these new values. Rather than the popular conception of Jackson bringing this about, it was due to social forces of which Jackson took advantage. He was a backcountry aristocrat, a "nabob" in Tennessee who fought the democratic forces of Grundy and Carroll, and a Mason as was Van Buren, who originally opposed the nominating conventions initiated by the Anti-Masonic party, the real party of egalitarianism. No period in our history, perhaps, better illustrates that the "hero" cannot alter these forces, but only use them more efficiently than can others.

There were other important institutional changes: land grant colleges with an emphasis upon practical subjects; frontier revivalism and the creation of new sects around personalities such as William Miller and John Smith; the breakdown of the authoritarian structure of the family. Perhaps the most important result was our inability to nominate and elect a really strong President after Jackson until the twentieth century with the lone exception of Lincoln, who could be considered almost an accident.

One important result of such an approach is that it breaks down the dichotomy between Western migration and industrialization. The values of the frontiersman were remarkably similar to those of the early industrialist. The former we forget bought land for speculation, too, and behaved as a good capitalist. In fact, one could view the industrialist as simply another type of pioneer, and industrialization as an economic frontier. If we view both as a social process, we can salvage some of the Turner thesis.[5] Of course, the student has to understand that the results are only intelligible if he keeps in mind the values brought to the frontier: the democratic beliefs of the radicals in the Revolution which, in turn, can be traced to seventeenth-century England, the Puritan emphasis upon an emotional experience of conversion, and the "Protestant ethic."

This conceptualization of change can constantly be referred to in later units. The student should be asked to analyze later changes in terms of these traditional sources of change. In looking at the New Deal, he should be able to see its relationship to technological changes known as the industrial revolution and accompanying migration to urban centers, and to visualize how these social forces would alter values and lead to institutionalized change. The less obvious and less concrete changes brought about by industrialization are too often overlooked in the classroom. The student should be made aware of what migration into the city meant in terms of total dependency upon wages; lack of personal satisfaction and identification working on an assembly line; effect of the premium placed upon physical space; the transition of the family from a producing unit to a consuming one. I have witnessed lessons in high school classrooms on the standardization of goods without a single mention of the concomitant standardization of life itself, or on increased economic specialization without the direction of the students' attention to the fact that this increases the dependency of members of society on each other to satisfy their wants. The booms, crashes, panics and depressions are recorded in the classroom in good chronological order without any consideration of how it must have increased the feeling of insecurity as men faced more abstract, complex economic forces over

---

[3] Alexis de Tocqueville. *Democracy in America.* Vol. II. New York: Vintage Press, 1954. p. 99-103.
[4] Martin Trow. "Small Businessmen, Political Tolerance and Support for McCarthy." *American Journal of Sociology* 64: 279-80; 1958. See also S. M. Lipset. "The Sources of the 'Radical Right,'" in Daniel Bell, editor. *The New American Right.* New York: Criterion Books, 1955. p. 166-219.

[5] See George Wilson Pierson. "The Frontier and American Institutions." *New England Quarterly* 15:224-255; 1942. For an excellent criticism of the Turner thesis and an attempt to salvage it as a migration thesis. See also David Potter. *People of Plenty.* Chicago: University of Chicago Press. Chapter VII.

which they had less control. Taught correctly, the student quickly sees how technological and ecological changes can greatly alter values. The response was a collectivistic one on all levels. That is, the industrialist formed pools and then trusts to mitigate the effect of competition and business cycles. The distributors formed associations and were perhaps, more instrumental than any other group in bringing about railroad regulation and the Interstate Commerce Act. The workers formed unions and the farmers cooperatives. All of these organizations sought government aid, both state and federal, at one time or another. The very density of population in cities would necessitate greater group cooperation in areas such as crime prevention and fire and health controls. All this would have to affect values associated with rugged individualism. With such an understanding, it would be difficult for the student to view the New Deal as a betrayal of Jeffersonian liberalism, or a left wing plot hatched in the economics department at Harvard.

Current events can be analyzed with the same conceptual model. For example, the student could be asked to analyze today's increased Negro militancy in terms of these traditional sources of change. It would be difficult for him to view it as the result of a Yankee or Communist plot. A more fruitful approach would be apparent in the migration of Negroes into cities during the two world wars. In the cities the Negro is less dependent upon the white man than he was as a sharecropper, and even has greater economic power as a consumer due to his higher wages. All this will alter his values. He no longer accepts Uncle-Tomism or displaced aggression against his own, or humor as the only responses to Jim Crow. He is now in a position to demand more, and the timing of this demand at the very moment when we are competing with Soviet Russia for the allegiance of the underdeveloped world inhabited largely by non-Whites sensitive to the racial issue, has put the whites in a position which makes it difficult to refuse him his demands. Lastly, ideas associated with Christianity and democracy have afforded him powerful arguments with which to irritate the conscience of the white man. In other words, traditional sources of change, i.e., migration, effect of neighboring states, and ideas, have altered to a degree the values of both the Negroes and the whites on this issue. With this understanding, the debate, fostered largely by the White Citizens Council, over whether or not Martin Luther King is a card-carrying Communist becomes totally irrelevant.

Medicare may well be "creeping socialism," but the student is made aware that changing values are behind it and not a left wing plot pulling the wool over our eyes. Since 1880 the percentage of people over 65 in our population has increased from 3.4 to 8.1 in 1950.[6] This means that more families support people over 65 whose social security checks hardly begin to cover their medical bills. A few heavy bills from a nursing home will quickly alter their attitudes toward a collective plan which will offer them relief. Increased medical costs are in turn partially due to technological changes in the field of medicine.[7] If they continue to increase at the same rate, it is not inconceivable that our values will change enough to permit some sort of health plan similar to the one in the United Kingdom. If it comes, it cannot be attributed simply to the administration that initiates it, but to social forces now in operation.

This is, of course, only one of the many possibilities in utilizing the approach of the anthropologist and sociologist to social and cultural change. It can provide the teacher with a valuable pedagogical tool permitting him more efficiently to organize a mass of material. It also is a better approach to the period discussed than the usual broad coverage that includes "locofocos," "barnburners," "hunkers," and such, in that it more clearly illustrates cause and effect relationships. Moreover, such a conceptualization avoids the liberal or conservative indoctrination that often takes place in the social studies classroom. The teacher does not have to assign moral values to these events but simply stick to the cause-and-effect relationships, much the same way a teacher of physics would do. It is immaterial whether the teacher approves or disapproves of the current Negro militancy. Given the social forces that have brought it about, there is little we can do beyond slowing down or speeding up the social process by which Negroes are achieving equal status. One can discuss plans to make this transition more orderly and less costly for all concerned,[8] but we cannot prevent it. Lastly, this conceptual model not only provides the student with too much sophistication to swallow a silly conspiracy theory of history and social change,[9] but it also equips him to anticipate change. In other words, such a model may help him to see what Robert Heilbroner calls "the forward edge of history."[10]

---

[6] Warren Thompson. *Population Problems.* New York: McGraw-Hill Book Company, 1953. p. 95.

[7] See *The New Republic.* November 9, 1963. p. 9-12. Almost this entire issue was allocated to an excellent discussion of the problems facing both the doctors and the patients (p. 5-43).

[8] For example, see Morton Grodzins. "The Metropolitan Area as a Racial Problem." In *American Race Relations Today.* Edited by Earl Raab. New York: Doubleday and Company, 1962. p. 85-123. See also Ingle Dederer Gibel. "How Not to Integrate the Schools." *Harper's.* November 1963.

[9] This is not to imply, of course, that the teacher using a strictly disciplinarian approach inculcates such interpretation. But it does suggest that the usual, bland description of the past with little real analysis leaves the student more vulnerable to the plot thesis of either right or left wing variety, depending upon his own political predilections.

[10] Robert Heilbroner. *The Future as History.* New York: Harper and Brothers, 1959. p. 13-58.

The Common Denominator of Cultures
By GEORGE PETER MURDOCK

MOST of anthropological theory has revolved about the interpretation of the similarities and differences between the various cultures of mankind. Cultural differences, perhaps because they are more immediately obvious, have received especially close attention. They have been variously explained in terms of distinct stages of postulated evolutionary series, of allegedly disparate racial endowments, of diverse geographic or economic conditions, of nonrepetitive historical accidents, of endlessly varying social contexts, of unique configurations of like or unlike elements, of divergent personality characteristics created by differential childhood training, and so on. Cross-cultural similarities have received theoretical consideration, in the main, only when they have been confined to a limited number of particular cultures, in other words, when they could be regarded as exceptions in a universe of cultural diversity. Such instances of similarity have been explained in terms of the transplantation of culture through migration, of cultural diffusion through contact and borrowing, of parallel development from similar cultural backgrounds, of convergent development from unlike backgrounds, of the independent burgeoning of hereditary potentialities, or of the allegedly determining influence of like geographical factors. In comparison, universal similarities in culture, the respects in which all known cultures resemble each other, have received relatively little theoretical treatment. It is this subject—the common denominator of cultures—with which the present paper will be exclusively concerned.[1]

Early reports of peoples lacking language or fire, morals or religion, marriage or government, have been proved erroneous in every in-

[1] The views of the author have been significantly influenced by John Dollard, Clellan S. Ford, Clark Hull, Albert G. Keller, Ralph Linton, Bronislaw Malinowski, John Whiting, Earl Zinn, and others of his present and past colleagues of the departments of Anthropology and Sociology and the Institute of Human Relations at Yale University. So great is the personal interdependence in scientific endeavor that he is incapable of isolating those portions of the present contribution which are independently his own from those which he has acquired from others, much less of distributing adequately the credit for the latter. Since he is writing from his post in the naval service he is unable even to cite supporting bibliographical references.

The Science of Man in the World Crisis,
Columbia University Press, Linton Edition,
1945, pp. 123-125.

stance. Nevertheless, even today it is not generally recognized how numerous and diverse are the elements common to all known cultures. The following is a partial list of items, arranged in alphabetical order to emphasize their variety, which occur, so far as the author's knowledge goes, in every culture known to history or ethnography: age-grading, athletic sports, bodily adornment, calendar, cleanliness training, community organization, cooking, coöperative labor, cosmology, courtship, dancing, decorative art, divination, division of labor, dream interpretation, education, eschatology, ethics, ethnobotany, etiquette, faith healing, family, feasting, fire making, folklore, food taboos, funeral rites, games, gestures, gift giving, government, greetings, hair styles, hospitality, housing, hygiene, incest taboos, inheritance rules, joking, kin-groups, kinship nomenclature, language, law, luck superstitions, magic, marriage, mealtimes, medicine, modesty concerning natural functions, mourning, music, mythology, numerals, obstetrics, penal sanctions, personal names, population policy, postnatal care, pregnancy usages, property rights, propitiation of supernatural beings, puberty customs, religious ritual, residence rules, sexual restrictions, soul concepts, status differentiation, surgery, tool making, trade, visiting, weaning, and weather control.

Cross-cultural similarities appear even more far-reaching when individual items in such a list are subjected to further analysis. For example, not only does every culture have a language, but all languages are resolvable into identical kinds of components, such as phonemes or conventional sound units, words or meaningful combinations of phonemes, grammar or standard rules for combining words into sentences. Similarly funeral rites always include expressions of grief, a means of disposing of the corpse, rituals designed to protect the participants from supernatural harm, and the like. When thus analyzed in detail, the resemblances between all cultures are found to be exceedingly numerous.

Rarely if ever, however, do these universal similarities represent identities in specific cultural content. The actual components of any culture are elements of behavior—motor, verbal, or implicit—which are habitual, in the appropriate context, either to all the members of a social group or to those who occupy particular statuses within it. Each such component, whether called a folkway or a cultural trait or item, can be described with precision in terms of the responses of the behaving individuals and of the stimulus situations in which the responses are evoked. Eating rice with chopsticks, tipping the hat to a woman, scalping a slain enemy, and attributing colic to the evil eye are random examples. Any such specifically defined unit of customary behavior may be found in a particular society or in a number of societies which have had sufficient contact to permit acculturative modifications in behavior. It is highly doubtful, however, whether any specific element of behavior has ever attained genuinely universal distribution.

The true universals of culture, then, are not identities in habit, in definable behavior. They are similarities in classification, not in content. They represent categories of historically and behaviorally diverse elements which nevertheless have so much in common that competent observers feel compelled to classify them together. There can be no question, for example, that the actual behavior exhibited in acquiring a spouse, teaching a child, or treating a sick person differs enormously from society to society. Few would hesitate, however, to group such divergent acts under the unifying categories of marriage, education, and medicine. All of the genuinely widespread or universal resemblances between cultures resolve themselves upon analysis into a series of such generally recognized categories. What cultures are found to have in common is a uniform system of classification, not a fund of identical elements. Despite immense diversity in behavioristic detail, all cultures are constructed according to a single fundamental plan—the "universal culture pattern" as Wissler has so aptly termed it.

The essential unanimity with which the universal culture pattern is accepted by competent authorities, irrespective of theoretical divergences on other issues, suggests that it is not a mere artifact of classificatory ingenuity but rests upon some substantial foundation. This basis cannot be sought in history, or geography, or race, or any other factor limited in time or space, since the universal pattern links all known cultures, simple and complex, ancient and modern. It can only be sought, therefore, in the fundamental biological and psychological nature of man and in the universal conditions of human existence.....

An attempt to present a complete analysis of the universal culture pattern, with a full consideration of the factors underlying each category, would far exceed the limits of the present paper. The author's primary purpose has been to indicate the general lines along which such an analysis might be undertaken and to present a few illustrative examples. The principal conclusion has been that the common denominator of cultures is to be sought in the factors governing the acquisition of all habitual behavior, including that which is socially shared. Among these the most important are those which bear directly upon the incidence of reward. To the extent that these conclusions prove valid, one brick will have been added to the scientific edifice of the future, in which anthropological and psychological theory will be united in a broader science of human behavior.

Lawrence Senesh
Purdue University

Organizing a Curriculum Around Social Science Concepts

For years professional associations and social science educators have defined and redefined the objectives of social studies education. Volumes have been written about the behavioral changes, the skill objectives, and the changes in attitudes that social studies education is expected to achieve. Many of the statements emphasize that the purpose of social studies education is indoctrination of values. The National Council for the Social Studies has emphasized for years in its publications that the ultimate goal of education in the social studies is the development of desirable socio-civic behavior and the dedication of youth to the democratic society. Fundamentally, nobody would object to these goals if the students could achieve this behavior through the rational analysis of society. But in most of the statements indoctrination of values is emphasized at the expense of analysis.

The Need for Analytical Thinking

The primary function of the development of analytical thinking is to help our youth understand the structure and the processes of our society. With possession of analytical tools, our youth will be able to understand the dynamic changes of our society and the problems created by science and technology. In the final analysis, the purpose of social science education is the development of problem-solving ability. By acquiring the analytical tools and the skill to apply the tools to the problems, our youth will feel that, as adults, they can participate intelligently in the decisions of a free society. The development of the problem-solving ability will help our young people to gain respect for social sciences as an organized body of

Concepts and Structure in the New Social Science Curricula, Holt, Rinehart & Winston, Morrisett Edition, 1967, pp. 21-38.

knowledge and will motivate them to choose social science as a professional career. This emphasis is neglected in the guidance programs in our schools.

The correct use of analytical tools and the discovery of the ideas underlying the social process require a particular mode of analytical thinking. The development of analytical thinking requires a long process of conditioning. Such conditioning should start in grade one of the primary grades.

The present social studies program does not offer the proper intellectual framework to develop the analytical faculties of our youth. Social studies educators who have tried to identify generalizations for the social studies curriculum have suppressed the unique characteristics of the individual social science disciplines and formulated concepts so general that they are without analytical content. Since social scientists have not yet achieved a unified theory of society, economists, sociologists, political scientists, and anthropologists observe society from different points of view, and their findings have to be superimposed on each other before social change can be understood. Since all the social science disciplines are necessary to explain social phenomena, the fundamental ideas of all the disciplines should be introduced in the school curriculum. Why not in grade one?

Grade Placement of the Social Sciences

Some academicians interested in the social science curriculum have raised the question many times whether social science instruction should not begin with geography and history. In an article, "The Structure of the Social Studies,"[1] Professor Scriven recommends that social science education start with geography and history in grade one. He justifies beginning with history and geography because the generalizations are less "high-falutin' " and nearer to common sense. He would rather introduce a "low-falutin' " approach in the lower grades, hoping that "high-falutin' " understanding will develop later. The history of the social studies curriculum indicates that a curriculum begun as "low-falutin' " will remain "low-falutin'."

Professor Scriven does a disservice to geography and history when he assumes that a geographic or historical phenomenon can be explained meaningfully without the aid of the various social science disciplines. Primary school children study Indians and the colonial period, but since they do not possess the fundamentals of economics, political science, sociology, and anthropology, their learning is trivial. It would make more sense if geography and history were culminating courses in high school. In the intervening years the children could have learned the fundamental ideas of the various social sciences, thereby enriching the geography and history courses.

The Organic Curriculum

A team of social scientists has worked with me during the last two years to outline the fundamental ideas of the various social sciences. This team includes Professor David Easton, Political Science Department, University of Chicago; Professor Robert Perrucci, Sociology Department, Purdue University; Professor Paul Bohannan, Anthropology Department, Northwestern University; and Professor Peter Greco, Geography Department, Syracuse University. These fundamental ideas of the various social sciences represent:

a. a logical system of ideas;
b. the cutting edge of knowledge; and
c. an organization of ideas that can be used at every grade level.

Presenting the structure of knowledge in this way challenges popular curriculum practices based on minimum understandings broken up and parceled for different grade levels.

Our team has been guided by the awareness that we are training children for an age which we don't even foresee. We are giving the children knowledge that we want them to use in the 21st century. A hundred years ago the idea that our children are a generation ahead was a platitude. Today it is a drama. No longer can parents understand their children when they come home from modern mathematics or modern science classes. The stage where parents will not understand their children when they talk about the nature of society will soon be reached.

After we had formulated the fundamental ideas of the social sciences, I visited first grade classes to find out how many of these ideas could be related to the first graders' experiences. I found that the children's experience in social matters is potentially so meaningful that the fundamental structure of knowledge can be related to their experience.

After we found this out, we formulated the next question. If we teach all these fundamental ideas in the first grade, what can we teach in the second grade? The same structure of knowledge, only now with increasing depth and complexity. And in the third grade we teach the same structure but with still greater depth and complexity, as the child's experience grows.

On a scope and sequence chart, all concepts are listed vertically, and all grades are shown horizontally. Since every concept is taught in every grade, the scope and sequence chart should show in the first column, for the first grade, very pale checkmarks. In each grade the intensity of the checkmarks is increased until the darkest color is used for the twelfth grade, indicating that the same concept has been taught with increasing depth and complexity. The question arises as to how this can be done.

How can political science, sociology, economics, and anthropology be taught all in one grade, particularly the first grade? This is a new art, I think, which I call the orchestration of the curriculum. Units have to be constructed in such a way that different units give emphasis to the different areas of the social sciences. In some units the sociologist plays the solo role while the other social scientists play the accompaniment; then the economist is the soloist, then the anthropologist, and so on.

The first element of my approach, taking the fundamental concepts and teaching them with increasing depth and complexity, I call the organic curriculum because these concepts are not presented atomistically between grade one and grade twelve. They are introduced all at once and grow with the child, as he moves from grade to grade. I call the second element the orchestration of the curriculum. The child may not know that the sociologist is talking to him, or the economist, or the political scientist, nevertheless he will be exposed to the social science disciplines in an undiluted form.

Fundamental Ideas in Economics

The solo role of the economist can be illustrated by the following development of fundamental economic ideas. The same ideas and relationships are shown in chart form in Figure 1.

1. The central idea of economics is the scarcity concept, namely, that every society faces a conflict between unlimited wants and limited resources.

2. Out of the scarcity concept a family of ideas emerge. Because of scarcity, man has tried to develop methods to produce more in less time, or more with less material and in shorter time. Various types of specialization were discovered in order to

Figure 1
FUNDAMENTAL IDEAS OF ECONOMICS

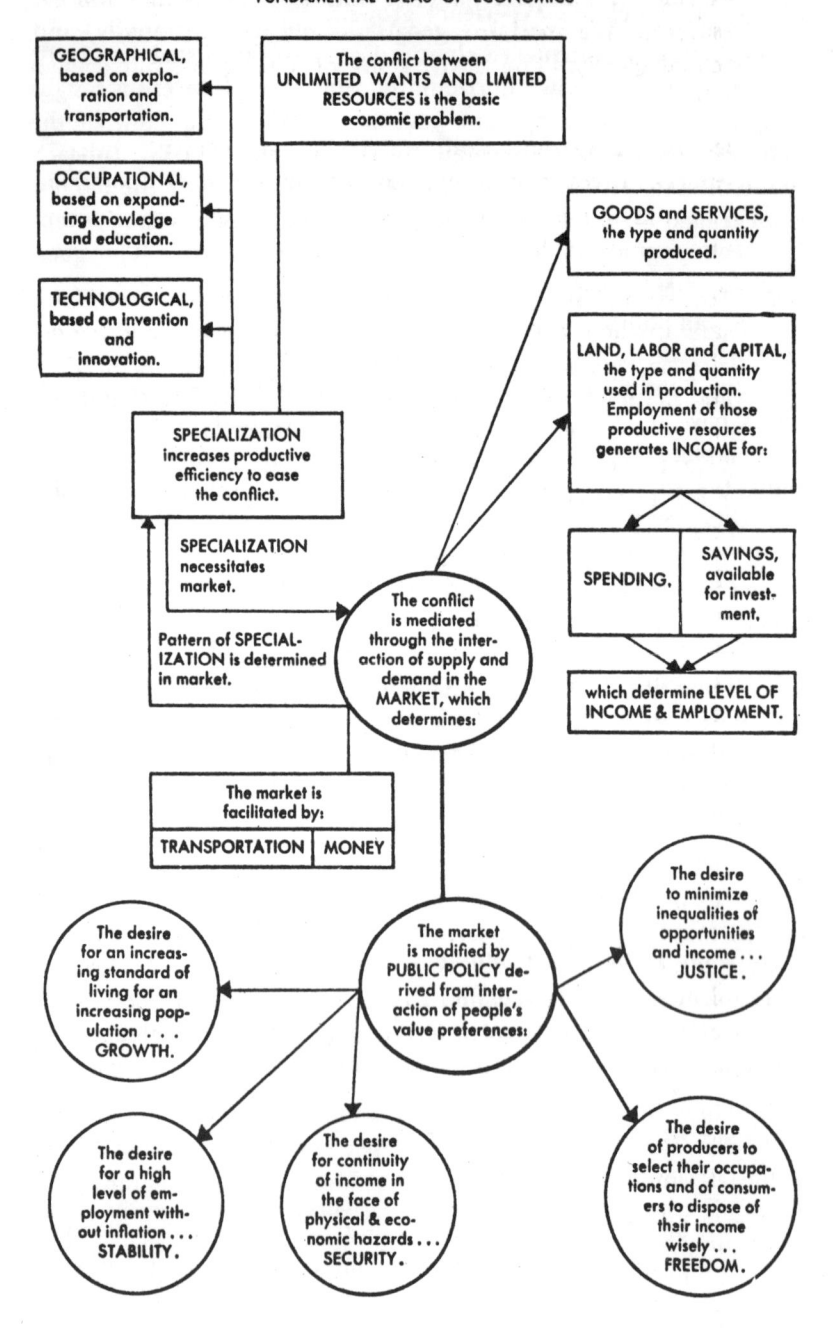

The conflict between **UNLIMITED WANTS AND LIMITED RESOURCES** is the basic economic problem.

GEOGRAPHICAL, based on exploration and transportation.

OCCUPATIONAL, based on expanding knowledge and education.

TECHNOLOGICAL, based on invention and innovation.

SPECIALIZATION increases productive efficiency to ease the conflict.

SPECIALIZATION necessitates market.

Pattern of **SPECIALIZATION** is determined in market.

GOODS and SERVICES, the type and quantity produced.

LAND, LABOR and CAPITAL, the type and quantity used in production. Employment of those productive resources generates INCOME for:

SPENDING,

SAVINGS, available for investment,

which determine **LEVEL OF INCOME & EMPLOYMENT**.

The conflict is mediated through the interaction of supply and demand in the MARKET, which determines:

The market is facilitated by: | TRANSPORTATION | MONEY

The market is modified by **PUBLIC POLICY** derived from interaction of people's value preferences:

The desire for an increasing standard of living for an increasing population ... **GROWTH**.

The desire to minimize inequalities of opportunities and income ... **JUSTICE**.

The desire for a high level of employment without inflation ... **STABILITY**.

The desire for continuity of income in the face of physical & economic hazards ... **SECURITY**.

The desire of producers to select their occupations and of consumers to dispose of their income wisely ... **FREEDOM**.

overcome the conflict between unlimited wants and limited resources. We specialize geographically, occupationally, and technologically. The third family of ideas grows out of specialization.

3. Because of specialization, we are interdependent; interdependence necessitates a monetary system and a transportation system. The fourth idea emerges from the first, scarcity, and from interdependence.

4. Men had to discover an allocating mechanism and this is the market, where through the interaction of buyers and sellers price changes occur. Prices determine the pattern of production, the method of production, income distribution and the level of spending and saving, which, in turn, decide the level of total economic activity. The fifth family of ideas grows out of the fact that the economic system is a part of political society.

5. The market decision is modified by public policies, carried out by the government, to assure welfare objectives. These welfare objectives are determined in the United States through the political interaction of 200 million people which generates thousands of welfare objectives which I have reduced to five: our attempts to accelerate growth, to promote stability, to assure economic security, to promote economic freedom, and to promote economic justice.

These are the fundamental ideas of economic knowledge which we try to incorporate at every grade level, always with the objective in mind that these analytical tools should help the students analyze the cause of a problem, to measure its scope, to develop some solutions, and to measure the dislocations which have been caused by the attempt to solve it. We try to put the problem in a dynamic context and then see what other dislocations are created.

Teaching Applications of Economics

Now I would like to present a few ideas on how I relate these economic concepts to the child's experience. The first grade child recognizes the scarcity concept beause he lives it. He goes to the A&P and he recognizes that he cannot have everything which is on the shelves. The "three wish" fairy tales reflect men's yearning to close the gap between unlimited wants and limited resources.

Cut-outs from the *National Geographic Magazine* and other pictorial material can dramatize the different degree to which nations have satisfied their people's wants.

Division of labor can be dramatized with the children by using simple experiments in the classroom. The class may organize two teams. One team executes a production process, such as making gingerbread boys on an assembly line, while the other makes them without using the division of labor. The time keeper decides which of these teams has been able to produce a given amount in less time and with less waste of tools and materials. Children discover division of labor in the home (where each family member does a particular job), in the neighborhood, in the city, in the nation, and in the world. Children discover the division of labor between men and machines. All these kinds of specialization introduce to children the ideas of international trade and mass production. In many classes, the teacher associates the children's discoveries with those of Professor Adam Smith and Mr. Henry Ford. Such identification of the child's experience with the experience of the big society is necessary to the success of this program.

Children's literature is full of delightful stories that can underpin specialization and the resulting interdependence. Through stories and games the children learn that trading would be much more complex if we could not use money as a medium of exchange.

In the second grade, the children can develop models for perfect and imperfect competition, and they can simulate the operation of the market. To dramatize the principle of perfect competition, the children may become wheat farmers one morning. Each child can represent the farmers of the different wheat-growing countries. The teacher can play the role of the broker whose task is to sell the farmers' wheat at the best possible price. At the end of the harvest the farmers report to the broker how much they have produced. The weather was good throughout the world, and since the game limits each country's production to two truckloads, the farmers from Australia, Canada, U.S., U.S.S.R., and Argentina ask the broker to sell their two truckloads at the best possible price. The broker starts an auction among the rest of the class who are the buyers. Their ability to bid has been limited by the toy money the teacher has given them. The bidding starts at a low price and as the buyers bid for the ten truckloads, the price moves up toward an equilibrium price at which all the wheat that has been offered for sale can be sold. The children discover the most important characteristic of perfect competition—the lack of control of the market by producers and consumers. The class may extend to another period when the harvest was twice as good as before. The children will be surprised to learn that the equilibrium price will be so low that the farmers' earnings will be smaller than previously when the farmers brought the smaller quantity to the market. This activity introduces to the children the concept of elasticity of demand without its being identified as such.

To dramatize imperfect competition, some children in the class may play the role of inventors, manufacturers, and owners of grocery stores. The game will help children discover that all these producers can control the market in different degrees. The class discussion can bring out how these different degrees of control affect the producers' power to set prices.

Discussion finally gets to public policy, where the children decide what goods and services will be purchased together. Many goods and services are not purchased by each family but purchased together. The Mayor, the Governor, and the President of the U.S. each prepare a long shopping list. Discussing the lists, some people think they are too long and others think they are too short. When they agree upon the proper length of these shopping lists, taxes are collected. The people may decide to pay for a part of the list from tax monies, and to pay for the rest by borrowing money. If they don't want to pay taxes, they have to go into debt to buy goods and services together.

Fundamental Ideas in Political Science

The important idea relationships of political science were defined just as with economics. Figure 2 shows the systems analysis of political life which Professor David Easton of the University of Chicago has developed. This chart contains the following ideas:

1. Members of society have many wants which they hope to satisfy.
2. Some of these wants will be satisfied through the economic system, family system, educational system, and religious system. Wants that cannot be satisfied by any of these systems are channeled to the political system.
3. As the people's wants enter the political system for satisfaction, they become demands. These demands are screened.
4. The screening process operates through formal or informal organizations. These organizations act as gate keepers. Some

Figure 2

SYSTEMS ANALYSIS OF POLITICAL LIFE

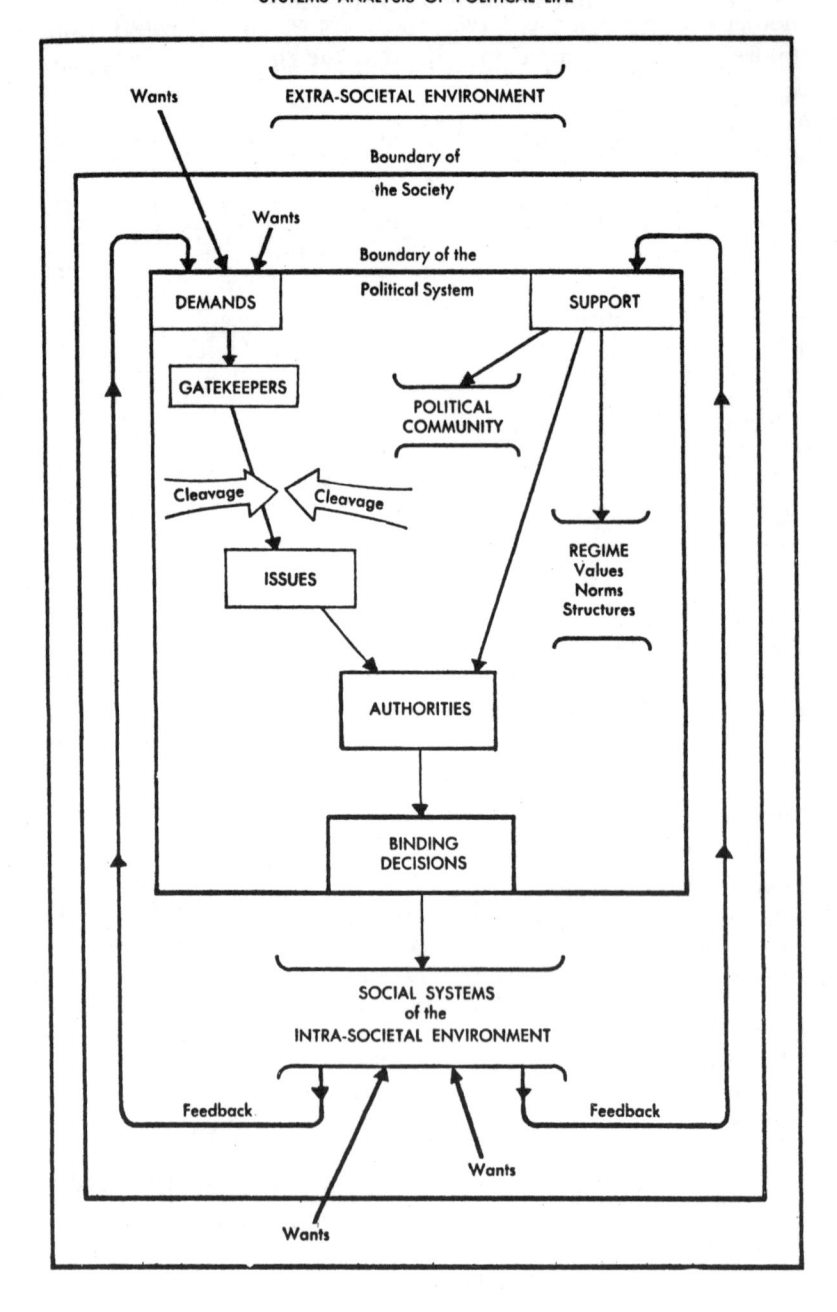

of the demands vanish. Others become issues debated in the political community (a group who share a desire to work together as a unit in the political solution of problems).
5. The issues are molded by cleavages in the political community and by the authorities which translate these demands into binding decisions.
6. The binding decisions affect the social systems and the participants in them, generating positive or negative support.
7. The support may be directed toward the political community, toward the regime (a political system which incorporates a particular set of values and norms, and a particular structure of authority), and/or toward the authorities (the particular persons who occupy positions of political power within the structure of authority).
8. The binding decisions generate new wants which appear again at the gate of the political system asking for recognition.
9. The source of the support for the political community, regime, and authorities may originate from the social systems in the form of education, patriotism and other mechanisms.

Teaching Applications of Political Science

In the same way that the fundamental ideas of economic knowledge can be related to the child's experiences, we can also relate the fundamental ideas of political science on every grade level. The home is a good example of how the innumerable wants of the family are satisfied through the various institutions, and of how many of the wants are exposed to the political scrutiny of the members of the family before they become the rules of the home. The discussion about the various forces which keep the family together has a striking resemblance to the different types of supports which keep the political society together. Looking upon the political system in this way is a fundamental departure from the present civics curriculum where the main emphasis is on description of the legislative, judicial and executive branches of the government.

Fundamental Ideas in Sociology

Professor Robert Perrucci of Purdue University has developed a fundamental structure of sociology which is already in use in experimental classrooms. The core idea is that of values and norms. The system is illustrated in Figure 3.

Figure 3

FUNDAMENTAL IDEAS OF SOCIOLOGY

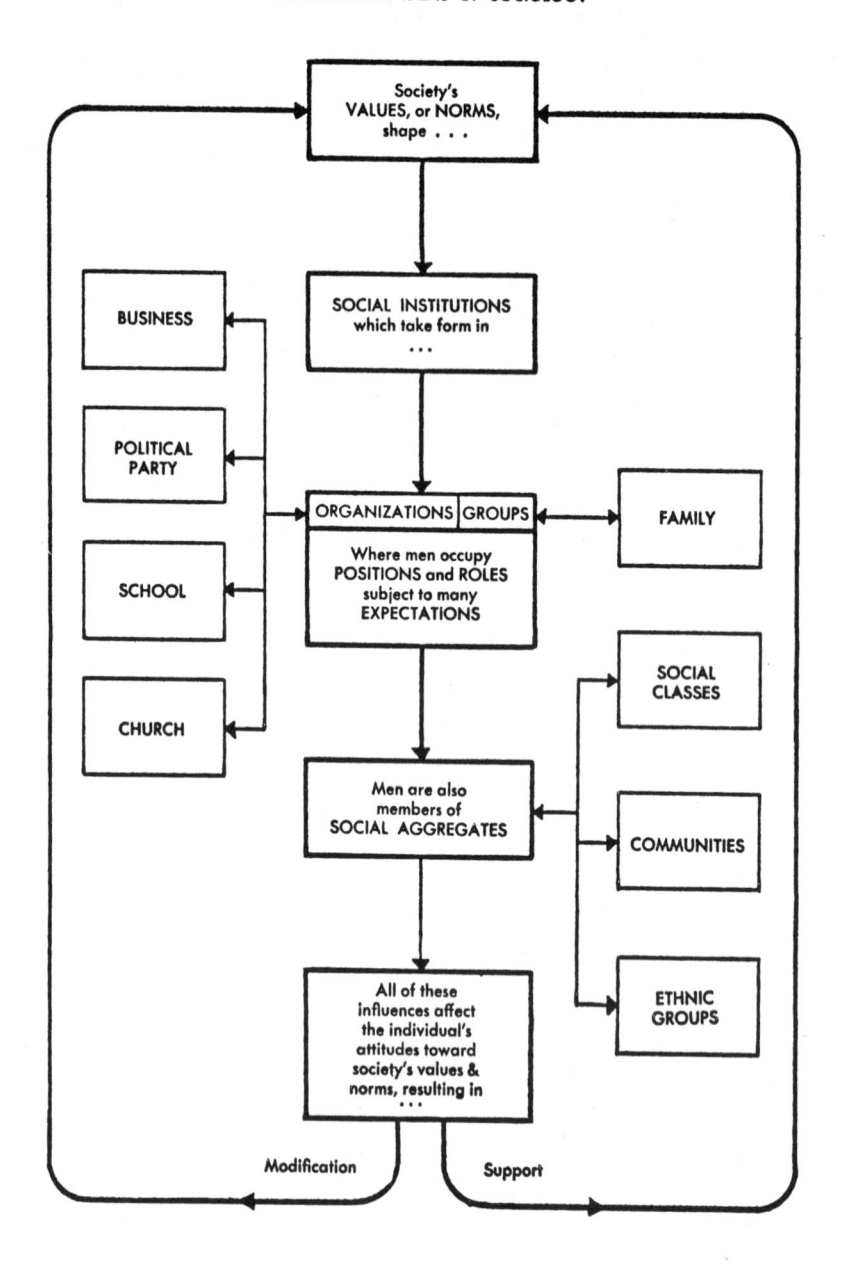

```
                    ┌─────────────────┐
        ┌──────────→│    Society's    │←──────────┐
        │           │ VALUES, or NORMS,│           │
        │           │    shape . . .   │           │
        │           └────────┬─────────┘           │
        │                    ↓                     │
        │           ┌─────────────────┐            │
        │           │SOCIAL INSTITUTIONS│          │
        │           │ which take form in│          │
        │           │       . . .      │           │
        │           └────────┬─────────┘           │
        │                    ↓                     │
┌──────────┐                                       │
│ BUSINESS │──┐                                    │
└──────────┘  │                                    │
              │                                    │
┌──────────┐  │   ┌──────────────────────┐    ┌────────┐
│ POLITICAL│  └──→│ORGANIZATIONS│ GROUPS │←───│ FAMILY │
│  PARTY   │─────→│ Where men occupy     │    └────────┘
└──────────┘      │ POSITIONS and ROLES  │
                  │ subject to many      │
┌──────────┐  ┌──→│ EXPECTATIONS         │
│  SCHOOL  │──┘   └──────────┬───────────┘
└──────────┘                 │
                             │
┌──────────┐  ┌──────────────┤           ┌────────┐
│  CHURCH  │──┘              ↓       ┌──→│ SOCIAL │
└──────────┘       ┌─────────────────┐   │ CLASSES│
                   │  Men are also   │   └────────┘
                   │   members of    │   ┌────────┐
                   │SOCIAL AGGREGATES│──→│COMMUNI-│
                   └────────┬────────┘   │  TIES  │
                            │            └────────┘
                            ↓            ┌────────┐
                   ┌─────────────────┐──→│ ETHNIC │
                   │  All of these   │   │ GROUPS │
                   │ influences affect│  └────────┘
                   │ the individual's │
                   │attitudes toward  │
                   │ society's values &│
                   │norms, resulting in│
                   │      . . .      │
                   └────────┬────────┘
                    ↙              ↘
              Modification        Support
```

84

1. Values and norms are the main sources of energy to individuals and society.
2. Societies' values and norms shape social institutions, which are embodied in organizations and groups, where people occupy positions and roles.
3. People's positions and roles affect their attitudes toward society's values and norms, and result either in support of the existing values and norms, or in demands for modification of them, and the circle starts again.

Teaching Applications of Sociology

The conceptualization of sociology makes it possible to develop units in the primary grades which will make children aware of the importance of predictable behavior among people. Units may show how the ability to predict human behavior creates orderliness in the family, neighborhood, city, and the world. The teacher can demonstrate through experiments how unexpected situations have both very funny and very sad consequences. Children's plays can bring out that the school, business and family could not exist without predictability and order in human behavior.

The many positions men take in society can be observed at home. The children may prepare charts showing the different positions fathers, mothers, and children take and the difficulty of fulfilling all the expectations attached to the positions. The children can show that, depending on which positions we think more important or less important, and depending on our ability, we can fulfill some positions better than others. The story of *The Ant and The Grasshopper*[2] points out effectively the value preferences of the two. The children can also observe and experiment in the classroom how men's positions, due to science and technology, and due to change in ideas, have changed during history.

Laying the foundation of sociological concepts in the primary grades helps children to understand later how interplay between values and institutions brings about social reforms.

Fundamental Ideas in Anthropology

Fundamental ideas of anthropology have been developed by Professor Paul Bohannan of Northwestern University. Figure 4 shows the following idea relationships.

Figure 4

FUNDAMENTAL IDEAS OF ANTHROPOLOGY

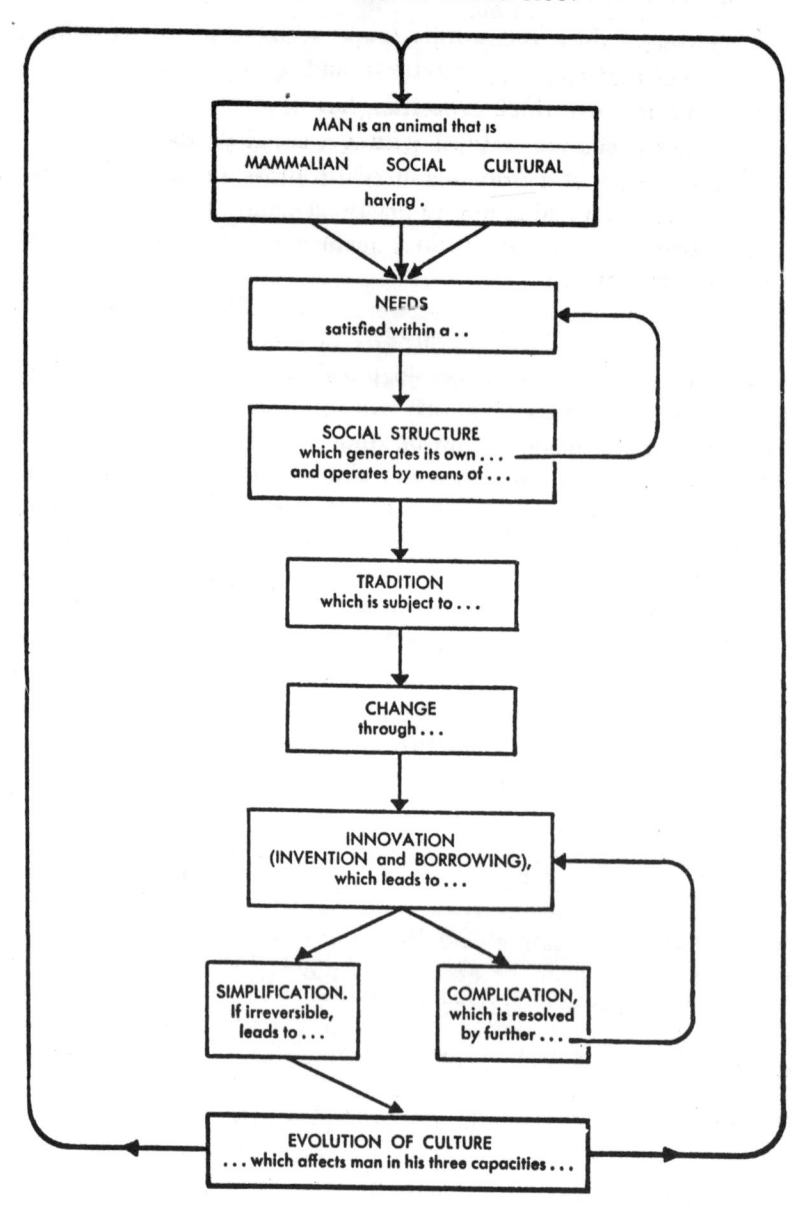

```
MAN is an animal that is
MAMMALIAN   SOCIAL   CULTURAL
having ..
         │
         ▼
       NEEDS
  satisfied within a ..
         │
         ▼
   SOCIAL STRUCTURE
which generates its own ...
and operates by means of ...
         │
         ▼
      TRADITION
  which is subject to ...
         │
         ▼
       CHANGE
      through ...
         │
         ▼
     INNOVATION
(INVENTION and BORROWING),
    which leads to ...
      /        \
     ▼          ▼
SIMPLIFICATION.   COMPLICATION,
If irreversible,  which is resolved
  leads to ...    by further ...
         \        /
          ▼      ▼
    EVOLUTION OF CULTURE
... which affects man in his three capacities ...
```

86

1. Man may be looked upon as a
   a. mammalian animal,
   b. social animal, and
   c. cultural animal.
2. Man, in these three capacities, has needs.
3. Man's needs are satisfied within a social structure.
4. Social structure itself has needs (called "requisites") which must be satisfied if it is to persist.
5. Needs are satisfied within a particular set of patterned behavior: tradition.
6. All traditions leave some wants unsatisfied.
7. Dissatisfaction leads to changes in traditions.
8. Changes take the form of invention and borrowing: innovation.
9. Innovation leads to complication and simplification.
10. Complication leads to social dislocations. Problems caused by dislocations may be resolved through further innovations.
11. If simplification is of such a magnitude that it forms an irreversible base for man's behavior (for example, the use of fire), it leads to evolution of culture.
12. The evolution of culture affects man in his three capacities as a mammalian, social, and cultural animal.

Teaching Applications of Anthropology

The conceptualization of anthropology in this way will enable the elementary school curriculum builder to develop meaningful units on such conventional subjects as the Eskimos and the American Indians.

A unit on the Eskimos, for example, demonstrates how acceptance of the idea of money changed the life of the Eskimo. The Eskimo in our unit acquired his food, clothing, and part of his shelter from caribou. The scarcity and his nomadic life affected his value system. Then he found out that far away there was a trading post where Eskimos could trade silver fox pelts for articles which he had never had before. Our Eskimo family stopped hunting and started to trap silver fox to use as a medium of exchange. The family settled down near the trading post in an Eskimo village. There was less uncertainty here. This story presents to the children evolution in the Eskimo culture. Living together with other Eskimos created new problems. The family's needs changed. Their desire for learning increased. The changes came about because money as a medium of exchange had been accepted by the Eskimo family.

In the higher grades, the conceptualization of anthropology will help the curriculum builders to develop units which will show how the development of underdeveloped areas and the pursuit of nationalism affects people's tribal loyalties and changes their physical, social and cultural needs.

These are the four areas of social science in which we have tried to formulate the fundamental idea relationships. Deliberately, we are leaving the areas of history and geography to the last stages of our inquiry. The reason is that these two areas have a different character from the other social sciences. They have to borrow many of the analytical tools of the other areas of the social sciences to explain a geographic area or the processes of history. Until now history and geography in the elementary and secondary school curriculum have been mostly a narrative of men's actions and a description of their environment. Now, our team of social scientists hope to use their analytical tools to explain cause-effect relationships in man's actions in time and place. Using the analytical tools of social scientists, the children can begin to simulate the historians' and geographers' methods of inquiry.

Fundamental Ideas in Geography

The scope of the geographers' inquiry has been worked out by Professor Peter Greco of Syracuse University. The fundamental ideas in geography are shown in Figure 5, and described below.

1. Every geographic area is affected by physical, biotic, and societal forces.
2. The impact of these forces on a geographic area creates similarities among areas. These similar areas are called uniform regions. They are static in character.
3. The similarities among different areas have been brought about through different combinations of physical, biotic, and societal forces.
4. An area may be kept together through a pattern of circulation binding the area to a central place. This area is called a nodal region, held together by functional relationships. The nodal region is dynamic in character.
5 Uniform and nodal regions are often related to each other through gravitation to the same central place.

Figure 5

FUNDAMENTAL IDEAS OF GEOGRAPHY

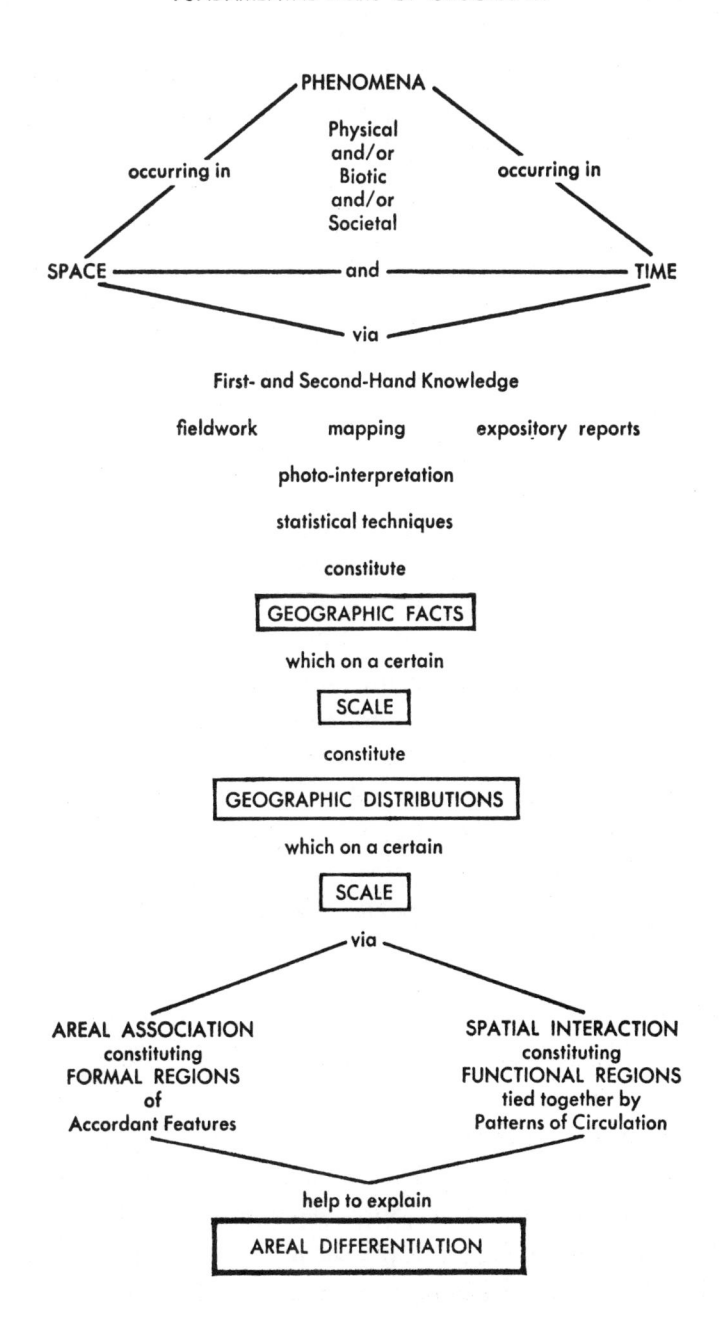

PHENOMENA
Physical and/or Biotic and/or Societal

occurring in SPACE — and — occurring in TIME

via

First- and Second-Hand Knowledge

fieldwork   mapping   expository reports

photo-interpretation

statistical techniques

constitute

GEOGRAPHIC FACTS

which on a certain

SCALE

constitute

GEOGRAPHIC DISTRIBUTIONS

which on a certain

SCALE

via

AREAL ASSOCIATION
constituting
FORMAL REGIONS
of
Accordant Features

SPATIAL INTERACTION
constituting
FUNCTIONAL REGIONS
tied together by
Patterns of Circulation

help to explain

AREAL DIFFERENTIATION

Teaching Applications of Geography

The classroom applications of geography are now in preparation. Activities are being constructed to show the many ways in which the surface of the earth may be divided by geographers, depending upon the objectives of their inquiries. Units are also being constructed to show how the shape and size of the divisions of the earth's surface are influenced not only by natural forces but also by the state of science and technology. Deserts and cold lands, which in the past have been unproductive, may now become productive through scientific progress; for example, irrigation or the discovery of oil can make a desert productive, and the discovery of minerals in Alaska and the Antarctic can increase the usefulness of those frigid lands.

In defining and studying regions, geographers are concerned with physical, economic, sociological, anthropological, and political facts. The regions defined by physical, economic, sociological and anthropological factors seldom coincide with the boundaries of the political systems that men have set up to solve some of the most important social problems. The resulting dissimilarities between political and non-political regions have been the cause of many problems. For example, if a river basin or an ethnic group is bisected by a political boundary, serious political tensions may result. Such problems may be "solved" by war, by international agreements, or by other social mechanisms. The approach we are taking, as shown by this brief description, provides a partial synthesis of political science, economics, sociology, and anthropology with geography.

Conclusion

The development of the organic curriculum and its orchestration is not a crash program. It is a lifetime commitment. It is the job of the academic departments of universities to stimulate more social scientists to pay attention to the problem of structuring the knowledge of their own discipline. Such logical patterns of ideas will serve the social scientist as a map to identify new areas of research, and will serve the curriculum worker as a guide to build a curriculum which can be adjusted to incorporate new ideas as the frontier of knowledge expands.

■

[1] In G. W. Ford and Lawrence Pugno, *The Structure of Knowledge and the Curriculum* (Chicago: Rand McNally, 1964).
[2] *The Ant and the Grasshopper; A Georgian Folk Tale*, translated from the Russian by Fainni Solasko (Moscow: Foreign Languages Publishing House, no date).

A Case for Anthropology in Public School Curricula

By ROBERT A. HELLMANN

IN recent years, not only has paleoanthropological research proceeded at an increased rate (thanks to such sources as the Wenner-Gren Foundation), but also it has become increasingly popular with the general public. At first Darwin's *The Origin of Species* and *The Descent of Man* rocked the foundations of the Holy See of Canterbury. The pronouncements of the Archbishop of Armagh on the age of the earth were cast in doubt. Bishop Wilberforce vigorously assailed these new heresies in the famous debate with Thomas Huxley in words so caustic as to be improper to the dignity of his episcopal office. But today few doubt the validity of the principle of organic evolution and its application to man.

Increasing numbers of popular accounts of human beginnings are appearing on the market, and highly authoritative ones, too.[1] Fascination for the story of our origins has merit in itself. It is a basis of "pure" intellectual inquiry, a foundation of academic pursuit. As Emerson said of beauty, it is its "own excuse for being." But is there a future significance to the study of human evolution? Professor Raymond Dart, of the University of Witwatersrand, gives us a clue in his recent book, *Adventures with the Missing Link*.[2] In the chapter, "How Man Got Off His Knuckles," he describes the protohuman as an ape-like creature assuming an erect posture, peering over the tall veldt grasses, and carrying a stick in his hand for self-defense. He ate meat, relentlessly hunting down his prey and clubbing it to death. That prey consisted of birds, tortoises, antelopes, hyenas, and even his own fellows. Furthermore, he killed not only for food, but also for bones, horns, and teeth to be used as weapons for killing and dismembering more prey. Professor Dart argues that "The blood-spattered, slaughter-gutted archives of human history, from the earliest Egyptian and Sumerian records down to the most recent unspeakable atrocities of World Wars I and II," accord with a wide variety of cruel practices, such as head-hunting, sacrifices, and body mutilation, and represent the essentially cannibalistic nature of mankind, as distinct from his vegetarian relatives, the apes.

Had man's ancestors not become predaceous, it is doubtful if they would successfully have invaded the grasslands, at least without such specializations (e.g., hoof-like feet for flight) as would have precluded culture. Significant about man, of course, is his plastic generalized nature. Culture has done for him what morphological adaptation has done for other creatures. Culture has the advantage that it can be undone or radically altered at will, without wasteful genetic mutations and the long gruelling process of natural selection. However, the predaceous, even cannibalistic and destructive nature of man is a biological heritage which must be understood *now* if we are to proceed successfully into the coming age of mass world populations, high technological development, and the space age. How will we harness this psychobiological force and bring it to fruitful sublimation? It cannot be ignored, ostrich-like; it cannot be submerged, driven into the cultural subconscious to erupt unexpectedly in some hideous form such as the recent Nazism and the cruel suppression of peoples behind the Iron Curtain. In his *The Story of Man*,[3] Dr. Carleton S. Coon remarks, " . . . once a species has evolved, it will not change into another species for a long time. That is why the biological capacities of man are geared to the life of a hunter, and hence why the most satisfactory civilizations are those that permit the full expression of those capacities."

Dr. Dart has proven that man as a successful and vicious predator has existed for a full million years, and for the same period has had the capacity to build at least the rudiments of material culture. Dr. L. S. B. Leakey, of Nairobi, has

---

MR. HELLMAN *(Theta 1282) is a lecturer at the Institute of Education, Makere College, The University College of East Africa, Kampala, Uganda. He took the assignment last year through the Teachers for East Africa Project, Teachers College, Columbia. This project is supported by the U.S. government's Agency for International Development.*

[1] In America a good example is Ashley Montagu's *Man: The First Million Years*.
[2] Raymond Dart, *Adventures with the Missing Link*. New York: Harper, 1959.
[3] Carleton S. Coon, *The Story of Man*. New York: Knopf, 1954.

provided substantial evidence of hominid existence of almost twice this age. Thus the nature of man is well established and paleontologically authenticated. It might well be that the new generations of national leaders all over the world should be educated in their zoological origins and their cultural diversities.

In view of this, it would seem that there is a valid case for inclusion of anthropology in the public school curriculum. This would include human evolution, constitutional anthropology, and ethnology. Human evolution would be intended to develop an understanding of our anatomical and behavioral characteristics as animals, as well as some of our psychological needs. Dr. Coon said, in the aforementioned book, " . . . we can live and work most happily and efficiently if we reproduce, with modern improvements, some approximation to our ancestors' living conditions. A hunter needs space to move around in. He needs trees and grass and rocks and streams; he needs the presence of birds and animals. . . . " If these needs are to be met, they must come sharply into focus as part of the cultural value system.

Constitutional anthropology, being related to health education, might actually replace the latter, not by arbitrary substitution, but by evolution. Thus the traditional program of teacher-training in the area of health could be altered to give it an anthropological emphasis, and the change would not involve any serious personnel or curriculum dislocations. Such an approach would include blood groupings and their significance in modern medicine; body types and their relation to personal health and physical limitations; sex education; and much of the present material on nutrition and personal hygiene.

Ethnology is at present almost taught—partly as geography units in social studies and partly as history units, including studies of the American Indian. In my experience with New York City school classes and teachers, with whom I had contact while with the Department of Education of the American Museum of Natural History, I found such studies much too superficial to be of lasting value in helping growing citizens understand our neighbors abroad. The children are usually given a random assortment of details of material cultural traits, such as how pottery is made, how weaving is done, and what crops are grown by this or that particular tribe or society. A conscious study of family organization, value systems, world views, and other fundamental principles is not undertaken. Children need to understand the concept of ethnocentrism before they become as ethnocentric as their teachers. In all fairness to the teachers, of course, we must realize that most of them have had no formal training in anthropology.

With Tokyo only a few hours away from New York, and London but a short hop from Nairobi, we can no longer peer curiously at pictures of exotic peoples in peculiar dress and consider them as oddities of far-away lands. It takes less time for us today to fly from Boston to Bombay than it did for Audubon to walk from Louisville to Chicago. Tomorrow "foreign" will be an archaic word, and "air pollution" may well be a pan-world crisis. At this point in history, when man reaches out into new dimensions, new realms, new environments, will his wisdom and self-understanding be equal to his intelligence in technical spheres?

Political Science in the Social Studies

By Robert E. Cleary and Donald H. Riddle

THE STUDY OF POLITICAL PHENOMENA

A DEMOCRATIC PEOPLE must understand and appreciate the character of their society, its goals and purposes, its limitations, its methods of operation, and the boundaries of reasonable choice in their nation and the world of which they are a part. Every country requires people with certain kinds of knowledge and particular skills, but if a democratic nation is to exist, its citizens must have an understanding of their political system and its setting. The people of a democracy play an active role in public affairs. At times, they virtually set national policy. As a consequence, they must be acquainted with ways of gathering, ordering, and using knowledge about matters political.

In the complex world of the twentieth century the elementary or secondary school social studies teacher has an extremely difficult job to perform. The editors of this yearbook feel that the discipline of political science can be of considerable assistance to teachers of social studies courses. Political science is an intellectual discipline that is

NCSS Thirty-Sixth Yearbook, 1966, Chapter 1, pp. 1-13.

primarily concerned with the question of how man governs himself. It includes the analysis of informal interaction within government; interaction among governmental officials, individual citizens, and interest group representatives; along with the study of the visible organizational structure of government.

Political science is concerned with the study of government, but it is by no means restricted to the study of the formal structure that is usually called government. Students of political science go beyond the study of governmental structure to concern themselves with the processes and the goals of politics: with techniques of government, methods by which decisions are made, and the bases of decisions. In so doing they pose questions such as: Who has the ability to influence others in the determination of policy choices on matters of public concern, and to secure the enforcement of his policy preferences through government? How is such influence exerted? For what purpose is it employed? In other words, who has power in a given situation, how is it exercised, to what ends, and with what results?

Students of American politics should supplement their study of governmental structure through analysis—even if only on an elementary level—of such topics as the nature of the American party system, the role of political parties, party operation, voting behavior, the role of the independent voter, interest groups, the role of a particular interest group, public opinion, political campaigning, and the nature of representative government. It is also useful to examine the social structure of a society, for often goals and means alike are influenced or determined by it. Class discussions, library research, and individual involvement on topics such as those presented here allow attention to the nature and the purpose of the political process, as well as emphasis on political behavior, thus amplifying the study of the "who" and the "what" of government with the "how" and the "why."

Political studies of this nature do not focus on factual knowledge for its own sake, but attempt instead to use facts to help achieve understandings. After all, facts as such are easily forgotten. They also become obsolete rather quickly in our constantly changing world. Furthermore, any body of knowledge encompasses more information than can possibly be learned in a school year or, for that matter, in a lifetime. In recognition of these facts, social studies courses with a political content are increasingly concentrating on central ideas, basic generalizations, and methods of inquiry that will be of assistance in the development of understandings and appreciations.

Political analysis in the elementary and the secondary school increasingly involves an attempt to help students develop a way of thinking that will give them the knowledge and the techniques necessary to arrive at reasonable answers to given questions. Such tasks as forming generalizations, making inferences, predicting possibilities, and explaining new phenomena involve skills that can be developed with practice. These skills take time to mature, but students can learn to group and to classify facts and to make generalizations on the basis of the evidence available.[1]

Along with the functioning and the processes of American government, the role and the purposes of government in our nation might well be emphasized in this connection in elementary and secondary school. History indicates that it is impossible for any society to maintain itself over a long period of time if it fails to pass a major portion of its basic heritage on to at least some key members of the younger generation. As a result, every nation must build an effective method of transmitting a deep appreciation of its underlying values to the young people who will be its future leaders.

Political studies in the United States have long been concerned with the necessity to help young people acquire certain knowledge, attitudes, and understandings with regard to the nature of their national community. Yet many American students have never undertaken an examination of the functioning and the processes of government in the United States, or a meaningful treatment of the underlying values and goals of the American society in a conscious effort to familiarize themselves with the roots of our heritage and the reasons for our basic beliefs. As a result, many Americans cannot place a specific situation in the perspective of a total picture by relating it to the overall goals of America. How many of our readers' students, for example, can even outline what the basic goals of the United States as a nation might be? Do we want an orderly society? How much order is desirable and how far should the government go in enforcing order? Do we want a society in which government interferes with individual action only when interference is absolutely necessary? When is interference absolutely necessary? Do we want a society that reaches a balance between the needs of order and of individual freedom? How do we reach such a balance? Is justice to be the measuring stick? What is just, and who determines it? Do the people make decisions of this nature in a democracy? If so, can the majority override the

---

[1] For a good discussion of these points see Taba, Hilda, *Curriculum Development: Theory and Practice.* N. Y.: Harcourt, Brace and World, 1962. Chapter 12.

rights of the minority? If not, are we a democracy? In sum, what might our goals be, and how can we attain them?

One basic listing of American goals can be found in the Preamble to the Constitution of the United States:

> ... to form a more perfect union, establish justice, insure domestic tranquility [i.e., order], provide for the common defense, promote the general welfare, and secure the blessings of liberty to ourselves and our posterity. ...

Such goals, however, penetrating as they are, are not self-defining. Does liberty include equality, or does promoting the general welfare include federally paid rent supplements in private housing? Furthermore, the goals may conflict with one another. An attempt to insure domestic tranquility can collide with the need to secure liberty. A political studies program might well include, therefore, an emphasis on the nature, the extent, and the interrelationships of equally desirable but conflicting American goals.

Careful attention to the question of how our basic national goals can be achieved and preserved also seems to be in order. What are the responsibilities of the individual citizen in this regard? What limits on conduct should he recognize? What positive obligations must he accept? Is it enough for him to obey the law and to pay his taxes? Moreover, what is his responsibility in so far as obeying the law is concerned? Should he, for example, refuse to buy merchandise offered for sale on Sunday in violation of a local blue law? Then, is there a higher order of responsibilities beyond observance of the law, particularly for the citizen in a democratic society? Must he vote? Keep informed on political affairs? Participate in party politics? Act in the general interest rather than in the specific interest? What does action in the general interest mean? Supporting zoning regulations that will limit the value of property the citizen owns? Supporting the reduction of tariffs when this will hurt his business? Supporting foreign aid when it will increase his taxes?

Queries of this nature are the heart and soul of government and politics, and should constitute a basic part of any political studies program. It is extremely difficult to teach about values and goals in a complex society, particularly one that is undergoing rapid technological and social change. There are no final answers to questions like those cited above. This is no excuse, however, for ignoring such queries. After all, people are more likely to be able to arrive at reasonable answers to these questions if they have some understanding of the nature of the political process, of political behavior, and of the purpose of government and its role in their nation.

Yet social studies courses often ignore or deny problems like graft in government, civil rights and civil liberties violations, and the informal control exercised by powerful economic groups over a number of governmental decisions because of a fear of controversy. Controversy is the very essence of politics, however, and pupils must learn that there are honest differences of opinion on most political matters even among the well informed. In so doing, they should also learn to analyze problems, to evaluate arguments, and to come to their own decisions on recommended courses of action. This does not mean the classroom presentation of a controversy should insure that "equal time" is given to each of two competing sides. One argument may be more complex than another and may require a greater amount of time to present. Furthermore, there are not usually two sides to a controversy, but three, or seven, or even more that may well require at least a summary presentation. Reasonable discussion of possible alternative choices in a given situation, however, is basic to education as well as to democracy.

A few teachers attempt to handle controversial political problems by dressing up reality to paint a picture that is more attractive than what actually exists. Teachers should be wary of this temptation to give students "final" answers based on hope, particularly in situations laden with political and emotional overtones. A thinking individual is more likely to be the product of an education in which he is allowed to study relevant information and come to his own conclusion than of an environment in which an attempt is made to provide him with specific but necessarily limited answers. Scarcely an American is unfamiliar with the Pledge of Allegiance, but how many citizens can rationally apply in specific situations those words in the pledge that refer to our basic rights as citizens? It seems clear to us that the individual who has developed the ability to think analytically and who has an understanding and an appreciation of the basic values of America should be better able to apply such overall principles in a sound manner than someone taught by rote and indoctrination.

Moreover, the majority of American students have at least a nodding acquaintance with the truths of politics by the time they reach high school, and some are already developing a cynical attitude toward government. An attempt to persuade them that government is ever benevolent is merely likely to feed their cynicism and convince them that the teacher is part of the "system." What has been termed "the milk-and-water moralism" of the average civics text is frequently self-defeating.[2] Defects in the American system must receive recognition in the study of politics, but emphasis should be placed on the overall validity of our political arrangements, with weaknesses being handled as deficiencies that require correction. If our system of representative government is basically a valid method of achieving order with justice, greater attention to controversial issues in the classroom should result in a better appreciation of American politics on the part of all concerned.

The full and frank discussion of various social problems and of possible ways of resolving them should, therefore, be encouraged. The excesses of the McCarthy period in the early 1950's, as well as the prevalence of trial by newspaper in modern America, well illustrate that we cannot ignore controversial political issues if we are to maintain our basic values. Nevertheless, in many communities it is extremely difficult for a teacher to discuss the activities of interest groups, or the problem of illegal arrest, or even a liberal interpretation of the clause "to promote the general welfare." Those who may suffer from changes stemming from such discussions are frequently powerful enough to block debate on these matters. As John Jarolimek puts it in Chapter XV, "Not many teachers wish to personally fight the cause of freedom, to appear before school officials to respond to charges, or to become the objects of local controversy and publicity. As a result, the teaching of political matters has, through the years, been formal, bookish, and often not very interesting. . . . No one can contest such teaching; besides, the correct answers can be found in the book. It is unfortunately true that the main emphasis in political studies at the elementary school and junior high school levels has been and continues to be descriptive." The material emphasized in this kind of situation, however, often has little relationship to the overall objectives of political analysis. Understandings are not likely to result from study which overemphasizes description at the expense of investigation. The school is an agent of behavior change—in a desirable direction, it is hoped—as well as a guardian of our heritage and ought to be allowed to attend to both these tasks. The teacher should recognize that the alternative is another nudge by the school—and by the teacher himself—toward cynicism or apathetic withdrawal.

An emphasis in our schools on the free and open discussion of the basic goals of America and the ways that such goals might best be imple-

---

[2] Long, Norton E., "Political Science," in *The Social Studies and the Social Sciences*. New York: Harcourt, Brace and World, 1962. p. 97.

mented is necessary in order to allow students the opportunity to obtain a better understanding of our political system. We believe that the traditional civics course is completely inadequate in achieving the objectives of American political studies. The typical such course is too often a dreary collection of unrelated facts which do little to help achieve student understandings. Either a much broader course in government or a full treatment of political issues in a problems of democracy course is much to be preferred. Among the problems which might well be treated at length in such courses are the extent of civil liberties in the United States, along with limitations on their exercise; the role of Negroes in American society and their rights; the meaning of the phrase "due process of law"; the basic goals of the United States in international affairs; the ability of the American system to reconcile the interests of the diverse and conflicting groups in American society; the desirability of changes in the system as it operates; how the people of the United States go about handling issues of this nature; and the role of Congress, the President, and the Supreme Court in dealing with them.

In discussing matters such as these we are attempting to help educate individuals who are more than passive observers, who do more than mouth the right slogans without having an understanding of how to apply them in specific situations. In doing so, of course, we must exercise caution. We are not trying to teach specific attitudes or beliefs in and of themselves. We must draw a distinction between indoctrination and education, between attempts to implant ready-made conclusions and attempts to get individuals to think for themselves. It is sometimes argued that the demands of good citizenship require we "teach the virtues of democracy" along with the drawbacks of communism in our schools. This misses the point that in attempting to infuse a respect for freedom we may effectively destroy freedom. How can we tell people to "appreciate the American way of life" without violating the free and open consideration of issues that are essential to that way of life? A true appreciation of the nature of freedom is not learned very easily. Freedom must be examined, discussed, and even lived if its meaning is to be understood. Rote learning and memorization of its principles are not likely to result in their comprehension. An atmosphere in which the individual can question, experiment, and investigate is of prime importance. The mere learning of facts will not develop desirable attitudes, for facts are simply tools which an individual employs to discover the larger and vastly more important ideas that are vital in a free society. We should not, therefore, be afraid to allow students to examine issues and draw their own conclusions. If we have taught them how to acquire knowledge and how to analyze it critically (even at relatively low levels of sophistication) they are more likely to make sound choices and reach defensible conclusions. They will also know how democracy works and will be able to help actively to preserve it.

The Objectives of Political Studies in the School Curriculum

The social studies teacher has a responsibility to acquaint students with methods of gathering information, as well as with the uses of knowledge—with ways of understanding, viewing, and evaluating the world in which we live. He is expected to go beyond facts, to be able to place discrete information in perspective by giving it order and by fitting it into a structure which will assist in understandings and appreciations. Above all, he must help students develop habits of critical thinking about political phenomena which will enable these future citizens to participate meaningfully in the political life of their society.

A basic controversy exists, however, over the primary purpose of political studies in elementary and secondary school. The editors of this yearbook feel that politics should be studied, in the final analysis, for the same reason other areas of knowledge should be studied: to acquaint an individual with information, to allow him to expand his ability to reason, to give him every opportunity to be a thinking, functioning individual—in short, to allow him to become an educated man. Within this framework, a second order goal of political studies is to acquaint students with the nature of government and politics, especially American government and politics.

A number of educators have argued that the immediate objective of political studies in the schools is carefully oriented toward a related but somewhat different goal. Good citizenship is so important to our nation and is so difficult to structure, it is declared, that the making of good citizens must be the immediate objective. While the editors sympathize with this argument, they disagree with it. Good citizenship is extremely important in a democracy. Americans are far from agreement, however, on what it involves. Who is to define good citizenship? One man's good citizen is another man's criminal. What about civil rights demonstrations, sit-ins, and the whole role of peaceful protest in American society, for example? Even if good citizenship were to be defined, how can it be attained? Not only is the concept a nebulous one, but it involves attitudes and values that are extremely difficult to structure. It may even be self-defeating in many situations to attempt to structure them.[3] Moreover, good citizenship is likely to be influenced more by developments outside the school than by those in the classroom, for academic instruction plays only a small role in the formation of the attitudes and habits of citizenship (See Chapter XIV on political socialization.)

To the extent that the values of citizenship can be developed in the classroom, it is the belief of the editors that an honest inquiry into the nature of government and political interaction is more likely to result in good citizenship than a controlled attempt to develop particular attitudes and ideas. Good citizenship is a goal of political study, yes, but it is our feeling that the way to achieve this goal is through an effort to enlarge student horizons. In this sense there is nothing unique about the study of politics as compared with other social sciences, and no need to orient instruction to conform to a particular mold.

What, then, is the place of political science as a discipline in the elementary or the secondary school classroom? A number of educators and political scientists have argued in recent years that pre-college students should become familiar with the nature of political science as a discipline. For example, Jerome Bruner, in his book on *The Process of Education*, develops the thesis that the structures of the various intellectual disciplines should form the framework for the elementary and secondary school curriculum.[4]

Evron M. and Jeane J. Kirkpatrick, in their article on political science in *High School Social Studies Perspectives*, argue that:

> One of the most important responsibilities of the secondary school teacher is to inform students about the existence of a field of inquiry into government and politics and to give them some indication of the complexity and difficulty of many public problems. . . . [While it is not] possible to make political scientists out of secondary school students . . . it is possible to teach secondary school students something about political science: what it is, what it does, the complexity and the difficulty of the problems it deals with.[5]

Norton Long, in his chapter on political science in *The Social Studies and the Social Sciences*, declares that education in the social studies has a threefold objective: acquainting students with

---

[3] For an excellent discussion of the complexity of desirable civic attitudes see Almond, Gabriel A., and Verba, Sidney, *The Civic Culture: Political Attitudes and Democracy in Five Nations*. Boston: Little, Brown, 1963.

[4] Bruner, Jerome, *The Process of Education*. Cambridge, Mass.: Harvard University Press, 1960.

[5] Kirkpatrick, Evron M., and Jeane J., "Political Science," in *High School Social Studies Perspectives*. Boston: Houghton Mifflin, 1962. p. 122.

factual knowledge and a means of ordering it, imparting an understanding of the methods of inquiry and verification, and imparting an appreciation of the basic values of our society.[6]

Bruner feels, then, that the disciplines should provide the framework for social studies education, the Kirkpatricks believe pupils should know what political science is, and Long feels that the student should be acquainted with the broad outline of political science as a discipline along with its methods of inquiry. The editors agree, but only with an important qualification: students should know what political science is and they should be acquainted with its scope and methodology, but they should also know what it is not. One thing it is not is a unified science with an agreed-upon structure, in Bruner's use of the term. Political science *may* provide a useful framework for political studies in the elementary and the secondary school. There are a number of approaches and concepts which *can* provide unity and give order to political studies (See Unit I of this yearbook). The focus of study, however, should not be on political science as a discipline. The main ideas of the discipline might form the framework for study, but the overall purpose of social studies education is not to acquaint young people with the existence of various disciplines such as political science. Rather, within the framework of a cultivation of the intellect, the purpose of political studies is to acquaint young people with an understanding of the nature of government and its methods of operation.

As Long points out, the social studies educator is attempting to acquaint students with various means of pursuing knowledge, ordering it, and evaluating it. It is not information about political science *per se*, however, which is central to the elementary or the secondary school student. With rare exceptions, he is not a scholar attempting to expand the boundaries of knowledge. Instead, he is attempting to expand *his* knowledge about and understanding of government and politics. In this endeavor political science is a tool to be used by the teacher according to the capabilities of the students concerned. Knowledge and understanding are best imparted in a framework, rather than in bits and pieces. Political science can offer a framework that students might employ to organize their study of government. (Actually, it presents a choice of frameworks for such a purpose.)

As students expand their horizons and develop their understandings of the political world, it is likely, then, that they will gradually be-

---

[6] Long, *op. cit.*, pp. 88-89.

come acquainted with the existence of the discipline of political science, as well as with some of the leading methods of inquiry used by political scientists. This is desirable, for students should know that the discipline exists and should have an idea of how political scientists are attempting to expand their understanding of government. It is our feeling, however, that this is not a goal in itself at the pre-college level, but a means to an end—the improvement of the political understanding of the average student. In doing this, social studies teachers might well utilize much of the information and many of the techniques of political science. A primary by-product of such an emphasis is quite likely to be the development of better citizens who are knowledgeable about their rights, their duties, and the limitations of reasonable choice in their society and their world.

Plan of the Book: What We Are Trying to Do

In some ways the title of this yearbook is a presumptuous one. The editors would like to point out, however, that we have no intention of attempting to offer a definitive study of the function of political science as a discipline at various levels of elementary and secondary education. Even if political science were developed as a discipline to the point where such a study were possible, the school curriculum is in too great a state of flux to permit anything like final formulations of course objectives, content, placement, and methods. As a result, it is the intention of the editors to limit themselves to outlining possibilities and to discussing what seem to be the more important possibilities.

The editors hope the information and the ideas discussed will prove of assistance to teachers of courses with a political content. The yearbook includes basic facts about government and politics, with emphasis on the United States. More than this, it provides an overview of the major ideas, underlying generalizations, and leading methods of gathering, ordering, and employing knowledge used by political scientists in order to improve their understanding of political phenomena. It is our hope to acquaint social studies teachers with a number of ways of thinking about government so the teachers can be in a better position to help their students understand their nation and the world in which they live, accommodate to it, and perhaps even improve it.

We trust, then, that this book will accomplish a number of different purposes, and have organized it accordingly. The first major section of four chapters deals with political science as a discipline in an attempt to give non-specialists an overview of its nature along with some methods of approaching it for study. It is our sanguine expectation that enough information about the nature, the content, the scope, and the methodology of political science is provided here so that the interested social studies teacher will obtain a sufficient acquaintance with the discipline to enable him to enhance the study of government in his classroom.

The information included in social studies courses is drawn largely from the social sciences—those intellectual disciplines which deal with the behavior of man in organized groups. Ideally, classroom teachers and curriculum specialists do not select course content at random. Rather, they abstract from the disciplines the information that is felt to be most useful in educating beginning students. In order to do this well, teachers should be acquainted with the overall structure of the disciplines concerned. Chapter II of this yearbook deals specifically, therefore, with political science as a discipline. Chapters III, IV, and V outline three approaches to the study of the discipline: the legal-institutional approach, the behavioral approach, and the process approach.

Widespread disagreements exist within the discipline of political science over methods of studying the phenomena that comprise it. Not all political scientists would agree that these three approaches represent a proper breakdown of the leading ways to study the discipline. A number who are behaviorally inclined would be likely to argue for a greater emphasis on the study of political behavior, perhaps with separate chapters on such methods of study as surveys and model-building. Other members of the discipline might argue for a separate chapter on the philosophical approach to the study of political phenomena, while still others might argue for a historical approach. No matter what approach or approaches are employed, however, all offer the advantage of structuring knowledge so that it can be better understood.

The next two major sections of the yearbook, encompassing eight chapters, deal with subject matter. Here the editors are attempting to provide a broad overview of the substance of political science. Areas emphasized include the changing nature of international relations, the place of the United States in world affairs, and the politics of the emerging nations of the world; along with the nature of American government, the meaning of the Bill of Rights today, intergovernmental relations in the United States, the government of metropolitan areas, and government as an initiator of social change.

The last major section of the yearbook, including another eight chapters, is largely method-oriented, dealing specifically with political science in the school program, as well as with teaching techniques and sources. One chapter, Chapter XIV, is devoted to a summary of recent research on the political socialization of children, on how young people acquire attitudes and standards of evaluation concerning their political system. The yearbook is divided, then, into four sections; with one dealing with political science as a discipline, two with the substance of the discipline, and the final one with teaching methods and learning materials.

It is not our intention in this book to attempt to make political scientists out of social studies teachers. While we would applaud any teacher who would like to train himself as a political scientist, the book is not oriented toward this goal. The footnotes and bibliographies in Chapters II through V include references to a number of sources better suited for such a purpose. It is our hope in these pages to provide enough of an overview of political science as a discipline so that social studies teachers will be in a better position to help students acquire an understanding of the political environment as they try to carry out the primary task of education: assisting individuals to live up to their potentialities, particularly their intellectual potentialities, in order that they may have fuller and more meaningful lives. It is clearly the classroom teacher who is the key to an upgrading of political studies in elementary and secondary school. There are, however, a vast number of questions and an even greater number of answers concerning education about politics. We are certainly not under the illusion that we have been able to deal with anywhere near all of these matters in this yearbook, but we have at least discussed a number of the more important questions along with some possible answers. As a result, we hope that the book will prove of value to the teacher of courses with a political content.

New Viewpoints in Sociology

E. Merle Adams, Jr.

THE title "New Viewpoints in Sociology" is fortunate because it suggests that educators are concerned with perspectives, with new ways of looking at things in the field of sociology rather than simply the addition of new facts to a relatively infinite collection. The new data referred to will be selected on the basis of whether it "makes a difference" in the way we understand social systems and the organized human behavior of which they are constituted. Of special interest are those new viewpoints which can contribute to the insight of the social studies teacher regarding modern American social life and its problems.

The Study of Patterns of Behavior

Single sentence definitions are of doubtful utility; nevertheless, sociology may be defined briefly as the empirical scientific study of the structure and process of systems of interaction among humans ("social actors," as many sociologists tend now to call them). On the most general level, this means that the sociologist observes the consistencies or patterns of behavior which humans manifest as they are oriented to each other and as they share common values. These patterns of interaction may be analyzed as *systems;* that is, sociologists are better able to understand and, to a certain degree, predict behavior if they regard it as made up of units or "parts" all of which are interrelated. Thus a society is analyzed as a system made up of units which, at the appropriate levels, are institutions, groups or "collectivities," ecological complexes, and status-roles. More will be said about the idea of "system" shortly; the important point is that sociologists tend to look at any specific pattern of social interaction as part of a larger whole.

When the sociologist is engaged in studying the units or parts of a system of action, it is said that he is analyzing its *structure*. For example, in the analysis of a family system, the structural aspect involves a description of the status-roles of its members, their responsibilities, rights, and rewards. When he proceeds to the analysis of *process*, the sociologist studies the relationships among these status-roles in the family and their modification through time.

It is important to note that the behavior which sociologists study is *motivated* behavior; it reflects certain need-dispositions within the per-

NCSS Twenty-Eigth Yearbook, 1958, pp. 95-102.

sonalities of the members of an action system. This is another way of saying that the same basic data are shared by the psychologist and the sociologist; the psychologist analyzes behavior in terms of its relevance for the personality system. Thus the interest of the sociologist and the psychologist overlap in an important way, and it is crucial for the sociologist to know something of the way in which need-dispositions develop and are satisfied or frustrated within the status-roles of an action system.

It is also important to note that the behavior which the sociologist observes is patterned in part because it is *value-oriented*. The values to which the members of an action system are oriented are to some degree shared, are always learned through experience, and are to some degree passed on to the succeeding generation. That is, the value-orientations constitute a *culture*. This is another way of saying that the same basic data are shared by the anthropologist and the sociologist; the anthropologist analyzes behavior as it is oriented to a cultural system of values. Thus, the interests of these two also overlap.[1]

From the broad definition of sociology which we have developed it may be inferred that a wide variety of patterned behavior must be studied by the sociologist; such is certainly the case if the list of topics or "sections" is examined in which scientific papers will be read at the national meetings of the American Sociological Society in August 1958. The sections include sociological theory, methodology, social psychology, sociology and history, military sociology, political sociology, industrial sociology, criminology, sociology of science, sociology of medicine, sociology of the arts, race and ethnic relations, the family, population, sociology of education, sociology of religion, social stratification, sociology and ecology of urban life, sociology of complex organization, sociology of small groups, sociology of international relations, sociology of communications and opinion, the teaching of sociology, social disorganization and deviant behavior, sociology of mental health, sociology of occupations, rural sociology, collective behavior, socialization and personality, and sociology of aging.

THE LEVEL OF THE LOCAL COMMUNITY

Although all these areas in the field of sociology are potentially of interest to the teacher of social studies, some have a more direct bearing on his professional functions than others. In focusing on a few of the

---

[1] For an extensive discussion of these relationships of sociology, psychology, and anthropology, see Parsons, Talcott, and Shils, Edward A., editors. *Toward a General Theory of Action*. Cambridge: Harvard University Press, 1951. 506 p. (Note especially the section, "Values, Motives, and Systems of Action.")

new viewpoints in sociology which are most pertinent—in order to make the most headway and avoid randomness—a particular level for discussion should be selected. It seems that the level of the *local community* will be the most useful for purposes here, especially when the strong links between the public schools and the community are considered.

In America there is still a strong element of control of public education retained by local school boards with respect to finance and policy. The teacher plays a professional role in an organizational structure which is an integral part of the total community system. As a consequence, he needs to understand the whole community in order to understand the part played by education. Further, a comprehension of the community is essential if he is to understand his students, their backgrounds and aspirations as these are related to the community in which they will live as adults. It is particularly crucial for the social studies teacher to know the community because it is his responsibility to help his students know it as a most significant segment of their social world. Finally, the teacher has an important role outside the school as a professional person and citizen who has something to contribute to his community and the solution of its problems. It is not necessary to go to the extremes of some recent philosophies of the "community-centered" school to make a case for the significance which the local community has for the social studies teacher.

We shall approach the community as a local system of action made up of certain basic institutions. This analysis will apply primarily to "urbanized" communities, since, with 64 percent of our population living in such communities, they have become a most significant phenomenon. According to the Bureau of Census, an "urbanized area consists of one or more cities of 50,000 or more and all the nearby closely settled suburban territory, or urban fringe."[2] This is a new definition of "urban" population and reflects the necessity to adjust the classification of population data so that recognition can be given to the rapid growth of settled areas surrounding cities. Increasingly, our population has become not so much city dwellers as "suburban dwellers" and the prospect for the future is that this trend will continue.[3]

---

[2] U. S. Bureau of the Census. *1950 Census of Population.* (Vol. I.) Washington, D.C.: Superintendent of Documents, Government Printing Office, 1953.

[3] For a discussion of this trend see Bogue, Donald J. *Population Growth in Standard Metropolitan Areas.* U. S. Housing and Home Finance Agency, Washington, D.C.: Superintendent of Documents, Government Printing Office, 1953. See also Bogue, Donald J. *Metropolitan Decentralization: A Study of Differential Growth,* 1950.

Bogue, Donald J. "Urbanism in the United States." *American Journal of Sociology,* 60:471-86; March 1955.

Analyzing the community as a local system of action does not imply that it is an isolated or self-subsistent entity. It must be recognized that there are numerous relationships between the institutions of a given community and those of other communities. There are significant governmental, economic, and cultural relationships among communities. Further, there is considerable movement of population between communities although the extent is only recently becoming known. Actually, the local community should also be analyzed as a sub-system within a larger regional or national system. Nevertheless, the local urbanized community contains enough of the essential life activities of its members to constitute a meaningful unit of study.

Before listing the basic institutions essential to the functioning of a community as a system, we need to consider briefly what is meant by the term "institution": First, an institution is a pattern of behavior which has a certain probability of occurrence; that is, the behavior in question occurs over and over again given the appropriate conditions. For example, young people in our communities "leave home" when they become socially mature; they nearly always marry and/or take jobs and set up a place of residence apart from their original family. Although this is not legally compulsory, it is consistent enough to be considered a significant part of the institutional structure of the family.

Second, institutionalized behavior is, as Parsons points out, "legitimately expected," that is, it is considered morally right and members of an action system have a right to expect the behavior to be forthcoming.[4] Thus, in the example of the family, we say that young people have a right to "get out on their own" and have their own family, and that their parents and others may expect this of them.

Third, institutionalized behavior is behavior which has become a matter of self-expectation. This means that the social actor not only feels the pressure of others' expectations of him but that he also expects it of himself. It has become a part of the controlling mechanisms of his personality, of his "super-ego" in psychoanalytic terms. Thus, in the example of the family, the young person who does not achieve some independence from the family in which he grew up will, unless there are special conditions such as the necessity of care for an invalid parent, suffer from internal pressures.

Fourth, the pattern of behavior may be considered an institution if it is a significant part of the structure of the local community system; that is, the functioning of the rest of the institutions in the system

---

[4] Parsons, Talcott. *Essays in Sociological Theory Pure and Applied.* Glencoe, Ill.; Free Press, 1949. p. 276.

would be seriously disturbed if the pattern in question were to disappear or be materially altered. Thus, to return again to the example of the family, if young people did not "get on their own" and establish their own families, it is doubtful whether they would be able to achieve the degree of job mobility which seems to be demanded by our occupational structure. This would be a serious consequence for our industrial system.[5]

The Eight Institutions of a Local Community System

We may consider a local community system to be made up of the following eight institutions which are necessary to its functioning:

1. kinship (or family)
2. occupation
3. exchange
4. property
5. authority
6. stratification
7. education
8. religion

These institutions are defined in terms of the functions which they serve for the community; each institution solves certain basic problems which must be faced if the community system is to exist and grow.[6] Thus the institution of *kinship* or family takes account of the basic human factors of age, sex, biological relatedness, and the considerable care necessitated by the helplessness and plasticity of the newborn child. Our kinship system is distinctive by reason of the small size and independence of its basic unit, the "conjugal" or "nuclear" family, consisting of father, mother, and immature children.

The institution of *occupation* refers to the organization of work or "job" roles in the community. The occupational structure in American communities is characterized by a high degree of division of labor, elaborate specializations, and a complex organizational structure. *Exchange* as an institution represents the manner in which things of value are regularly transferred from one individual or group to another. Our institution of exchange is characterized by a market system and media of exchange which make for easy transfer of goods and services. *Property* refers to the way in which individuals or groups hold and exercise rights in things of value. Three types of property rights should be distinguished: control, use, and disposal. With respect to

---

[5] For a discussion of the relationship of family and occupation see Parsons, Talcott. "The Social Structure of the Family." *The Family: Its Function and Destiny*. (Edited by Ruth N. Anshen.) New York: Harper and Brothers, 1949. 443 p.

[6] For a discussion of the "functional prerequisites" of action systems see Parsons, Talcott. *The Social System*. Glencoe, Ill.: Free Press, 1951. 575 p.

See also Levy, Marion. *The Structure of Society*. New Jersey: Princeton University Press, 1952. 584 p.

any given item of property, these rights may be vested in one person or group as in the classical case of "private property," or distributed among different persons and groups as in the case of modern "corporate property."[7] The three institutions of occupation, exchange, and property are often grouped together by sociologists under the heading of "economic institutions." There is considerable basis for such grouping since they are in fact always closely interrelated. However, the use of the term "occupation" here is somewhat broader than that usually implied by the label "economic organization." As herein defined, work roles in the areas of business and industry, education, government and even religion would be considered occupations if the division of labor is carried to the point where the holder of the role devotes a major portion of his time to it and relies upon it for his "living."

Authority as an institution in the community refers to the recognized right exercised by certain individuals in controlling or influencing the behavior of other individuals. If it is to be stable and effective, authority must be recognized as legitimate by those subject to it. Control which is effective but not recognized as legitimate or "right" may be termed "power." The institutionalized patterns of authority include not only those formally structured arrangements which are usually subsumed under "government," but also those informal patterns of control and influence which are not legally or officially designated. Our communities characteristically show an informal pattern of authority of broad scope while, at the same time, formal structures have been greatly elaborated. *Stratification* refers to the differential distribution of prestige among persons in the community. Some persons and families are always ranked higher than others on a scale of relative evaluation. The criteria upon which such ranking is based always involve both "ascribed" and "achieved" elements in varying degrees. Family background and inherited wealth and position are the principal elements of ascription; they involve an evaluation of the person on the basis of "who" he is rather than what he can do and how well. Achieved elements include any evaluation of the person based on his performance which can be altered through effort; the principal modern example is that of ranking based on occupational performance. Our communities show a stratification pattern in which considerable stress is placed upon occupational achievement and social mobility, "being a success and rising in the community," although family background and differential opportunities, particularly in education, play a large part in the rank which any given person enjoys.

The institution of *education* is the pattern of deliberate and system-

---

[7] Moore, Wilbert E. *Industrial Relations and the Social Order.* New York: Macmillan Co., 1946. 555 p.

atic facilitation of the learning process beyond that provided in the kinship structure and in general participations in the community. Here the meaning of the term is somewhat more restricted than is often the case in common usage which would include under "education" all learning, whatever the conditions. However, some restriction is necessary if we are to distinguish adequately between institutional structures and the vastly differing conditions for learning which they provide. Education in the present sense refers to systematic training provided in a separate organizational context, for example, a school in which the teacher as an occupational specialist functions. Many communities, particularly those which are primitive, limited in size and changing very slowly, have managed to get along with a minimum of such educational structure. Our modern communities, however, show a high degree of development of formal educational organization and we expect a wide variety of functions to be handled by such procedures.

Finally, *religion* as an institution refers to the pattern of beliefs and rites to which community members adhere. The beliefs define the ultimate nature of the world and man's place in it; they define what the social order should be and why it is right. They provide interpretations of the basic crises of life, such as birth and death; in short, they provide answers to fundamental moral questions which underlie the institutional structure of the community. The rites, or religious ceremonies and observances, are standardized behavior on special occasions which express the moral and ideological commitments contained in the religious beliefs. Our communities manifest a large number of religious sects and denominations representing a wide variety of organizational types; yet, there is a relatively low level of religious conflict.

New Viewpoints on the Eight Institutions

The basic institutions which form the backbone of any community system have been outlined here. Each is necessary to the functioning of the system and all are interrelated so that a change in one involves changes in the others. We are now ready to consider some of the new viewpoints which have developed in sociology regarding each of the eight community institutions. However, it should be pointed out that what we have discussed thus far is a "new viewpoint" in sociology, namely, the increasing tendency to analyze behavior as constituting a "system." We are applying this concept to the local community; there are several other levels of society at which this concept is now being applied such as the family,[8] the small work group or committee,[9]

---

[8] Parsons, Talcott, and Bales, Robert F. *The Family: Socialization and Interaction Process.* Glencoe, Ill.: Free Press, 1955. 422 p.

[9] Homans, G. C. *The Human Group.* New York: Harcourt, Brace and Co., 1950; Bales, Robert F. *Interaction Process Analysis.* Cambridge: Addison-Wesley Press, 1950.

and the level of the total society which will now be discussed.[10]

Turning first to the institution of kinship or family, perhaps the most important new perspective is the tendency to reject the idea that the family is in a process of breakdown or disintegration as an institution and to regard it instead as in a process of adjustment to other community institutions. Even before Ogburn's classic analysis[11] of the family's loss of such functions as production, recreation, and education, sociologists had tended to interpret changes in family structure as symptomatic of its decline. The average family was becoming smaller due partly to the increasing isolation of the conjugal unit and also because of a gradually declining birth rate which meant that families contained fewer children. Another telling point was the increasing rate of divorce. Finally, there was a tendency to blame family weakness for a number of social problems such as juvenile delinquency.

There are now signs that a somewhat different perspective of the family is developing as a result of new data on family trends as well as from a better understanding of the family's relationships to other institutions. The functional significance of the small size of the basic family unit has been pointed out by Parsons.[12] It seems crucial that our family units be independent to a considerable degree if they are to be socially mobile as our industrial and occupational system requires. Such independence also means that it is more feasible for the breadwinner of the family to be promoted and to move with his dependents up the social scale. When family units are large and extended, it is virtually impossible for a member to be upwardly mobile even if his achievements should warrant it; he must carry the whole extended family with him. If the family structure were to turn in the direction of a more extended unit, there would be a much less open class system in our communities than there is now. Inheritance of prestige rank would have to be stressed to a much greater degree....

---

[10] Parsons, Talcott, *The Social System. Op. cit.*
See also:
Parsons, Talcott, and Shils, E. A., editors. *Toward a General Theory of Action. Op. Cit.*
Levy, Marion. *The Structure of Society. Op. cit.*
[11] Ogburn, William F. "The Family and Its Functions." *Recent Social Trends in the United States.* New York: McGraw-Hill Book Co., 1933, p. 664-72.
[12] Parsons, Talcott. "The Kinship Structure of Contemporary United States." *Essays in Sociological Theory, Pure and Applied.* Glencoe, Ill.: Free Press, 1949. 379 p.
See also:
Parsons, Talcott. "The Social Structure of the Family." *The Family: Its Function and Destiny. Op. cit.*
Parsons, Talcott, and Bales, Robert F. *The Family Socialization and Interaction Process. Op. cit.*

CONTENT AND CURRICULUM

FABLE OF THE ACTIVITY CURRICULUM

Once upon a time the animals decided they must do something heroic to meet the problems of a brave "new world." So they decided to organize a school. They adopted an activity curriculum consisting of climbing, swimming, running, and flying, and to make it easier to administer, all the animals took all the courses.

The duck was excellent in swimming, better in fact than his instructor, and made passing grades in flying, but he was very poor in running. Since he was slow in running, he had to stay after school and also drop swimming to practice running. This was kept up until his web feet were so badly worn and he was only average in swimming. That average was acceptable in school so nobody worried about that except the duck.

The rabbit started at the top of the class in running but had a nervous breakdown because of so much make-up work in swimming.

The squirrel was excellent in climbing until he developed frustration in the flying class where his teacher made him start from the ground up instead of from the tree top down. He also developed charley horses from over exertion and so got C in climbing and D in running.

Now the eagle was a problem child and was disciplined severely. In the climbing class he beat all the others to the top of the tree but insisted on using his own way to get there.

At the end of the year, an abnormal eel that could swim exceedingly well, and also run, climb, and fly a little, had the highest average and was valedictorian.

The prairie dog stayed out of school and fought the tax levy because the administration would not add digging and burrowing to the curriculum. They apprenticed their child to a badger and later joined the groundhogs and gophers to start a successful private school....

Has this fable a moral?

Anonymous.

What Are We Teaching in Social Studies and Science?

DONALD L. BARNES
Associate Professor of Education, Ball State Teachers College
Muncie, Indiana

In the heat of argument surrounding present controversies over curricular offerings in American schools, zealots on all sides frequently resort to sweeping statements based upon limited observations.

The two national surveys reported in this article were conducted in an effort to piece together a more accurate picture of current offerings in social studies and science in cities and towns throughout the United States. Sixty-two cities in forty-two states from Maine to California co-operated in the study.

Social Studies

Completed tabulations in social studies reveal that there is much similarity among the programs on various grade levels. Programs begin with studies of people and things close at hand and expand as children's interests expand. The percentage of school systems offering each topic at each grade level is as follows:

Grade One: Family, 30 per cent; Home, 84 per cent; School, 82 per cent; and Other, 16 per cent.

Grade Two: Community, 42 per cent; Neighborhood, 44 per cent; Community Helpers, 44 per cent; and Other, 20 per cent.

Grade Three: Indians, 22 per cent; Pioneers, 10 per cent; Food, 24 per cent; Shelter, 24 per cent; Clothing, 26 per cent; Transportation and Communication, 22 per cent; Our City, 68 per cent; and Other, 18 per cent.

Grade Four: Our State, 40 per cent; and Beginning Readiness for History and Geography, 78 per cent.

Grade Five: United States, Past and Present, 90 per cent; Western Hemisphere, 12 per cent; and Other, 4 per cent.

Grade Six: Old World, 42 per cent; Other Nations, 42 per cent; Eastern Hemisphere, 12 per cent; and Other, 14 per cent.

Grade Seven: U. S. Geography, 24 per cent; World Geography, 48 per cent; State Geography, 24 per cent; State History, 26 per cent; and Other, 24 per cent.

Grade Eight: U. S. History, 82 per cent; Citizenship, 14 per cent; and Other, 16 per cent.

Grade Nine: World Geography, 18 per cent; World History, 26 per cent; Civics, 58 per cent; and Other, 8 per cent.

Grade Ten: World History, 88 per cent; World Geography, 28 per cent; and Other, 4 per cent.

Grade Eleven: U. S. History, 82 per cent; Sociology, 10 per cent; Government, 16 per cent; and Other, 27 per cent.

Grade Twelve: Economics and/or

Education, October, 1960, pp. 121-123.

Sociology, 54 per cent; Government, 60 per cent; and U. S. History, 26 per cent.

In the absence of a centralized governmental control agency similar to those found in European countries, it is surprising to find such great similarity among the offerings in the various school systems. A partial explanation of the phenomenon may lie in the fact that most large publishers in the United States enjoy nation-wide distribution of their school-texts—a reflection of common values held by citizens throughout the country.

Approximately 90 per cent of the cities in the study indicated that they used the unit method in teaching social studies. The units incorporated panels, group and committee work, films, pupil-teacher planning, audio-visual materials, and trips through the city or area in which the school was located. Most units consisted of an introduction, a study or mastery period, and an evaluation period. The length of units varied from two to six weeks.

Science

The cities surveyed also reflected similarity among their science offerings on each grade level. All of the school systems inaugurated their science programs at the first-grade level. The topics under common headings appeared as follows:

Grade One: Living Things, 88 per cent; The Earth, 76 per cent; The Universe, 40 percent; Natural Forces, 67 per cent; Machines, 58 per cent; Physical and Chemical Changes, 27 per cent; and Other, 5 per cent.

Grade Two: Living Things, 85 per cent; The Earth, 80 per cent; The Universe, 42 per cent; Natural Forces, 45 per cent; Machines, 33 per cent; and Physical and Chemical Changes, 27 per cent.

Grade Three: Living Things, 88 per cent; The Earth, 79 per cent; The Universe, 54 per cent; Natural Forces, 45 per cent; Machines, 54 per cent; Physical and Chemical Changes, 21 per cent; and Other, 1 per cent.

Grade Four: Living Things, 79 per cent; The Earth, 76 per cent; The Universe, 82 per cent; Natural Forces, 61 per cent; Machines, 37 per cent; Physical and Chemical Changes, 24 per cent; and Other, 6 per cent.

Grade Five: Living Things, 88 per cent; The Earth, 85 per cent; The Universe, 39 per cent; Natural Forces, 54 per cent; Machines, 46 per cent; Physical and Chemical Changes, 45 per cent.

Grade Six: Living Things, 60 per cent; The Earth, 85 per cent; The Universe, 67 per cent; Natural Forces, 64 per cent; Machines, 45 per cent; Physical and Chemical Changes, 36 per cent; and Other, 18 per cent.

Grade Seven: General Science, 70 per cent; Other, 21 per cent; no course, 9 per cent.

Grade Eight: General Science, 85 per cent; Other, 12 per cent; no course, 3 per cent.

Grade Nine: General Science, 87 per cent; Biology, 18 per cent; and Other, 12 per cent.

Grade Ten: Biology, 100 per cent; and Other, 21 per cent.

Grade Eleven: Physics, 76 per cent; Chemistry, 64 per cent; and Other, 42 per cent.

Grade Twelve: Chemistry, 76 per cent; Physics, 70 per cent; and Other, 45 per cent.

Forty-two per cent of the schools reporting indicated that, where possible, science was correlated with other subjects, particularly with social studies. Six per cent of the schools surveyed indicated that they had no formal course of study for science, but provided a source book of science experiences to be used in the development of the core areas.

The data collected did not indicate whether science was taught as a method of investigation or simply as a study of natural phenomena. The study of living things received the greatest stress up through the fifth grade.

Conclusions

Much has been said about life-adjustment courses in the social-science curricula and about watered-down science courses in flycasting or photography. The present survey failed to uncover evidence of degenerate curricular offerings. Simple physics, chemistry, and biology have been added to the curriculum, along with jets and rockets, beginning at the sixth-grade level. It might be concluded that our curricular offerings have remained far too stable over recent years of rapid change.

By HUBER M. WALSH

Elementary Social Studies: *Content Plus!*

Huber M. Walsh is associate professor at the University of Toledo, Ohio.

IN RESPONSE TO THE WIDELY RECOGnized need for broader content emphasis in elementary social studies, teachers, curriculum workers and professors are effecting searching analyses and extensive revisions of existing programs. A result of this activity has been the emergence of a "new look" in elementary social studies in which programs are based (more distinctly than before) upon content drawn from the social sciences. In general this approach focuses upon major understandings or generalizations which are widely applicable key ideas taken from academic disciplines such as geography, history, sociology, anthropology, political science and economics.

Many persons welcome this approach for it promises to advance elementary social studies in several significant ways. *First,* this plan permits a more direct relationship between elementary social studies instruction and the parent social sciences—a relationship long in coming. *Second,* instruction built upon major understandings from the social sciences holds the promise of generally up-grading content coverage in the elementary school. *Third,* instruction in key ideas, according to authorities, can promote deeper comprehension, result in better transfer of knowledge and facilitate subsequent learning (2,4). Perhaps the greatest value of such instruction is that it prepares the learner for independent study (1).

Worthwhile though it is, this instructional plan may not be the panacea which many persons are seeking. Indeed, if made the sole basis for teaching, it could produce an undesirable imbalance in the social studies program. Present society demands that the schools of today equip future citizens with two essential ingredients for successful living: *knowledge* and *skill in working effectively with others.* Bringing youngsters into contact with big ideas from the disciplines will expose them to basic knowledge about man and his interrelationships. But, the acquisition of such information does not *ipso facto* insure the pupil will then apply appropriate aspects of this knowledge to improve *his own* human relationships. Teachers know that sometimes the child most able to verbalize eloquently about desirable behavior (*e.g.,* feelings of tolerance, patience with others) proves to be most inept in practicing what he preaches; obviously he has not learned beyond the level of sheer verbalism. If children are to extend knowledge beyond verbalism they must put it to work in

Childhood Education, 1966, No.43, pp. 124-126.

120

deeds. This requires systematically planned learning experiences in which the pupil has the opportunity to *apply* what he has learned about desirable human behavior. These kinds of learning activities are the essence of what is commonly referred to as *social education*. Content alone, without provisions for social education, is not enough.

Content Plus

The child needs content *plus* social education. Content *alone* cannot constitute the whole social studies program any more than social education alone—both are essential and complementary; both must be in sensible proportion in a sound program designed for society's needs.

The present emphasis on subject matter does not automatically imperil acquisition and practice of important social learnings; but in some situations this stress on subject matter has been accompanied by a devaluation of social education. One reason is that educational respectability attaches more to the teaching of content than to the development and practice of social education. The danger is that social learnings in the elementary school will continue to receive diminished attention. If certain critics have their way, social education will be abandoned despite society's needs to the contrary (6). In some classrooms acquisition of information is regarded as an end in itself. Comprehension of key ideas and concepts is seen as the principal and exclusive instructional outcome. Little or no attention is given to providing social settings which give children opportunity to apply some of this knowledge in their day-to-day relationships under the guidance and direction of the classroom teacher. When this happens, teachers can miss determinate kinds of learning contacts in which the child's skill in human relations can be appraised, diagnosed and improved.

Overemphasis on content could now weaken the effectiveness of social studies programs in much the same way as overemphasis on social education did in the past. The former cry of critics was that the elementary child was being "socialized to death." Unless we avoid rushing to the opposite extreme, their future criticism may well be that the child is being "intellectualized to death." Why should we sacrifice either when we can have both? There is no reason to make it an "either/or" case. A sensible middle course can be maintained—*both* subject-matter and social learnings can be developed simultaneously without sacrificing either. They are compatible and complementary. Many social learnings taught and practiced in the elementary schools are predicated upon human relations skills closely allied to the funded knowledge in the social and behavioral sciences. Consider, for example, the major idea in political science: every known society has made rules on how its members should get along together and instituted coercive sanctions to help insure that rules are obeyed (3,5). This idea is germane to the classroom social context in which teacher and pupils together formulate guidelines and sanctions essential to their getting along together.

Specific social learnings in the classroom depend upon a variety of considerations. Examples for developing behaviors are: being a worthy group member (participating in discussion and resolution of questions and issues); practicing social amenities; communicating effectively (listening and speaking); respecting one's own rights and responsibilities and those of others.

These objectives can be served simultaneously through learning experiences in *both* subject-matter and social learnings. Illustrations of both follow.

Teacher-Led Group Discussions: Discussions with the entire class afford the teacher the opportunity to present new human relations ideas. For the pupil, such teacher-guided activities give practice in some of the social skills.

John's group is of the opinion that the class has gathered sufficient information on the way of life in India, but Virginia's group believes further research is necessary. The teacher might ask: How shall we decide? What do we need to know in order to make a reasonable decision?

This activity can be a confluence of *both* content and social learnings. Social learnings deal with group processes in sound decision making, while content learnings involve subject matter which is the essence of the discussion. Exchange of ideas can be instrumental in developing skills associated with precise transmission and reception of ideas.

Study Sessions: Study sessions can be settings for social education while children investigate content — especially when the class is divided into study groups of four or five. These small groups give opportunity to practice sound *leadership* and *followership* skills.

Paul, as group leader, determines with the others how the day's work shall be carried on. Each person may contribute ideas during the planning phase. Following that, each has an opportunity to practice directing his individual efforts toward reaching the mark. Through combined effort a team can work together to achieve the common goal.

Reporting: Groups of children can report to others the results of their studies. Usually reporting deals with content; but since it involves people working with people, it can function as settings for social learning. A group must decide what data and information will be presented and how this knowledge can be communicated clearly to the audience. During reporting time youngsters in the audience can practice what they have learned about courteous listening, respect and tolerance for the persons in the spotlight.

Each content experience need not unfailingly have a social dimension any more than every social learning must have content. As indicated above, there are worthwhile learning activities in which the two can be combined in a mutually beneficial way. Surely both are compatible in the same social studies program.

Most of today's pupils are destined to spend the rest of their lives dealing with others. Ideally, youngsters should begin learning and practicing good human relations during the formative elementary years. Teaching content and developing social learnings are not antithetical. Neither need be neglected if social studies programs are to be effective in preparing our future citizens. Wise educators responsible for improving social studies programs will be successful in finding the middle course which sacrifices neither content nor social education.

References

1. BRUNER, JEROME S. *The Process of Education.* Cambridge: Harvard University Press, 1960.
2. KEISLAR, E. R., and McNEIL, J. D. "Teaching Science and Mathematics by Auto-Instruction in the Primary Grades: An Experimental Strategy in Curriculum Development." Los Angeles: The Authors, October 1961 (mimeographed).
3. LLEWELLYN, K. N. "Law and Civilization," *People, Power and Politics.* L. J. Gould and E. W. Steele (eds.). New York: Random House, 1961. Pp. 321-9.
4. PHENIX, PHILIP H. "Key Concepts and the Crisis in Learning," *Teachers College Record* (December 1956), 58:137-143.
5. RIENOW, ROBERT. *Introduction to Government.* New York: Alfred A. Knopf, 1956.
6. SMITH, MORTIMER. "Social Studies Challenged," *The Toledo Blade Sunday Magazine* (July 26, 1964). Pp. 4-5, ff.

Challenging the Expanding-Environment Theory

by RONALD O. SMITH AND CHARLES F. CARDINELL

DO CHILDREN have broader interests than the confines of the home, the neighborhood, and the community as they enter the elementary school? A committee composed of 18 teachers and administrators of the Portland (Oregon) public school system raised this question in February, 1963, when it met to examine the school's social studies sequence, built on the expanding-environment theory. It was the committee's opinion that the children entering our elementary schools today have had far broader experiences, both real and vicarious, than the children for whom the expanding-environment program was created. Supporting this contention is the fact that many American children now entering the elementary schools have traveled throughout the 50 states of their own country with their parents, and some have even been all around the world. The county seat is no longer the far limit it was for many Americans of the early twentieth century. And even those children who have stayed at home have been transported from their own neighborhood to many distant corners of the earth through the medium of television.

The mobility of Americans at mid-century prompts not only Portland teachers, but teachers throughout America, to question the validity of the expanding-environment theory.

THE STUDY

In an attempt to determine to what extent elementary school children do have interests beyond their immediate environment, the members of the committee decided to examine their classes and explore the children's understanding of and reaction to certain words with which all of them were more or less familiar. The words selected for this purpose were *honesty, India, river, Washington,* and *world*.

A total of 81 classes participated in the study, with each class averaging about 30 pupils. As a result, approximately 2500 children were involved. The classes were distributed as follows: kindergarten (7), grade one (8), grade two (8), grade three (10),

grade four (9), grade five (10), grade six (12), grade seven (9), grade eight (8).

For several reasons, including the number of different people participating in this informal investigation, the committee did not expect to achieve any statistical exactness. Rather, it sought to determine the major responses of the various age groups. Although schools in various socio-economic areas of the city participated, no significant differences between schools were noted when the results of the study were compared. In fact, once the results from the first school had been recorded, all the other schools were found to have similar patterns of response.

As a common point of departure, teachers asked the children, "What does the word, [one of the five noted above] mean to you?" They urged the children to answer in one word or in a short phrase, and assured them that there was no "right" or "wrong" reply to the question. In some kindergarten and primary classes, the teachers obtained the responses through class discussion, while in other classes the children whispered their answers to the teacher. In the intermediate and upper grades the children wrote their responses on paper, with the result that their statements were longer and more sophisticated than those in the lower grades.

RESPONSES TO THE WORD *Honesty*

At all grade levels, the most consistent associations with the word *honesty* were: "telling the truth . . . being truthful [This was the most uniformly noted response of any of the five test items of this investigation] honest . . . God and love . . . not to lie . . . to be trustworthy."

Associations limited to the primary grades were "polite . . . being good." Children K-5 were concerned with the concept of "promise" and keeping it. Primary children also mentioned many negative attributes within their experience, e.g., "not to break toys," etc.

Intermediate and upper-grade children more frequently had these associations: "Scout's honor (5-8) . . . Abe Lincoln (4-8) . . . not to steal (4-8) . . . citizenship (6-8) . . . loyal (6-8) . . . sincere (6-8) . . . police (5-8)." Children beginning in grade 3 mentioned not cheating and good sportsmanship, as in games, etc.

This report of a committee project carried on last winter was prepared by RONALD O. SMITH, *Supervisor of Social Studies in the Public Schools of Portland, Oregon, and* CHARLES F. CARDINELL, *Assistant Supervisor.*

Social Education, March, 1964, No. 20, pp. 141-143.

Responses to the Word *India*

The most consistent associations with the word *India* for all grade levels were: "It is a country... wild animals... Indians [in terms of the North American stereotypes]... elephants... camels... jungle... desert... snakes and snake charmers... sunny and hot... missionaries at work."

Associations limited to the primary grades were: "it is a town... it is a state in the U.S. (K-5)."

Characteristic of the intermediate grades were such associations as "natives... jewels... tiger hunting... located in Africa (5-7)... wars (6 only)... pyramids (4-8)."

Upper-grade children more frequently had these associations: "starvation (4-8)... dark people (3-8)... country in the Far East... Eastern hemisphere... temples (3-8)... Taj Mahal (6-8)... wars (6-8)... overpopulation... spices... Red China... Marco Polo (5-8)... poverty (6-8)... [specific religions] Moslem... Hindu... Buddhist." Children in grades 7-8 attempted to give a more specific location for India. Many were oriented to visualizations from maps and mentioned "diamond shaped," or "below China."

Responses to the Word *River*

The most consistent association with the word *river* for all grades were: "fishing [with more emphasis at grades 7-8]... coolness... swimming... water... fish... boat... stream... water skiing."

The following associations were limited to the primary grades: "an ocean... place where fish live... place for big boats... lake (K-6)... hole with water in it... rain... clouds... weather... snow... sharks." "Whales" were associated with the word by kindergartners.

These associations were characteristic of the intermediate grades: "body of water (3-4)... electricity (3-8)... commerce, trade (3-6)... bridges (2-8) for drinking (3-7)... drowning, falling in (3-7)... [specific river names] Willamette (3)... Columbia (4) Mississippi (5)... Amazon (6)... [specific names of water animals]."

Associations more frequent among upper-grade children were: "flows, flowing (4-8)... transportation route (7-8)... valley (6-8)." Upper-graders became more specific in describing a river with a source, mouth, tributaries, and motion, using gradually more sophisticated terms.

Responses to the Word *Washington*

Most consistent associations for the word *Washington* for all grade levels were: "honest, great man... a good man... District of Columbia, D.C.... a city... President Kennedy... George Washington... President of the United States... a state [by grade 4 children began giving specific location of Washington]... Father of our Country... Seattle... World's Fair... White House... place where relatives live.

Limited to the primary grades were "Abraham Lincoln (K-2)... America... birthday... flag."

Intermediate and upper-grade children more frequently had such associations as: "war... Revolutionary War (5-8)... where presidents live (4-8)... cherry tree anecdote of Washington's boyhood (5-8)... first president (5-8)... George Washington Carver (5-8)... a general (5-8)... apples (6-8)... a leader (4-8)... capitol (3-8)... Congress and government (6-8)."

Responses to the Word *World*

The most consistent associations with the word *world* for all grade levels were: "people... like a ball... goes around and around... animals live on it... lots of countries... shaped like a globe... is round... space... where people live... a planet... God and His creation of the world."

The following associations were limited to the primary grades: "schools... our flag... sun... moon... sky... rockets... homes and houses."

Characteristic of the intermediate grades were: "a country... bigness of the earth (2-8)... universe (5-8)... land and water distribution [idea of the continents] (4-8)... Earth (3-8)." Children in grades 5-8 were profoundly concerned with the idea of world conflict, wars, communism, etc.

Upper-grade children more frequently had these associations: "the world is part of the solar system (6-8)... orbit of the world... shape of the earth [particularly that it is a modified 'pear shape']... rivers (6-8)." The children expressed ideas that showed they had a visualization of the world based on maps and globes they had seen.

Observations and Conclusions

When the members of the committee chose the word *honesty* they did not expect that the children would be able adequately to verbalize their concepts of the term. However, instead of a diversity of responses, the 2500 children involved in the study generally limited their responses to those listed above. This was not as evident in regard to any of the other four terms.

As might be expected, the youngest children expressed their ideas about honesty by citing situations very real to them. Older children were more verbal in their responses and showed a stronger loyalty to their peer groups than the younger children. The older children also evidenced a concern for the control of violence, mentioning, for example, "not to steal" and "police."

The diversity of associations with the word, *India*, was surprising, for the study of India is not included in the elementary sequence of the Portland Public Schools. Despite the fact that their concepts were for the most part erroneous, the children seemed to have an interest in this part of the world. The need for some instruction on India early in school is indicated to prevent children from building these erroneous concepts.

Naturally enough, the upper-grade children were able to give a more specific location for India. Their concern with poverty, starvation, and overpopulation was surprising, considering that these problems are not normally emphasized in the elementary school curriculum.

The effect of television on children's social studies concepts is dramatically evident with this particular test item. When the committee sought for an explanation for the diversity of responses to *India*, someone recalled that an old Shirley Temple film with India as its locale had been shown on television the Saturday afternoon before the study took place!

Primary children attempted to describe the word *river* in terms of their direct experiences. They could not discriminate between rivers, lakes, and oceans. Progressing from grade to grade, the school curriculum made its contribution in terms of names, functions, and uses of rivers. Upper-grade children were more adept at defining the word. Children in grades 3-7 seemed to have a fear of falling in and drowning in the rivers they visualized.

Apparently even from an early age children have many associations with the word *Washington*. They associate the Presidents with Washington. Presidents Roosevelt, Kennedy, Lincoln, and Eisenhower were all mentioned. Washington and Lincoln are apparently confused images with primary youngsters. Nevertheless, the term *Washington* appears to involve intense patriotic feelings in younger children.

As children progress in school, they seem to enlarge their concepts of *Washington*. They become aware of the function of the city of Washington as the seat of the nation's government. They learn more, too, about the (for them) neighboring state of Washington, expressing their ideas in terms of the frequently used description, "the evergreen state," and the classic stereotype, "apples."

Children of all grade levels consistently associated Washington with monuments, statues, and the familiar painting of Washington crossing the Delaware.

Although children at all grade levels, including kindergarten, knew that the *world* is a spheroid and that it is a planet, too many described it only as a place for animals and peoples to live and as a grouping of many countries. While the responses indicated that children did acquire broader concepts of *world* as they progressed through the grades, the very real need for more effective teaching about geographical terms was brought out by the responses to this item and to the term, *river*.

This study cannot, of course, in any sense be considered scientific research, but it did prove of great value to the members of the committee who undertook it, and it does point to the need for more definitive studies in this field. It clearly indicates that children *do* have interests in things beyond their immediate environment; that television does have a great influence on children's outlooks; that there is a need for more effective instruction concerning geographic terms at an earlier grade level; and that children even in kindergarten have distinct, if often erroneous, concepts of some terms used in social studies.

The study has served, in our case, to inspire the committee to develop a broader curriculum for the elementary grades than the traditional program built on the theme of an "expanding environment."

The school not only provides instruction in important learnings but also serves as a proving ground for the application of these learnings. Within the school environment, problem-solving and decision-making situations can be carefully controlled. Errors in judgment or wrong decisions rarely have disastrous consequences. In life outside the school, however, decision making and problem solving are much more critical. The skills needed to resolve many of the problems encountered in life are the ones with which the social studies deal. Consequently, the school seeks to bring the student's skill development to a level that will make it possible for him to do creative problem solving on his own throughout his lifetime. Perhaps much of what the pupil learns in the social studies will wear thin or become obsolete. But skills learned in school continue to be functional indefinitely, or for so long as they are used. Skills are among the most permanent of the learnings.—From John Jarolimek, "The Psychology of Skill Development," in *Skill Development in the Social Studies,* the Thirty-Third Yearbook of the National Council for the Social Studies.

Clarifying Social Studies Terms

JOE PARK AND O. W. STEPHENSON

DURING the last few decades educators have exercised an unwarranted lexical license with respect to the use of certain terms. In fact, some words have been assigned meanings which no lexicographer ever intended they should have. Because of this arbitrary practice, confusion has resulted to such an extent that on hearing one of these words, or seeing it in print, one has to wait until the connotation has been completely revealed before he can be sure of the sense in which it is being used. It is true, of course, that a new concept justifies the creation of a new word, but too much authority is assumed when the generally accepted dictionary meaning of an old term is wrongfully elasticized to take care of that concept. In the interests of clarity of thought and expression it should be agreed that new words should be brought into existence only when there is a genuine need of them, and that dictionary definitions should be closely adhered to if there is no such need.

Confusion and ambiguity in key terms have long plagued the social studies field. The authors of this analysis are, respectively, critic teacher in the social studies department of the University High School, University of Michigan, and associate professor of the teaching of history in the School of Education and head of the social studies department of the University High School.

Perhaps there is no area in education where more liberties have been taken with word meanings than in the social studies. Great confusion exists in these fields, particularly as a result of the improper use of the terms *fusion, integration, correlation,* and *core* as these are applied to the organization of social studies materials. As T. H. Schutte points out:

... we have various proposals for meeting some of the shortcomings of our educational program. Prominent among these we find suggestions for correlation, for integration, for a central core, for unit organization, and so forth. The meaning of these plans is not always clear when they are discussed.[1] ...

The lack of clarity is also noted by E. B. Wesley, who writes that:

The student of education who seeks to find a clear definition of fusion will find it if he reads *one* writer; if he reads two or more, he will discover that fusion is practically synonymous with concentration, integration, problems, correlation, or almost any other type of organization.[2]

As an example of the implied confusion we cite the first paragraph of a recently published article, which bore the title "Fusion of Art and Social Studies."

Through art, it is possible for the teacher to create a sincere appreciation of the social studies, as well as to enrich the teaching of art itself. The teacher who inspires her pupils with a love for history and geography, and the desire to delve further into these subjects, is making a real contribution. There is no better way than through correlation with art.[3]

Thus the confusion in the use of terms has not gone unnoticed. It may be that the

---

[1] T. H. Schutte, *Teaching the Social Studies on the Secondary School Level.* New York: Prentice Hall, 1938, p. 285.
[2] Edgar B. Wesley, *Teaching the Social Studies.* Boston: Heath, 1937, p. 245.
[3] Elsa S. Saunders, "Fusion of Art and Social Studies," *Instructor,* April, 1937, p. 20.

Social Education, 1940, No. 4, pp. 311-319.

confusion and the attention drawn to it by such authorities as we have quoted caused Margaret Koch to write that, "In order to avoid confusion, definitions should in each case accompany the use of the term since the meanings vary so that the same statement may not or, in some cases, cannot be true of all."[4] In the light of her suggestion, it will be of interest to see how a few of these terms are used or defined, since to do so will bring out the need of agreement as to meanings.

Fusion

LET us begin with *fusion*. According to Charles A. Beard, fusion, or a synthesis of social science, could it be effected, "would be a skillfully wrought mosaic rather than a subliminal coalescence in which separate disciplines would disappear and completely lose their identity as law, politics, economics, geography, and history."[5] The disappearance of these disciplines also receives the attention of R. M. Tryon. At a "Conference Upon Desirable Adjustments Between History and Other Social Studies in the Elementary and Secondary Schools," he enumerated, among other types of adjustment,

> ... one that contemplates a combined course in these subjects. Some advocates of this adjustment would go so far as to supplant all the independent work now done in geography, history, and civics, with a new course made by a careful selection of material from the social studies field.[6]

What the resultant product would be, Tryon does not say, but we do not have to go far to find out. J. M. Gambrill not only furnishes us a description of what he considers fusion to be, but tells us what the organization of materials is like when fusion has been accomplished:

> Materials from history, geography, economics, political science, anthropology, sociology or any other field needed is drawn upon. Materials are then organized definitely in "problem-solving form." Common subject lines are wholly disregarded, yet the word "merge" is not used lest it suggest that the content of the "present school subjects" has been used in new combinations. "Only one criterion is employed in selecting the content of the course; its contribution to present living."[7]

The disregard for subject lines is, according to both D. C. Knowlton and Wesley, an essential characteristic of fusion courses. As the former sees them, such courses are neither history, geography, nor civics, but a synthesis of these that results in an approximation of a true social studies course because it does ignore subject boundaries.[8] He maintains, moreover, that such courses are organized according to the findings of modern psychology.[9] As Wesley understands them, there is "the complete negation of subject organization." In his opinion,

> The fusionist professes to meet the needs of the boys and girls rather than to maintain an allegiance to scholarship. He believes that a fused organization promotes this objective better than a subject organization. The proponents of subjects and the proponents of fusion agree as to the desirability of making their materials significant; both agree that units, problems, projects, and topics are possible within either organization; but the fusionist stresses the significance of his *organization*.[10]

It is also pointed out by Wesley that the fusionist regards the subject viewpoint as an impediment to learning.[11] Something of the same sort is set forth by H. O. Rugg in "A Preface to the Reconstruction of the American School Curriculum":

> We must invent a new synthesis of knowledge and make it the basis of the entire school curriculum. The conventional barriers between the existing subjects must be ignored in curriculum building. The *starting point* shall be the social institution, or the political and economic problem,—not the subject. Psychological forces must oust economic and political form as the directing themes of organization [p. 607]. The first change ... imperatively needed in the school curriculum is a change in the character of the content. Paralleling this there is a second: the critical need for a sweeping reconstruction of the *organization* of our entire school curriculum [p. 606].[12]

---

[4] Margaret Koch, "Social Studies and the Correlated Course," *Progressive Education*, November, 1935, p. 460.
[5] Charles A. Beard, *A Charter for the Social Studies*. New York: Scribner, 1932, p. 21.
[6] Rolla M. Tryon, "Desirable Adjustments Between History and the Other Social Studies in the Elementary and Secondary Schools," *Historical Outlook*, March, 1922, p. 81.
[7] J. M. Gambrill, "Experimental Curriculum-Making in the Social Studies," *Historical Outlook*, December, 1923, p. 395.
[8] Daniel Knowlton, *History and the Other Social Studies in the Junior High School*. New York: Scribner 1926, pp. 2-3.
[9] *Ibid.*, p. 3.
[10] Edgar B. Wesley, *op. cit.*, p. 245.
[11] *Ibid.*
[12] Harold O. Rugg, "A Preface to the Reconstruction of the American School Curriculum," *Teachers College Record*, March, 1926, pp. 606-07.

As a result of his analysis of several so-called fusion courses, H. E. Wilson makes three statements to which the fusionist doubtless would subscribe. These statements, he says, "are not to be regarded as separate from one another but as closely integrated to form in mutual support, the platform of the fusion movement." According to these statements,

> 1. Only such material as has direct value in developing in pupils intelligent understandings and tolerant, and cooperative appreciations fitting them to engage in the activities of the life of the time shall be taught.
> 2. Selected subject matter in the social sciences must be organized in units of experience, psychologically appealing and learnable, and corresponding as closely as possible to life situations.
> 3. Traditional subject boundaries shall be ignored in the construction of the social-science curriculum; subject fields not only fail to achieve the purposes of education but interfere with the selection and organization of a curriculum which will achieve these purposes. The current problem rather than the subject fact is the heart of the functional unit.[13]

The word *fusion* was chosen to describe this "new synthesis of knowledge" because the word means, among other things, a "union or blending of things as if melted together by heat." In the strict dictionary sense of the word there can be no such thing as fusion, nor can there be, perhaps, in the elasticized sense in which the word is used by the authors we have quoted; it is not possible to consider all aspects of a situation at one and the same time. However, this need not concern us here; what we need is a definition of fusion which will be acceptable to everyone and which will rid us of some of the confusion which now exists in the social studies. By bringing together the various essential characteristics emphasized by these authors, fusion may be defined as *the organization of worthwhile, life-like experiences and materials into psychologically sound learning units which take no account of social studies boundaries as such.*

See also Ernest Horn, *Methods of Instruction in the Social Studies* (New York: Scribner, 1937), p. 12, for recognition of loss of identity of subjects as a fundamental assumption in unification, fusion, or integration.

[13] Howard E. Wilson, *The Fusion of the Social Studies in the Junior High Schools.* Cambridge: Harvard Univ. Press, 1933, p. 61.

INTEGRATION

INTEGRATION is another word which has been given various meanings by writers in the social studies, though the standard dictionaries agree on the essential idea that it is a process of uniting parts into a larger whole. Wesley defines integration as an organization of subject matter which emphasizes the social studies field as a whole rather than the separate subjects which compose this field. The subjects are recognized, it is true, but they are freely ignored in selecting and arranging materials for teaching purposes.[14] In the writers' interpretation, the term applies only to materials drawn from the social studies. To M. J. Stormzand and R. H. Lewis, however, integration is the bringing "to bear upon a life situation knowledge, skills, habits, and attitudes from all pertinent fields of learning,"[15] while to the Nortons it is merely the uniting of all school subjects.[16]

What the Nortons meant may be much the same as the writer of the preface to the seventh-grade social studies course of Aliquippa, Pennsylvania, had in mind when he described the integrated course of that city:

> The major field of concentration in the Junior High School of Aliquippa is an integrated learning unit in social sciences including all materials in the following fields: history, geography, health, English expression (oral and written), reading, spelling, vocabulary development, art and industrial arts, related music, related mathematics, [and] homeroom guidance.[17]

In similar vein is the description of the Los Angeles integrated course for the seventh and eighth grades, "The American Epic":

> This double period unified English-social studies course involves certain relevant and meaningful descriptive phases of music, art, and science. Skills in the use of language, both oral and written, are taught largely through practice in the enunciation of ideas in

[14] Edgar B. Wesley, *op. cit.*, p. 245.
[15] M. J. Stormzand and R. H. Lewis, *New Methods in Social Studies.* New York: Farrar and Rinehart, 1935, pp. 152.
[16] John K. and Margaret A. Norton, *Foundations of Curriculum Building.* Boston: Ginn, 1936, pp. 193.
[17] "Integrated Learning Units for Seventh Grade," Aliquippa Public Schools, Aliquippa, Pennsylvania (Mimeographed).

the social studies field. Literature is not necessarily confined to social studies content. In fact, teachers are urged to encourage pupils to establish habits of reading worthwhile selections quite unrelated to the social studies field. An activity type of teaching procedure is employed.[18]

The descriptions of a number of other courses of study emphasize the same broad concept which runs through the two excerpts just quoted. It would seem, therefore, that because of its completeness and conciseness the definition of integration given by A. C. Bining and D. H. Bining will be generally acceptable: The word integration is "used to connote units of understanding that consist of integrated materials of instruction from several fields in order to present a whole picture of a phase of knowledge rather than a part of it." [19]

The main difference between fusion and integration seems to be one of the negation of subject-matter boundaries in the one case and the recognition of them in the other, a distinction which many curriculum workers fail to take into account.

CORRELATION

A THIRD word around which much confusion centers is *correlation*. As understood by Stormzand and Lewis, it is the "process of arranging the content of related fields in such a manner that each of the fields is mutually contributory to the other." [20] The same idea is expressed by the Nortons when they say that "history, geography, civics, and economics [there is no mention of sociology] are organized as separate subjects, but interrelations and connections are strongly emphasized." [21]

In the mind of Wesley there are two kinds of correlation, *incidental* and *systematic*. He describes incidental correlation as made up of "occasional associations" and says it is "used to relate not only the various social studies but also to connect each of them with science, literature, and other fields." Systematic correlation, on the other hand, is a device by which each subject is made to yield its values for every other subject. Two subjects may be taught with alternating attention to each. Sometimes cross references may be made between two subjects in the social studies, or between one of the social studies and a subject in some other field.[22]

This matter of correlation and cross references is also discussed by D. G. Fancler and C. C. Crawford. As worked out in practice,

The equipment necessary for some project in the social studies is built in the manual arts classes; the scientific information involved in the study of some civic problem is more fully developed in natural science classes; the same papers may be submitted for correction and credit in social studies, English, science, art, and music courses.[23]

The descriptions of correlation given here are characteristic of those given by other writers in the field of the social studies. Most of them, however, are content with descriptions of correlation rather than giving a definition of it. But Bining and Bining have defined it. Indeed their definition is so good that its acceptance is urged. According to these authors, "Correlation means the seeking and utilizing of points of contact and relationships between subjects in order to bring about associations in the general field of knowledge and to some degree among the various parts of the curriculum." [24]

By comparing this definition with the definitions of fusion and integration which have been suggested for general acceptance, the differences in the concepts will be seen. If the words are used according to the sense of these definitions, there will be much less confusion as to their meaning.

---

[18] *World Cultures*, Part I, Los Angeles City School District. School Publication No. 283. Los Angeles, 1936.
[19] A. C. Bining and D. H. Bining, *Teaching the Social Studies in the Secondary Schools*. New York: McGraw-Hill, 1935, pp. 213.
[20] M. J. Stormzand and R. H. Lewis, *op. cit.*
[21] John K. and Margaret A. Norton, *op. cit.*, p. 192.

[22] Edgar B. Wesley, *op. cit.*, pp. 242-43. Wesley's distinction between incidental and systematic correlation follows Henry Johnson. See *The Teaching of History in Elementary and Secondary Schools*. New York: Macmillan, 1915, chapter XV. Johnson identifies systematic correlation with efforts "to unify the curriculum" (p. 389).
[23] D. G. Fancler and C. C. Crawford, *Teaching the Social Studies*. Los Angeles: C. C. Crawford, 1932, p. 247.
[24] A. C. Bining and D. H. Bining, *op. cit.*, p. 213.

Core Curriculum

THE fourth word which is greatly abused is *core*, as used in connection with the word *curriculum*. Any standard dictionary would define a core as the central part of anything, especially as being enveloped by parts of a different character, or as being the essential or vital part. But as conceived by P. W. L. Cox, the core curriculum is "purposeful, cooperative, living," [25] whatever that may mean. A more recent writer defines such a curriculum as the "organizing of a common core of experiences drawing content from all the major areas of human living, a curriculum which disregards subject matter lines and which is generally required of all pupils a substantial part of each school day." [26]

After considerable study of such definitions and so-called core curricula, a group of graduate students working in the curriculum workshop in Ann Arbor, Michigan, during the summer of 1938, described a core curriculum as

an attempted means of enabling the child and the teacher to see life and live it in school, home, and community as a unified experience. The subject matter for such a course is based on the expressed and implied needs of the individual. Whenever it is necessary, use is made of English, History, Biology, art, music, or any other material, but only as they clarify, amplify, illustrate, or enrich the solution of the life problem under consideration.

In practice, the core may involve several teachers who work together without regard to subject-matter distinctions. They plan the work among themselves and with the pupils and bring to the students the opportunity to engage in activities which will allow each one to participate according to his ability and arrive at some fulfillment of his own needs.[27]

These students recognized nine principal characteristics of a core curriculum:

1. It draws from all subject-matter fields as they contribute to the needs and interests of the pupil.
2. It places the emphasis on the functional organization of learning experience.
3. It is built on the democratic way of life; that is, the pupils actively and purposefully participate in planning, carrying out, and evaluating the activities, both as a part of the group and as individuals.
4. It emphasizes the growth of the individual as well as the growth of the group.
5. It encourages cooperation in planning, teaching, learning, and evaluating by teachers within the school.
6. It makes use of the educational agencies of the community, is based directly on the vital problems of the community, and will probably be different for each school.
7. It is always in a process of change.
8. It stresses desirable attitudes and ideals.
9. It is evaluated in terms of its clearly formulated purposes.[28]

Examples of such core courses are not difficult to find. In Tulsa, Oklahoma, the Central High School developed a core curriculum which includes such objectives as, "building and maintaining physical and mental health; an understanding of the fundamental principles and institutions of a democratic society; knowledge of the interaction between man and the natural environment; fundamental skills and knowledge of communications; acquaintance with and opportunities for self-expression through creative activities; and individual guidance and counseling." [29]

A second example is found in the East High School of Denver, Colorado, where for several years the pupils have been taking a "core course." This course covers much of the work commonly taught in English and social studies classes. The teachers in charge of the course usually have remained with the same classes throughout all three years of the senior high school. As a result of the experience with this old core course it has been proposed that a new core course be organized which will include teachers of other subjects than English and the social studies.[30]

By comparing the characteristics claimed for integrated material with those claimed for the core curriculum, it appears that there are no fundamental differences between them. The integrated program has in view

---

[25] Philip W. L. Cox, "The Changing Core Curriculum," *Junior-Senior High School Clearing House*, January, 1929, p. 32.
[26] William B. Brown, "The Core Is Not All of the Curriculum," *Curriculum Journal*, May, 1938, p. 210.
[27] "Source Materials for the Development of Core Courses Assembled by the Core Group," Cooperative Secondary Curriculum Workshop, Michigan Study of Secondary School Curriculum, Ann Arbor, 1938, p. 31 (mimeographed).

[28] *Ibid.*, p. 4.
[29] "News Notes," *Curriculum Journal*, May, 1938, p. 193.
[30] T. D. Rice, "A High School Core Program," *Curriculum Journal*, May, 1938, p. 201.

the union into large wholes or units, parts chosen from all areas of knowledge, and the core curriculum contemplates the same type of content and organization. In other words, the terms *integration* and *core* as applied to the organization of material for teaching purposes are practically synonymous. However, if we accept Wesley's idea of integration, a definition of the term would confine us to the field of the social studies, and it would not be broad enough to include branches of knowledge outside of this field. On the other hand, if we accept the idea of integration as conceived by the other writers we have quoted, the definition must be broad enough to comprehend all branches of knowledge. Thus the definition of integration as quoted from Bining and Bining serves also for a definition of the word "core."

If the terms *fusion, integration, correlation,* and *core* are used in the respective senses urged in this article, there will be less confusion among educators, the terms will be properly applied, and it will not be necessary in the future to take such liberties with the dictionary as many have taken in the past.

There is no reason for assuming that any deterministic science of human affairs or any part of them is possible. It follows also, that there are no exact subsidiary social sciences, such as economics, politics, or sociology, despite much display of learning under these heads. Each of them deals with the same indeterminate, man, and besides rests upon assumptions respecting related fields over which neither it nor its subject matter can exercise effective control. That is, a science of the State assumes the existence and continuance of economy and yet it cannot assure . . . the perdurance of the economy upon which it depends for its life blood. The science of economics, in turn, assumes the existence of order on a large scale and yet economy cannot assure the order necessary to its efficient functioning (Charles A. Beard, *The Nature of the Social Sciences,* Report of the Commission on the Social Studies. New York: Scribners, 1934, p. 37).

A PROBLEM IN DEVIATION

by
M. Kleg

The family is the basic social unit in our society; however, there is no universal structure of the family in American society. Some families lack one or more of the classic characters. An example of this would be the family without a father. In such cases, the mother may assume a dual role, while in other circumstances the role of the father is assumed by one of the siblings. With the emergence of A.D.C., the paternal role may be completely unassumed.

In an impoverished area it is not surprising to find children from backgrounds without any family structure in accordance with a functional definition. In such situations, the mother and father may not be assuming their responsibilities toward the creation of a functionally defined family. Often the father may be unemployed, alcoholic or even incarcerated; a mother may be nothing more than a harlot. Obviously, a child from such an environment finds the conceptual and functional definition of the middle class family usually presented in the classrooms and by "Dick and Jane" somewhat phony or unreal to say the least.

If we are in agreement then in order for learning to take place, communication between the child and the learning environment (ergo teacher, curriculum, etc.,) is imperative, then the teacher must be aware of the child's home environment and adopt a meaningful curriculum. There is no universal curriculum which is meaningful to all subculturals in American society or even in any one community. Therefore, regardless of what the printed curriculum guide may be, the teacher must recognize that he or she is the final word in curriculum development. The educator may find no written guide to solve a particular problem, thus, leaving the teacher to recognize the problem, make an estimate of the situation and finally to take action on her own.

In the final analysis, the purpose of a curriculum guide is to supply "food" for thought before action. The guide is not a terminal point but rather a pivotal point for further inquiry, investigation and development.

Original Manuscript.

EDWIN FENTON

Professor of History, Carnegie-Mellon University

Social Studies Curriculum Reform: An Appraisal

If you find new developments in the social studies bewildering, I bid you welcome to a very large club. Experiment has been piled on experiment in confusing disarray. In order to make sense of these changes, I spent a leave from Carnegie Tech during the academic year 1965-66 visiting social studies projects throughout the country and reading the thousands of pages of material they have produced.[1] No generalizations hold for all of the more than fifty social studies projects established during the past five years. They vary in almost every dimension: objectives, teaching strategies, types of materials, patterns of pupil deployment, evaluating instruments. I could cite a half dozen exceptions to every generalization which I am going to make. Let me make generalizations anyway, in order to indicate dominant trends which I have detected.

The purpose of the new social studies is to make the child a useful, independent citizen through helping him attain four types of objectives: attitudes, values, inquiry skills, and knowledge. The major criterion for the selection of content is the structure of the disciplines. The major teaching method is directed discussion. The dominant types of material consist of data in virtually every form except the traditional textbook. Let me discuss each of these four generalizations in turn, leaving the most significant of all—objectives—to the end. I shall begin with structure.

In his influential little volume, *The Process of Education,* Jerome S. Bruner failed to give a clear and specific definition of structure.[2] Although he hints that structure involves both attitudes and inquiry skills, he limits his examples in the social studies to substantive generalizations: "That a nation must trade in order to live." Bruner's definition has touched off heated controversy about whether the social studies have a structure. I have read twenty-seven books and a number of articles written during the past five years about this subject. Most have not been illuminating.[3] The long

---

[1] A full account of what I have learned is in my book, *The New Social Studies* (New York Holt, Rinehart and Winston, 1967).
[2] Vintage Book (New York Random House, 1963), pp. 6-8 and elsewhere.
[3] Among the best of these volumes are two produced by curriculum projects: Roy A. Price, Warren Hickman, and Gerald Smith, "*Major Concepts for Social Studies*" (Social Studies Curriculum Center, Syracuse University, Syracuse, New York, 1965); Irving Morrissett, ed., *Concepts and Structure in the New Social Science Curricula* (Social Science Educational Consortium Inc., Purdue University, West Lafayette, Indiana, 1966).

California Social Science Review, June, 1967, No.6, pp. 23-33.

lead article by Professor Mark Krug in the September, 1966, edition of *Social Education* is the most recent contribution to the controversy, a contribution which confuses more than it clarifies, because neither Bruner nor Krug has a sound conception of structure.[4]

What is structure? The most useful definition I know, that of Joseph J. Schwab, argues that structure has two parts: ". . . the body of imposed conceptions which define the investigated subject matter of that discipline and control its inquiries," and " . . . the pattern of its procedure, its method, how it goes about using its conceptions to attain its goal."[5] In layman's language, structure consists of a method of inquiry made up of two parts: hypothesis formation and proof process. Let me examine each, beginning with hypothesis formation.

Facts mean nothing by themselves. They assume meaning only as part of each person's frame of reference. The same piece of data can have quite different meanings to two people with contrasting views of the world. Moreover, a person's frame of reference inclines him to notice some facts and to overlook others. Marx's firm conviction that class struggle explained history caused him to select certain facts as he read and to use them in particular ways as evidence for his argument. Adam Smith's dedication to the theory of the free market would condition him to note other facts in the same body of data and to use them as evidence for very different arguments. The way in which a person selects facts to note helps to determine the kinds of hypotheses he forms. His "body of imposed conceptions" conditions him to ask certain questions and to seek answers to particular problems. The pedagogical issue can be stated simply: How can we help a student to develop a "body of imposed conceptions" which will help him to formulate useful hypotheses about a variety of problems?

Bruner's generalizations are not very helpful. Generalizations lead to teaching social studies as product, as information known to scholars which students should learn. One school system after another has indulged in the vain pursuit of a small body of generalizations to cram into children's heads. Professors Hanna and Gross of Stanford University together with ten of their graduate students identified more than 3200 generalizations.[6] Both the California and the Wisconsin State Social Studies Committees have issued well-known lists.[7] None of them is very useful, primarily

---

[4]Mark M. Krug, "Bruner's New Social Studies: A Critique," *Social Education,* 30:400–406, October 1966.

[5]Joseph J. Schwab, "The Concept of the Structure of a Discipline," in *Educational Record,* 43:199, 203, July 1962.

[6]See a condensation of their work in the following article: Paul R. Hanna and John R. Lee, "Content in the Social Studies," in John U. Michaelis, ed., *Social Studies in Elementary Schools,* National Council for the Social Studies (Washington, D.C., 1962), 62–89.

[7]*Report of the State Central Committee on Social Studies to the California State Curriculum Commission* (Sacramento, 1961); *A Conceptual Framework for the Social Studies in Wisconsin* (Madison, 1964).

because a generalization is inert. Teaching product becomes the major objective, and product in the form of generalizations—many of which may be proved incorrect in another decade or so— are not very useful as a body of imposed conceptions to control inquiry.

The best of the new social studies projects identify the hypothesis-making aspect of structure with concepts. By a concept they mean a category: social class, leadership, culture, or supply-and-demand may serve as examples. A number of curriculum centers have tried to identify a small number of analytical concepts from all the social sciences. Although each has developed a workable list, the lists are not identical. This result suggests that the social studies do not have a single structure inherent in the discipline. Each person brings his own "imposed conceptions" to the task of selecting concepts. Hence, each person has his own structure. The problem for each of us, like the problem for curriculum centers, is to develop a structure based on the social sciences which will help us to analyze problems in such a way that our answers have a high probability of accuracy.

Let me examine the way in which concepts make up a body of imposed conceptions which will help a student learn to develop fruitful hypotheses. Suppose that a student knows four concepts from sociology—social class, role, status, and norms—and wants to investigate a problem in history or in contemporary society, say, to describe the social structure of Boston, Massachusetts, in the middle of the eighteenth century. As he reads diaries, autobiographies, newspaper accounts, and similar source material, his knowledge of social class, status, role, and norms will help to guide his search for data. He will ask himself how many social classes existed in the society. He will try to learn what relative position on the social scale each occupational, racial, and religious group occupied. He will examine the roles of many groups and individuals in society to determine, for example, whether housewives in seventeenth-century New England had the same roles as housewives in our own world. He will be alert to pick up clues about norms, the behaviors expected of various people of different status and roles. Knowing these concepts guides his search for data along productive lines which social scientists have found extremely useful for the scientific analysis of society. Concepts are an extremely useful body of imposed conceptions because, unlike generalizations, they are useful tools of inquiry. Generalizations become ends in themselves; taught properly, concepts become means to an end.

Some concepts are more useful for the analysis of society than others. Let us consider five types as examples: historical periods (the Renaissance), historical topics (the growth of parliamentary government), concepts requiring historical definitions (democracy), concepts involving methods of procedure (multiple causation), and analytical concepts (leadership). Only the last of these five can be used as a source of analytical questions to guide the search for data in any study of any political system at any time or place. Many lists of concepts jumble several types together indiscriminately. With our growing knowledge of the nature and purpose of structure, we should soon be able to do much better, eventually arriving at several alternative lists of analytical concepts which can guide the search for data along productive lines.

Analytical concepts imply questions. Let us use the concept of leadership as an example. Modern political scientists recognize the vital role which leaders play in any political system. They want to know a number of things about political leaders. How are they recruited? What are their personal characteristics? How do they gain and maintain support from their followers? How can a citizen get access to them? The overwhelming majority of analytical questions used in the social studies either come from social science concepts or can be related to social science concepts. Taken together, concepts and analytical questions constitute an extremely useful notion of the hypothesis-forming aspect of structure. They are tools, a part of the process of inquiry. Generalizations, on the other hand, are product and are learned for their own sake.

The remaining part of structure, as Schwab defines the term, consists of proof process. Once a person has developed a hypothesis, he must revise, reject, or validate it. Within the past decade a number of scholars, both within and outside of the curriculum projects, have worked hard to develop schemes of validation. Much of their work stemmed originally from the model of reflective thinking posed by John Dewey in his classic volume *How We Think*.[8] The projects have refined and amplified this model to bring greater precision to the enterprise. They have identified each of the steps in the proof process and devised ways to teach individual skills of critical thinking on which these steps depend.

At Carnegie Tech we have integrated the teaching of structure defined as hypothesis formation and proof process into six major steps. They are:

1. Recognizing a problem from data
2. Formulating hypotheses
    a. Asking analytical questions
    b. Stating hypotheses
    c. Remaining aware of the tentative nature of hypotheses
3. Recognizing the logical implications of hypotheses
4. Gathering data
    a. Deciding what data will be needed
    b. Selecting or rejecting sources on the basis of a statement of the logical implications
5. Analyzing, Evaluating, and Interpreting the Data
    a. Selecting relevant data from the sources

[8](Boston: D. C. Heath and Co., 1933), p. 106.

      b. Evaluating the sources
         (1) Determining the frame of reference of the author of a source
         (2) Determining the accuracy of statements of fact
      c. Interpreting the data
   6. Evaluating the hypothesis in light of the data
      a. Justifying the hypothesis
      b. Modifying the hypothesis
         (1) Rejecting a logical implication
         (2) Restating the hypothesis

    The process I have been describing makes structure something useful to teach. A discipline is not so much a body of knowledge as a method of inquiry. Hence, the structure of a discipline is not a group of generalizations; it is a tool which can be used to analyze problems—contemporary, historical, personal—which interest the student. Whether or not the solution he arrives at will be useful will depend upon the skill with which he uses the mode of inquiry, the attitudes he brings to the endeavor, and the knowledge he amasses as he develops and validates his hypothesis.

    Let me now turn to teaching strategies. The major teaching method of the new social studies is directed discussion. Most of the projects, however, do not rely solely on one teaching technique. They employ a range of techniques, each one directed toward a specific group of objectives.

    Teachers sometimes find it useful to think of teaching strategies as if they were ranged along a continuum. At one end of the continuum lie expository techniques—techniques such as the lecture in which the teacher gives all the cues, that is, all the generalizations and all the evidence for the generalizations which the student is supposed to learn. In most expository classes students listen, take notes, memorize them, and give them back to the teacher often in the same form on examinations or in class discussions.

    Several hundred pieces of research done with superior senior high school students and college students indicate that students master just as much content from a discipline by listening to lectures as they do by discussion.[9] Notice several aspects of that statement. The generalization is confined to senior high school and college students and the objective is confined to knowledge of content. Nevertheless, if a teacher's objective is to have students be able to recall or state a definite body of facts and generalizations and the students are fairly sophisticated and at least fifteen years old, then the weight of evidence indicates that the lecture is a suitable teaching technique.

    At the other end of the continuum lie discovery exercises in which the teacher gives no cues at all. He provides the data—a group of quotations, some tables, simply an assignment in the library—and then gets out of the way. Classroom interaction proceeds from student to student with the

---

[9] John W. Kidd, "The Question of Class Size," *Journal of Higher Education*, 23:440-44, November 1952, summarizes the results of some of these studies.

teacher acting only as a referee, leading the students neither by expository comments nor by questions which point the way toward data. I am referring to the sort of discovery exercise described by Byron G. Massialas and Jack Zevin.[10]

I find discovery exercises of this type useful for two purposes. First, they are an excellent evaluating device. If we want to learn whether or not a class can isolate a useful problem from data we can present them with a diary, an autobiography, or a group of tables and see what problem they identify for discussion. If they cannot formulate a worthwhile problem, they have not learned the first of the six steps in the mode of inquiry which I outlined. I'm sure any teacher can think of a number of other variables that could be evaluated in this way. Secondly, discovery exercises like these may encourage the creativity of children because they are challenged on their own to think a problem through. Creativity, however, does not spring full-blown from the mind of a child. The creative historians of recent decades have been among the best trained ones. They are men who know concepts and are in the habit of letting stubborn unexplained facts trigger new analytical questions, and they use these concepts and questions to develop new and interesting hypotheses. Nevertheless, discovery exercises may encourage creative thought by challenging students to use their resources to the limit.

Between these two poles on the continuum lie a variety of techniques which can be described as directed discussion. In directed discussion, the teacher asks questions. He does not give all the cues as he does in expository techniques nor does he withdraw almost entirely from the discussion as in a discovery exercise. Knowing exactly what he wants the student to learn by the end of the class period, he guides discussion by the questions he asks, helping students to learn how to put evidence and inference together in the process.

Directed discussion can be used for a great range of objectives. I find it indispensable, for example, for teaching students to use the mode of inquiry of the social studies, that is, to teach them to develop and validate hypotheses. As the work of Professors Lawrence Senesh at Purdue and [the late] Hilda Taba at San Francisco State College has proved, elementary school students can discover sophisticated social science concepts under the guidance of a skillful teacher.[11] These concepts can later be used as a basis for

---

[10]"Teaching Social Studies through Discovery," *Social Education*, 28:384-87, 400, 1964; reprinted in Byron G. Massialas and C. Benjamin Cox, *Inquiry in Social Studies* (New York: McGraw-Hill Book Co., 1966), pp. 136-52; and in Edwin Fenton, *Teaching the New Social Studies in Secondary Schools: An Inductive Approach* (New York: Holt, Rinehart & Winston, 1966), pp. 255-64.

[11]Lawrence Senesh, "Organizing a Curriculum Around Social Science Concepts," in Morrissett, ed., *Concepts and Structure*, pp. 21-38; Hilda Taba and James L. Hills, *Teacher Handbook for Contra Costa Social Studies, Grades 1-6* (Hayward, Calif: Rapid Printers and Lithographers, 1965).

hypothesis formation. Virtually all of the directors of projects agree that students can best be taught to learn the proof process of history and social sciences through directed discussion. Questioning, challenging, pointing out exceptions to a generalization, introducing new evidence which the students have not read in their homework assignment, a skilled teacher can emphasize over and over again the essential elements of inquiry skills.

Another sort of directed discussion can be used for another purpose: to teach students how to resolve value conflicts. The work of Donald Oliver at the Harvard Curriculum Center has been particularly concerned with this issue.[12] Oliver argues that the essential value of a democratic society is the belief in the dignity and worth of the individual. A truly democratic society tries to align its laws and practices with this value. Yet on many issues contradictory values are involved and need to be resolved. Americans have generally believed, for example, that the owner of a piece of property has the right to sell it to whomever he wishes. At the same time, we also believe that any individual of any race should be permitted to buy property in any neighborhood if he can afford it. What do we do when these two beliefs come in conflict? Which is more important, the property right or the human right? This is the specific sort of value problem which Professor Oliver argues should be discussed in the schools.

Oliver terms his type of classroom procedure Socratic-analysis discussion. He poses an issue such as open occupancy of housing and attempts to clarify both sides of the argument. Questioning one student at a time, he draws from the class the logical implications of each position and eventually tries to get each student to resolve the conflict in terms of a higher value, the dignity and worth of the individual. His objective is to teach students how to deal with public controversies involving conflicting values and conflicting policies. Socratic-analysis discussion in which the teacher plays an indispensable role as questioner and challenger lies at the heart of his teaching technique.

The entire matter of teaching strategies has been confused by the use of a variety of terms, most of which are not defined precisely. In contemporary literature the terms of discovery, inductive learning, inquiry, reflective thinking, directed discussion, Socratic-analysis discussion, and a half-dozen more all are used to describe varieties of directed discussion. Moreover, some teachers believe that people in curriculum projects endorse only one style of teaching to the exclusion of all others. For the Carnegie Tech group at least, this impression is completely wrong. We employ expository teaching for certain content goals with particular student audiences. We use nondirective discovery exercises for other goals, particularly evaluation. We use various sorts of directed discussion for still different purposes. At times,

---

[12] See the excellent account of the rationale for the Oliver project in Donald W. Oliver and James P. Shaver, *Teaching Public Issues in the High School* (Boston: Houghton Mifflin Co., 1966).

in the midst of a directed discussion, we employ recitation techniques to make sure that all the students in the class are dealing with the same body of evidence. Role playing and simulation also play a part in our teaching repertoire. There is no magic road to teaching. There are many roads each appropriate to different goals.

Most of the projects produce elaborate teacher's manuals to accompany their materials. For some of the courses produced at Carnegie Tech, the teacher's manual is as large as the collection of student material. Each manual contains a rationale for the entire four-year curriculum as well as a rationale for the particular course. These documents precede daily lesson plans which state specific objectives for each day's work, note the materials provided, and lay out a detailed teaching strategy which has been tested in the classroom. These elaborate aids are not designed to hamstring teachers; any instructor who wishes to do so may ignore them. Most teachers, however, welcome lesson plans. They provide the essential link between objectives, materials, and teaching strategy and help teachers to grasp principles which may be quite unfamiliar to them.

Now let me turn to teaching materials, the heart of the curriculum revolution. A few reformers still speak naively of "teacher-proof materials," an absurd notion. Teachers who do not understand the principles upon which materials are based can make hash of the most imaginative materials ever created. Moreover, the entire concept of teacher-pooof materials is unsound philosophically. Every teacher should adapt materials and teaching techniques to the particular needs of his own classroom audience. He should also adapt materials to his own personality and style of teaching. All these disclaimers aside, the new materials being produced by the projects stand at the forefront of the curricular revolution.

If the projects are the wave of the future, the textbook is dead. Only one or two projects produce materials in customary narrative textbook form. The rest have either abandoned conventional texts entirely or relegated them to a subsidiary position among a galaxy of diverse materials both written and audio-visual. In the past textbooks have been used primarily to teach the social studies as product. Teachers assigned as homework a few pages from a text. In class the next day they asked questions to determine whether students learned the facts and generalizations which they had studied. Texts remain a good way to convey information to students if the students under consideration are well motivated and have a conceptual apparatus to help them organize data from a textbook in meaningful ways. But conventional texts are not particularly useful for teaching the structure of a discipline nor are they as useful as many other materials to help form appropriate attitudes and to raise issues involving value conflicts.

If the textbook is on its way to the grave, what will replace it? An enormous variety of written, audio-visual, and manipulative materials. As the core of many courses, the social studies projects are putting together extensive collections of source materials each carefully designed for a specific function. Among these materials are diaries, letters, autobiographies, biographical sketches, pieces of fiction, government documents, business records, charts, tables, graphs, secondary accounts written by historians and social scientists—virtually anything, in other words, which contains data about society. For example, both of the one-semester ninth grade courses designed at the Carnegie Tech Curriculum Development Center contain between sixty and seventy readings each intended for one night's homework and one day's class discussion. A reading consists of three parts: an introduction which relates one day's work to that of the remainder of the course, three or four study questions guiding the student to the heart of the issue which is involved, and a document, article, collection of tables, or other written material which raises one or two points for students to think about. In addition to this written material, our project has prepared a large number of transparencies, tape recordings, single concept filmstrips, plays which the students can produce in class, simulations, and supplementary written material to be handed out in class, each piece carefully designed to make a specific point during a specific part of a class discussion. In our tenth and eleventh grade courses three days of source material like this are followed by a summary essay which analyzes in textbook style the main events in the history of western Europe or the United States and links one problem to the next. In this way students gain a grasp of continuity which often disappears when source materials are used entirely by themselves, and at the same time they learn the tools of inquiry through careful examination of documents.

Let me describe several innovations in materials which point in new directions. The Tech Center has developed a number of single concept filmstrips consisting entirely of pictures without captions. These filmstrips can be used to help students develop hypotheses, to give them data from which they can learn a concept, to introduce evidence which supplements written material in homework assignments, or for a variety of other purposes. An example may make the point clear. In our eleventh grade history course, we wanted students to develop a hypothesis about the cause of the Civil War before they began to study the Civil War in written materials. We made a filmstrip out of thirty pictures of maps, largely adapted from Paullin's *Atlas*.[13] The first four maps show physical differences between the North and South—such factors as rainfall, average yearly temperature, soil formations, and so forth. A second series contrasts the economies of the two areas, emphasizing agriculture, industry, trade, and commerce. A third series compares the societies by looking at a number of variables:

[13] Charles O. Paullin, *Atlas of the Historical Geography of the United States* (Washington, D.C.; Carnegie Institution of Washington, 1932).

number of slaves, number of immigrants, religious affiliation, number of colleges, and so forth. Finally, the fourth section concentrates on votes on various sectional issues beginning with the Missouri Compromise. At the end of each section of the filmstrip we ask students to write a couple of sentences indicating whether or not they see any major differences between the North and the South. For class preparation on the following day they are told to write a hypothesis from their notes on the subject, "What caused the Civil War?" They then spend the following three weeks in homework assignments and class discussions refining and altering the hypotheses they developed from the maps and discussing the advantages and disadvantages of beginning with a hypothesis based on such limited and controlled data.

Instead of single concept filmstrips, a number of projects have been developing film loops. A film loop consists of a continuous circle of film which projects through an 8mm. silent projector. Most of them last only four or five minutes. They are particularly useful, in my judgment, for helping students develop one single idea clearly. Suppose, for example, that a teacher wanted students to grasp the idea of cultural diffusion, the process by which ideas, institutions, techniques, and so forth are transferred from one culture to another. He might begin a loop with two-and-a-half minutes of film illustrating life in a major western city. The film would include pictures of housing, commerce, industry, transportation, clothing, recreation, and so forth. The next two-and-a-half minutes could be devoted to similar pictures from a city in a developing country. The teacher might then ask students which aspects of western culture had been diffused to the nonwestern city and encourage them to speculate about why some had been and others had not. He might also encourage students to think about the ways in which the culture of the west had been carried to other lands. An exercise such as this one encourages the student to observe carefully; it challenges him to be creative; it teaches him the concept of cultural diffusion; it breaks the deadly monotony of classroom recitation; it may even teach him how to look with a new perspective at his own city and at other cities when he sees them on television or on summer travel.

"But what's it all for?" you may well ask. What are the objectives of the new social studies? I have already suggested their essential purpose: to help the child develop into a useful, independent citizen. This general objective can be divided for purposes of discussion into four major parts: attitudes, values, inquiry skills, and knowledge. Let me get at each in turn.

A useful independent citizen has a set of cooperative attitudes towards society. He is a participant in politics, anxious to pull his oar. He wants to hear all sides of a debate and to make up his mind about an issue through a rational decision-making process. The new social studies tries to generate these attitudes and a number of others like them.

Many attitudes develop through the way in which a class is taught.

Calling on students whether or not they have raised their hands indicates that a student, like a citizen, should participate actively in the learning process. Requiring students to use a mode of inquiry from history and the social sciences may teach them to prefer a rational decision-making process to authority or superstition as a test for truth. Notice that these attitudes result from conduct in the classroom, not from the choice of teaching material. How silly talk of "teacher-proof materials" is in this context!

Many of the social studies projects assume a basic ethic based on the dignity and worth of the individual. With the exception of this basic value —and in a few cases without even this exception—the projects do not try to get students to internalize a specific set of policies toward controversial public issues. Instead the projects present materials and teaching techniques which consistently challenge students' values and encourage them to reflect upon them in the light of evidence. The goal is not consensus; the goal is reflection. If at the end of the year a student emerges with the same values he held at its beginning, he will still have amassed a body of evidence for his position, evidence which may support him in a crisis. He will also have learned something about techniques by which he can test his values. If, on the other hand, he finds that some of the values he held could not stand the test of evidence, he can abandon them for others. In either case he will be better off. By consistently raising issues involving values and by subjecting them to discussion under the rules of evidence, the projects are attempting to develop citizens who know where they are going in a world buffeted by change.

The projects are also trying to teach these students the skills of inquiry essential for independent learning. Robert Oppenheimer suggests that the total quantity of knowledge in the world doubles with every decade. Much of what we now accept as true will probably be proved wrong in the future. Learning a body of facts and generalizations cannot equip children to live intelligently ten or twenty years hence. In order to help them cope with the knowledge explosion, we must teach them how to learn for themselves. They must know how to inquire in a disciplined way to avoid being abandoned like worn-out automobiles on the human scrapheap.

Hence, the emphasis on inquiry skills, a phrase which, as I define it, is synonymous with structure. A child well-equipped with the skills of inquiry can develop hypotheses, drawing upon the conceptual apparatus which he has learned. He can also use a proof process with which he can validate, revise, or abandon the hypothesis he has formed. This mode of inquiry is a tool with which he can learn in the future. The facts gleaned from textbooks often disappear from a child's memory bank within a few weeks after the examination. The skills of inquiry, however, persist longer and are far more useful. Perhaps the major difference between the objectives of the new social studies and the old lies in the area of inquiry skills. In the past, courses of study have always bowed to something called "critical thinking." The new projects put inquiry in the forefront of their objectives. No one who cannot inquire independently and critically can survive well in the modern world.

Finally, let me turn to the last objective, knowledge of content from history and the social sciences. In the past what a textbook author thought was important was the major guide to content in the social studies. Teachers "covered the course;" students "read the whole book;" what lay between those grey flannel covers *was* the social studies to millions of children. The projects are much more self-conscious in their choice of criteria for the selection of social studies content. Most of them combine four criteria: what will help a student grasp the fundamental conceptual apparatus of a discipline; what interests a child and what he needs; what will help a student understand and cope with contemporary problems; and a certain indispensable corpus of knowledge which the curriculum developer feels every educated and intelligent American citizen should know. Establishing four criteria such as these implies an end to the dogma of coverage which is a ridiculous dogma to begin with. The projects leave out vast quantities of material which has been covered superficially and often badly in the past. Better to do a few things well, they argue, than to do more things poorly. Clearly a new day is coming.

Materials from the social studies projects have not yet been published commercially except in experimental units and a few paperback volumes. Within the next two or three years, materials will hit the market in a flood. It's time to get ready for them. I'd suggest several courses of action for any school system. Try to get teachers to an NDEA summer institute, many of which are stocking the materials from the projects which are already available. Buy the four new methods books which have come out during the past year or will appear next year for the professional book shelf in each social studies department and encourage teachers to read them.[14] Get hold of experimental editions from the projects.[15] Lists of these materials will appear from time to time in the pages of *Social Education*. Get a classroom set from a project and try it out on your own students to see how you like it before you plunge blindly into a new way of teaching. Start to work on your school administrators; let them know that you will need more money for materials, that you will require more audio-visual equipment, that every school should have a department chairman who devotes at least half of his

---

[14] See the volumes by Cox and Massialas, Fenton, and Oliver and Shaver cited above. A revision of the Hunt and Metcalf text, *Teaching High School Social Studies*, was published by Harpers in 1968.

[15] For example, experimental units from the Carnegie Tech project for the ninth, tenth, and eleventh grade courses are available free of charge in classroom sets from Marketing Manager, Social Studies, Holt, Rinehart & Winston, Inc., 383 Madison Avenue, New York, New York 10017.

time to keeping up with what's going on in the curriculum projects and to communicating this information to his colleagues. Finally, look at the new materials critically. Each teacher knows his own student audience far better than a college professor in a curriculum center. Decide which materials are most appropriate to your students and to their needs. Adapt what someone has written to your own particular circumstances. Keep the independence which teachers have always had to set their goals and choose their materials and ways of teaching for the needs of the boys and girls who are their charges. This is the thrill and glory of teaching. Don't let them take it away.

LEARNING ABOUT TIME ZONES IN GRADES FOUR, FIVE, AND SIX[1]

O. L. DAVIS, Jr.
Kent State University
Kent, Ohio

INSTRUCTION AND LEARNING in the social studies are highly verbal. Because of this, the development of accurate concepts is difficult, while nevertheless essential. Some authorities in the social studies maintain that too many concepts are presented too soon to pupils. They insist that the immaturity of children does not permit their development of clear concepts and that insufficient time is allotted to the slow process of concept formation.

Children's misconceptions of social studies' concepts long have been noted. Scott and Myers (8) reported many inaccuracies in concepts concerning common terms in history and geography. Confusion in geographic meanings held by elementary school children has been documented further by other studies, many summarized by Davis (1).

Concepts of time and space are two of the many social studies concepts which have received research attention. Location, distance, direction, orientation, and chronology are a few of the meanings involved in these concepts. Ideas concerning geographical time zones are related to concepts of both time and space.

Wesley and Adams, among others, unequivocally hold that learning about geographic time zones is too difficult for children until late in their elementary schooling (10, pp. 307-8). They hold that only the process of maturation will enable children to understand the sphericity of the earth. In programs for the development of the skills of effective map and globe interpretation, understanding geographic time zones is consistently placed in the upper elementary grades, six or above (5; 11).

Little classroom experimentation has been reported which reveals at which age and grade levels concepts of geographic time and space can be learned. Walker (9) found that seven- and eight-year olds could understand simple earth-solar system relationships. While unsubstantiated by statistical evidence, reports by Kelton and Hotchkiss (4) and Schaeffer (7) were enthusiastic about teaching these concepts to fourth graders. Forsyth (2) concluded that children of junior high school age can learn the concept of the sphericity of the earth in addition to certain map reading skills.

The available research, while meager and fragmentary, indicates that growth in the geographic time and space concept does occur and that children may profit from instruction in these concepts. The present study was designed to obtain additional evidence about the effect of instruction on the development of the geographic time and space concept.

Method

The purpose of this experiment was to determine if children in the fourth, fifth, and sixth grades could profit from instruction in concepts of time and space relating to geographic time zones. Five specific null hypotheses were tested. It was predicted there would be no significant interaction and no significant differences between grade levels and between experimental conditions with respect to performances on the criterion measure of time zone learnings:

1. at the conclusion of the experimental teaching period,
2. one month after the conclusion of the experimental teaching period, and with respect to the gain scores,
3. between the administrations of the pre-test and immediate post-test,
4. between the administrations of the pre-test and the test of delayed recall, and
5. between the administrations of the immediate post-test and test of delayed recall.

Subjects

Two classes each of fourth, fifth, and sixth

Journal of Experimental Education, Summer, 1963, No. 31, pp. 407-412.

grades were selected from six different Davidson County, Tennessee, elementary schools. One class at each grade level was designated as the experimental group, the other as the control group.[2] The subjects were white children determined as being members of the middle social class. At the beginning of the experiment, the following numbers of pupils were regularly enrolled in these classes: 4E, 32; 4C, 36; 5E, 34; 5C, 34; 6E, 34; 6C, 36. Because some children in each class were absent on testing days, it was necessary to eliminate their scores from the statistical analysis. Further, a few pupils were randomly eliminated in order to have the same number in each group, twenty-seven. All statistical analyses were made on the data provided by the twenty-seven pupils in each class. Data on chronological age, intelligence, and social studies achievement for the six classes are presented in Table I.

Instruments

Prior to the initiation of the experiment, IQ and social studies achievement scores were obtained. The Lorge-Thorndike Intelligence Test, Level 3, Form B, Nonverbal, was administered to all Ss. The Sequential Tests of Educational Progress Social Studies, Form 4A, was used to assess Ss' achievement in the social studies.

The criterion test employed in this experiment was a Test on Time Zones constructed by the experimenter. This test was composed of forty-six items. Questions related to direction, rotation of the earth, clock time, the International Date Line, and standard time zones in the United States and the world. Administration time was not limited, but all children in all grades finished it within thirty minutes. The reliability of this test was computed by the test-retest method using the scores of the three control classes made on the pre-test and the immediate post-test administrations. This overall correlation coefficient was .83; for grade four, .64; for grade five, .76; for grade six, .84. The test had acceptable content validity as judged by the experimenter and two competent authorities in the social studies.

This criterion measure was administered as a pre-test, an immediate post-test, and as a test of delayed recall. These administrations were designated as TZ1, TZ2, and TZ3, respectively. Data on the classes' performances on the criterion measure are presented in Table II.

Using a 3 x 2 factorial design, analyses of variance were computed for the groups' intelligence quotients, social studies achievement, and performance on the criterion pre-test, TZ1.[3] A summary of these analyses of variance is presented in Table III.

As Table III shows, there was no significant interaction and no significant differences between experimental and control conditions on any of these three measures. There was also no significant difference in IQ between grade levels. Obtained significant differences between grade levels with regard to social studies achievement and performances on the initial criterion test were further analyzed by means of t tests. With respect to social studies achievement, fifth grades scored higher than the fourth grades ($t = 3.07$); the sixth grades scored higher than both the fifth grades ($t = 2.58$), and the fourth grades ($t = 5.65$). On TZ1, likewise, the fifth grades scored higher than the fourth grades ($t = 4.98$) and the sixth grades higher than both the fourth grades ($t = 8.85$) and the fifth grades ($t = 3.87$).

Thus, prior to the experimental teaching period the experimental and control groups did not differ significantly in terms of intelligence, social studies achievement, and understanding of time zones. Differences between school grades on social studies achievement and understanding of time zones were what reasonably should have been expected.

Procedure

The experimenter met with the principals and the teachers of the classes and the intermediate grades supervisor in the second week of January, 1958. The design of the experiment was discussed and a schedule for the testing and experimental teaching was determined. It was agreed that the experimenter would be introduced to all the classes as a student teacher. The teachers of the control classes agreed that they would give their groups no specific instruction regarding geographic time zones during the experimental period except that which was a part of the normal program of study. It was further agreed that all of the pupils would not be told that there were other classes being taught by the experimenter. As far as it could be determined, none of the pupils had had prior instruction in regard to geographic time zones.

The experimental classes were taught a unit specifically embodying material relating to the development of an understanding of geographic time zones. The experimental unit was taught during the classes' regular social studies period. Each experimental group was taught each day for fourteen class days over a period of three weeks. The experimental classes were taught in the sequence of 5E, 4E, 6E. Alternation of times of instruction was not possible because of conflicts in regularly scheduled activities in all three schools. The period of daily instruction was approximately thirty minutes. The experimenter taught the unit to control for variations in teaching method, learning materials, and subject matter presented.

TABLE I

SUMMARY OF DATA ON CHRONOLOGICAL AGE, INTELLIGENCE QUOTIENT AND SOCIAL STUDIES ACHIEVEMENT FOR EXPERIMENTAL AND CONTROL CLASSES

Class	Chronological Age Yr.	Mo.	Intelligence Quotient M	SD	Social Studies Achievement M	SD
4E	9	10	101.74	12.18	244.85	6.37
4C	9	9	103.74	12.68	243.81	7.99
5E	10	7	104.04	13.39	253.40	12.00
5C	10	9	105.93	11.53	251.85	11.91
6E	11	8	104.22	14.42	261.89	10.60
6C	11	7	96.78	13.26	257.30	10.95

TABLE II

MEANS AND SDs OF THE THREE ADMINISTRATIONS OF THE CRITERION MEASURE

Class	TZ1 M	SD	TZ2 M	SD	TZ3 M	SD
4E	20.93	4.42	33.19	6.24	32.04	8.15
4C	18.52	5.42	20.81	6.03	22.74	5.54
5E	25.74	6.90	37.15	6.68	38.52	5.90
5C	25.96	5.85	27.00	7.23	29.00	6.60
6E	30.22	7.36	39.44	6.70	40.11	5.18
6C	31.00	7.40	31.30	6.70	32.74	7.33

Results

Data obtained from the administrations of the immediate and delayed post-tests and gain scores between the three administrations of the criterion tests were subjected to analyses of variance in a 3 x 2 factorial design. A summary of these analyses appears in Table IV.

Performances on Criterion Tests

As indicated in Table IV, the experimental classes performed significantly better than did the control classes on both TZ2 and TZ3. This indicates that the experimental classes significantly profited from the instruction about geographic time zones. There was no significant interaction. Differences between grade levels observed at the beginning of the experiment persisted. Comparisons of the means are given below. The critical value for the two-tailed test of significance is t = 2.01 (df = 156).

a. Immediately following the experimental teaching period, the fifth grades scored higher than the fourth grades (t = 3.99); the sixth grades scored higher than the fifth grades (t = 2.60) and the fourth grades (t = 6.59).
b. One month following the conclusion of the experimental teaching period, the fifth grades were still superior to the fourth grades (t = 7.17).

Analyses of the Gain Scores

With regard to gains between the administrations of the criterion test, Table IV shows that the experimental classes gained significantly more in understanding of time zones than did the control classes throughout the course of this experiment. There was no significant interaction at any point tested. On only one analysis, that considering the gain between TZ1 and TZ2, was there a significant difference between grade levels. Here, there was no significant difference between the gains of the fourth and the fifth grades (t = 1.07) or between the gains of the fifth and sixth grades (t = 1.67); the fourth grades indicated a significant gain over the sixth grades (t = 2.74). This finding may well have been due to the limitations of the criterion test, the upper limits of which may not have been high enough.

Discussion

The results of this study provide evidence that children, at a younger age than heretofore recognized by certain curriculum authorities, can profit from instruction about geographic time zones. Social studies curriculum theory which advocates deferment of certain concepts, such as those of time and space, has been justified on the basis of the slow maturation of children's concepts and the misconceptions found in children's thinking. If this present study is indicative of possible findings in other areas of concept development, a "deferment-of-instruction" theory needs radical revision.

This study cannot be interpreted as one that minimizes, to any extent, the importance of maturation in the development of concepts. It does indicate that substantial progress in understanding the complexity of geographic time zones can be made by children. A tentative hypothesis is advanced that the limits now believed imposed by maturation on the development of other concepts of time and space may not be as rigid as believed. Results of experimental research will substantiate or refute this hypothesis.

Intermediate grade children in this study learned about direction, sphericity of the earth, rotation of the earth, and earth-sun relationships relating to time, clock time, and time zones. Although outside the scope of this investigation, the investigator believes that some aspects of these concepts profitably can be learned earlier. Effective use can be made of the globe and various map projections, including a polar projection, in teaching these ideas in the intermediate grades. Firm and substantial beginnings can be made in the development of geographic time and space concepts as early as the fourth grade. During each subsequent year's program, provision should be made for additional opportunities to use these learnings in many and varied situations and for additional and progressively more complex learnings about such concepts.

Summary

Two classes each of fourth, fifth, and sixth grades were selected from six different Davidson County, Tennessee, elementary schools. One class at each grade level was designated as the experimental group, the other as the control group. The subjects were middle-class white children. At the beginning of the experiment, there were no significant differences between the experimental and control groups with regard to intelligence, social studies achievement, and understandings about time zones. The experimental classes were taught a unit specifically embodying material relating to the development of an understanding of geographic time zones.

All experimental classes profited from the instruction about geographic time zones. At all points of development observed, sixth graders demonstrated significantly better understanding than the younger children and fifth graders comprehended significantly more than the fourth

TABLE III

SUMMARY OF ANALYSES OF VARIANCE OF IQ, SOCIAL STUDIES ACHIEVEMENT, AND SCORES ON TZ1

Variable	Variance Components for the Several Analyses			
	Between Conditions df=1	Between Grade Levels df=2	Interaction df=2	Within df=156
Intelligence Quotient	56.89	271.13	396.72	167.52
Social Studies Achievement	232.33	3151.41* (F=30.16)	49.80	104.49
Scores on TZ1	8.92	1609.12* (F=39.09)	39.08	41.16

* The ratio between each of these variance components and its appropriate error term is significant at or beyond the five percent level.

TABLE IV

SUMMARY OF ANALYSES OF VARIANCE OF PERFORMANCES ON AND GAIN SCORES BETWEEN ADMINISTRATIONS OF CRITERION TEST

Variable	Variance Components for the Several Analyses			
	Between Conditions df=1	Between Grade Levels df=2	Interaction df=2	Within df=156
Performance on TZ2	4234.00* (F=96.84)	960.07* (F=21.97)	60.22	43.70
Performance on TZ3	3085.49* (F=72.26)	1164.24* (F=27.27)	18.84	42.70
Gain Between TZ1 and TZ2+	3755.55* (F=141.93)	100.26* (F= 3.79)	12.24	26.46
Gain Between TZ1 and TZ3+	2648.30* (F=90.76)	88.02	25.64	29.18
Gain Between TZ2 and TZ3+	93.39* (F= 5.08)	24.02	25.40	18.39

* The ratio between each of these variance components and its appropriate error term is significant at or beyond the five percent level.

+ A constant of 20 points was added to each true gain score for ease in calculation.

graders. The finding that fourth graders gained significantly more understanding as a result of instruction than did the sixth graders may have been spurious. All experimental classes gained significantly and equally well from the initiation of the experimental teaching period to the test of delayed recall. Too, they continued their significant gain of understanding following termination of instruction.

Interpretation of the results of this experiment raise serious questions about theories of instruction concerning the particular concepts considered in this study. Children may be able to profit from instruction in other geographic concepts earlier than thought possible. Questions are raised about the appropriateness of deferred instruction about other concepts. Much additional experimental evidence is needed about concept development in the social studies.

FOOTNOTES

1. This study was done at the George Peabody College for Teachers as part of a doctoral dissertation under the supervision of Harold D. Drummond.
2. All future references to these classes will be made in terms of their grade and experimental condition, i.e., Fourth Control, Fourth Experimental, Fifth Control, etc. At times, these references may be abbreviated, i.e., 4C, 4E, 5C, etc.
3. All data obtained in this experiment were treated by analysis of variance and, where appropriate, t tests. Two-tailed tests were employed and the five percent level of significance was used throughout. Hartley's test (3) was used to test for homogeneity of variance before proceeding with each analysis. In instances when the hypothesis of homogeneity of variance was not accepted, the departure was not so extreme as to have had appreciable effect on the assumption underlying the F-test (6, p. 86).

REFERENCES

1. Davis, O.L., Jr. Learning about Time Zones: An Experiment in the Development of Certain Time and Space Concepts, unpublished Ph.D. dissertation, George Peabody College for Teachers, 1958.
2. Forsyth, Elaine. An Experiment in the Teaching of Certain Map Reading Skills at the Junior High School Level, unpublished Ph.D. dissertation, Cornell University, 1943.
3. Hartley, H.O. "The Maximum F-ratio as a Short-cut Test of Heterogeneity of Variance," Biometrika, XXXVII (1950), pp. 308-12.
4. Kelton, Mary E., and Hotchkiss, Caroline W. "An Experiment in Fourth Grade Geography," Journal of Geography, XIV (1916), pp. 245-51.
5. Kohn, C.F., et al. "Interpreting Maps and Globes," in Helen M. Carpenter, ed., Skills in Social Studies. Twenty-fourth Yearbook of the National Council for the Social Studies (Washington, D.C.: The Council, 1953).
6. Lindquist, E.F. Design and Analysis of Experiments in Psychology and Education (Boston: Houghton Mifflin, 1953).
7. Schaeffler, Grace C. "An Informational Unit on Time," Elementary School Journal, XXXVIII (1937), pp. 114-17.
8. Scott, Flora, and Myers, G.C. "Children's Empty and Erroneous Concepts of the Commonplace," Journal of Educational Research, VIII (1923), pp. 327-34.
9. Walker, Helen E. Selected Time-Space Concepts of Seven- and Eight-Year-Old Children, unpublished M.S. in Education thesis. New Jersey State Teachers College, Glassboro, 1952.
10. Wesley, E.B., and Adams, Mary A. Teaching Social Studies in Elementary Schools, revised edition (Boston: Heath, 1952).
11. Whipple, Gertrude. How to Introduce Maps and Globes, No: 15: How To Do It Series (Washington: National Council for the Social Studies, 1953).

What Social Studies Content for the Primary Grades?

by RALPH C. PRESTON

IN RECENT YEARS the "readiness" problem in social studies has focused upon the question: Are children ready to study, formally and systematically, remote places and remote times (as opposed to the "here and now") at an earlier age than children of a generation ago? Are children, in short, more precocious?

Those who answer affirmatively point to studies which report that as a probable consequence of the advent of television, of expanded family travel, and of increased availability of children's books, children today have wider experiences than children of a few years ago. Other studies have shown that children are sometimes taught what they already know. For example, Lowry tested and interviewed second-grade children concerning concepts they were about to be taught.[1] She concluded that they knew on the average of from 64 to 85 percent of the concepts. Such studies bring out the ever-present danger of under-challenging children. It is all too easy to belabor the obvious. Although teachers should begin with what children know, they should drive steadily on to the unknown.

The issue becomes confused, however, if we jump to the conclusion that present social studies topics are necessarily inappropriate and if we overlook the strong probability that it is usually shallow treatment of topics rather than the topics themselves which result in failure of children to be challenged.

An example of the confusion of the issue is seen in studies which seem to proceed on the two-fold assumption that (1) new topics are needed, and (2) a way to determine these new topics is by investigating children's interests. In one such study, children's interests were determined by analyzing tapes of discussions attended by 715 children of all elementary grades who were divided into small discussion groups.[2] The children talked about social studies topics up to one hour per day for one month. The discussions were not free in that a framework of promptings was devised. Thus, the children in grades 1 and 2 were given the daily reminder to "talk about people of long ago, people who live today, (people) that you like. Talk about people in this land, places in other lands, (places) you like."

The following conclusion was drawn with regard to grade 1: "The geographic interests of first-grade children seem to center about environments different from their own. . . . Generally, first-grade children, at the conclusion of their first year at school, are interested in dry lands (the desert), wet lands (the jungle), hot lands (lands of the elephant) and cold lands (the country of the reindeer)."

The reader cannot help but wonder how the data imply a set of interests that so neatly and explicitly correspond to conventional social studies topics. As a matter of fact, "cold lands" came up in just one situation, was discussed by two sub-groups, and 24 first-grade children (out of 85) participated in the discussion for a total of approximately three minutes (or an average of about eight seconds per child).

The study's evidence for this and other designations of interests seems tenuous. Can we infer from children's expressed interests (even if validly identified) anything about the topics they should or should not be studying? Surely not, unless we wish to return to the curriculum chaos of the 1930's. If a new set of topics is required, it seems sounder to proceed according to a logical model.

There is a real possibility that we are exaggerating the apparent sophistication of today's children. We may be mistaking their verbal glibness on Topic A as a sign of readiness for Topic B. These possibilities were investigated by Mugge with second-grade children whose mean intelligence and whose socio-economic status were above average.[3] She found that they lacked precision of knowledge with respect to matters about the community, the farm, and other topics normally studied in first and second grades. On the topic of the post office, for example, very few children could tell how much it costs to mail a letter or why a stamp is cancelled. By way of further example, they had difficulty in keeping cities, states, and countries in their proper hierarchial relationship. Those children who had traveled did not know significantly more than those who had not traveled. The disparity between Mugge's results and those of investigators who have found modern children well

---

RALPH C. PRESTON *is Professor of Education and Acting Dean of the University of Pennsylvania's Graduate School of Education.*

[1] Betty L. Lowry. "A Survey of the Knowledge of Social Studies Concepts Possessed by Second Grade Children Previous to the Time When These Concepts are Taught in the Social Studies Lessons." Doctoral Thesis, State University of Iowa, 1963.
[2] J. D. McAulay. "Some Interests Related to the Social Studies of Elementary School Children." Mimeographed. December 1960.
[3] Dorothy J. Mugge. "Precocity of Today's Young Children: Real or Wishful?" *Social Education.* 27:436-39; December 1963.

Social Education, 1965, No.29, pp. 147-148.

informed is probably attributable to the fact that Mugge, when asking children for a definition, was not satisfied with vague synonyms, minor usage, or trivial attributes; when children offered her these, she probed further and often found a sea of empty concepts beneath a facile surface.

Further reason for caution against precipitating children too early into studies of remote places and times is found in the literature of child development. What is known about children's thought structures at various age levels? Piaget, the Swiss psychologist whose importance is now being acknowledged by his American colleagues, found that seven-year-olds, in structuring ideas, were tied to concrete content, still bound to the here and now. Data consistent with Piaget's findings have been reported by various investigators. To be sure, Piaget is more concerned with cognitive operations than with content, and the subjects of Piaget and of most other investigators whose conclusions are generally in accord with Piaget's were not reared in a television-saturated culture. Nevertheless, there are indications that the successive stages by which children structure their thought while growing up are independent to a surprising degree of the information and ideas to which they are exposed.[4]

How does Piaget's view relate to the view that, in Bruner's words, "there is no reason to believe that any subject cannot be taught to any child at virtually any age in some form"?[5] The views are complementary. As Bruner himself points out, "it is only when we are equipped with such knowledge [as produced by Piaget in the study of physical causality, of morality, of number, and the rest] that we will be in a position to know how the child will translate whatever we present to him into his own subjective terms."[6] There is no essential contradiction. A primary-grade teacher can assume, as would Bruner, that the geographical theme of man's adaptation to climate can be taught at any age. In applying the principle of readiness in accord with Piaget, the primary teacher may emphasize those applications which the child can observe and test at first hand. Without making formal study of the adaptation-to-climate principle as it applies to foreign lands and ancient times, the teacher can and should, nevertheless, make a number of comparisons and contrasts between the present scene and remote places and times.

The central problem of readiness is a question of fitting instruction—whatever its content may be—to the mental horizons and thought patterns of children at each successive stage of growth, whatever the pace of that growth. The point needs to be stressed that some elements of the "unknown" lie close at home. We should avoid being misled by children's glib talk about foreign places into concluding that they know all they need to know about that which is close at hand.

Rusnak has shown what is involved in teaching about the "here and now" in depth.[7] She experimented informally for three years with teaching children in the first grade about the home and community. Her report gives an apt illustration of how these important topics can be presented in a challenging way. Her pupils learned the profound aspect of home and community through analysis of historical sequence, cause-effect relationships, spatial relationships, environmental adaptation, and contrasts between simple and complex societies. They learned how to collect information, how to organize it, and how to report it. It may well be that the proper issue regarding readiness is not "here and now" versus "remote," but superficial study versus study which brings out underlying principles, relationships, and processes. Greater sophistication in the social studies on the part of today's children, if it exists, calls for teachers who know how to conduct studies in depth.

---

[4] Jean Piaget and Bärbel Inhelder. *The Child's Conception of Space*. London: Routledge and Kegan Paul, 1963. See also Piaget's many earlier works. Anselm Strauss and Karl Schnessler. "Socialization, Logical Reasoning, and Concept Development in the Child." *American Sociological Review* 16:514-23; August 1951. Ralph C. Preston. *Children's Reactions to a Contemporary War Situation*, Child Development Monographs, No. 28. New York: Bureau of Publications, Teachers College, Columbia University, 1942. Harold V. Baker. *Children's Contributions to Elementary School General Discussion*, Child Development Monographs, No. 29. New York: Bureau of Publications, Teachers College, Columbia University, 1942.

[5] Jerome S. Bruner. *The Process of Education*. Cambridge, Mass.: Harvard University Press, 1961. p. 47.

[6] *Ibid.*, p. 53.

[7] Mary Rusnak. "Introducing Social Studies in the First Grade." *Social Education* 25:291-92; October 1961.

TRENDS IN SOCIAL STUDIES

by
Roger E. Johnson
University of South Florida

During the past few years, several changes have begun to take place in the area of Social Studies in the elementary school. The importance of the various trends and which should receive the greatest emphasis will depend upon who is talking about them. Many teachers and producers of educational materials are already utilizing many of these "Trends." Regardless of this, several of the current trends in elementary social studies are listed below. They are stated in no order of importance since all of them are very important in the teaching of Social Studies today.

1. **Affective Objectives.** Affective learning is the goal of cognitive learning in current social studies programs. Cognitive learning includes concept attainment and the formation of generalizations, as well as the development of study skills and inquiry processes. Affective learning involves the development of feelings, attitudes, values and interests, and the application of those outcomes - as well as of concepts and generalizations, study skills, and inquiry processes - to life situations. By guiding pupils to explore values and to use them in making choices and decisions, a teacher helps the pupils link cognitive learning with affective learning. If a pupil's feelings, attitudes, values, and interests are developed and expressed in a cognitive learning situation, and if he transfers these to similar life situations, then well-rounded learning can be said to have taken place.

2. **Controversial Issues.** It is important that teachers and students discuss and investigate controversial topics. These issues have built-in motivation and will help students understand that there are usually two sides to an issue, often times neither side has to be the "Bad Guy," and that negotiation and compromise have always been present in our history. By studying controversial issues students will gain valuable experiences in the evaluation of events broadcast by the newsmedia, in magazine and newspaper articles, and the opinions from people with vested interests. It deals with, "What's Happening."

Original Manuscript.

3. _Evaluation_. All objectives are evaluated in new social studies programs - conceptual objectives, study-skills objectives, inquiry-processes objectives, and affective objectives. It has been found that evaluation is most effective when it is an integral part of instruction. Therefore, the teacher's primary responsibility in evaluating is conducting informal day-by-day observation as pupils are learning. Behavior can be observed as pupils use concepts; engage in inquiry; apply study skills; and express attitudes, values, and interests. At appropriate times, formal means of evaluation may be provided. At the beginning levels of instruction, formal evaluation may be in the form of planned questioning, picture tests, or chart making.

4. _Inner and Outer City_. Tell the story of how and where all people live as it is. Get away from the White Anglo-Saxon Protestant point of view. Not everyone lives in a white rambler with a fence and flowers. Investigate why people live where they do and how this influences their lives.

5. _Inquiry-processes_. This is to help insure that pupils will be able to apply effective inquiry processes in any learning situation. Pupils must observe, compare, and interpret factual eveidence before they can use it in making inferences, forming generalizations or making evaluations. The successful use of inquiry processes is directly related to the development of study skills such as planning, discusssing, and evaluating; interviewing and reporting; making and interpreting maps; and using time concepts.

6. _Multi-Ethnic Approach_. Emphasis is placed on showing that people other than the whites helped make America the great country it is. However, some people want to stress the importance of only the Negro, others the Mexican, some the Jew, etc. Social Studies should be taught truthfully and realistically, but not by teaching Negro, Jewish, or Mexican-American history separate from American History for this tends to further isolate these people. Destroy stereotypes where they exist. Not all Germans drink beer, all Jews do not make a fortune, all Dutchmen do not wear wooden shoes, and any American can and often does make mistakes.

7. <u>Multiple Sources of Content</u>. Current social studies programs draw core concepts and content from all of the social sciences, not just history or geography. The scope and sequence of a program's conceptual organization is based on the use of data to develop concepts and the use of concepts to develop useful generalizations. Pupil-developed inquiries call for the use of data and concepts from all the social sciences, as well as from other areas such as mathematics, science, literature, and art. Functional content is selected and used in terms of the subject being investigated.

8. <u>Multiple Sources of Data</u>. A well-established trend is toward the use of a variety of instructional materials. Learning involves TV programs, tape recordings, pictures clipped from magazines and newspapers, the telephone, and other materials the teacher can make available to her pupils. It also involves professionally produced materials such as filmstrips, films, recordings, overhead transparencies, and globes. Ideally, all materials should be selected and used to provide for systematic presentation or reinforcement of concepts and skills stressed in the school curriculum.

Varied materials are useful for meeting individual differences; for extending learning; and for obtaining higher-quality output in discussion, in individual and group work, in expression of new ideas, and in evaluation.

The use of multiple texts or no texts is being stressed because of the inability of one text to satisfy the needs of an entire class.

9. <u>Primary Source Material</u>. When possible, children should learn to use original materials or copies of them. Instead of just handing a child a copy of Lincoln's Gettysburg Address and reading it, go into such things as what had happened before, why the president was there, the type of people attending and even the weather conditions. Afterward, discuss the meaning of the various passages and what occurred afterward. Establish a background and/or setting for situations, documents, or speeches which are important enough to deserve study so students will be able to get a more true picture of what happened.

10. **Problem Approach**. Instead of trying to cover everything about a particular subject, select a few topics and concentrate on them. For example, instead of trying to cover all of American History in grade 5, select a few topics (or problems) and attack them from all sides, historical, geographical, sociological, etc. Such topics as colonization, Declaration of Independence and Constitution Westward expansion, Civil War, industrialization, and modern governments could take an entire year.

11. **Pupil Involvement**. Greater pupil involvement in learning is a characteristic of programs designed to promote inductive learning. Pupils themselves observe, interpret, and generalize with the help and guidance of the teacher. The teacher raises questions and stimulates pupils to raise additional ones and to seek answers to them.

Motivation is higher when pupils play an active role in learning experiences. In addition, the possibility of transfer of learning is improved. A pupil who has developed the word "group" by relating it to various school situations as well as to his group of playmates or to his family has a good basis for understanding people in communities as groups. Learning is more apt to occur and remain if children experience learning through all their senses, not just through their eyes by reading.

12. **Relate to World of Today**. No matter what topic is being discussed, it can be related to the modern life of the child. An Eskimo family can be compared to a family in Tampa, Florida, and an Indian Village and be compared to Minneapolis, Minnesota. People everywhere are concerned with food, clothing, and shelter. The geography of Mexico can be compared with that of California, and the Westward Movement in the 19th Century is similar to the migration happening today. Help children realize they, as individuals and members of groups, are important and that history is happening today.

These are some of the trends in elementary social studies today. They are suggestions to help you provide for every child and to make social studies real and meaningful to them.

METHODS AND MATERIALS

ART BUCHWALD

ADDING INSULT TO INJURY

Every time you think television has hit its lowest ebb, a new type program comes along to make you wonder where you thought the ebb was. The latest in TV wrinkles is what could be termed the insult interview show, in which the interviewer spends two or three hours insulting his guests. Joe Pyne is probably the master of this type of program, though, unfortunately, he now has many imitators. If you're lucky to live in a place that doesn't carry a show of this kind, they all go something like this:

Interviewer: "Our next guest on *Couth Wants to Know* is Professor Kowowski. What do you do, Professor?"

Professor: "I am making a study of the world population explosion."

Interviewer: "Well, that's the stupidest thing I've ever heard of. How did you ever get to be a professor?"

Professor: "I studied at Harvard, MIT, and did research at Stanford."

Interviewer: "We've had lots of nuts on this show, but you take the cake. Tell us about the world population explosion."

Professor: "It is getting very serious. There will probably be a terrible crisis by 1990 which should wreack havoc on all mankind."

Interviewer: "You sound like a pinko to me. Who gives you money for your research—the Soviet Union?"

Professor: "May I continue?"

Interviewer: "Sure. We may not get a kook like you again."

Professor: "The main problem is that the population is increasing at a much faster rate than our food production."

Interviewer: "Well, what about all those nutty kids at Berkeley?"

Professor: "I beg your pardon?"

Have I Ever Lied to You, Putnam, 1968, pp. 80-81.

Interviewer: "You're a professor. Why can't you keep those nutty kids on the campuses in line?"

Professor: "I'm not interested in that problem."

Interviewer: "Of course you're not. You're so wrapped up in your miserable statistics you don't even know what's going on in the world. You know what I would do if I was a professor and the kids got out of line?"

Professor: "What?"

Interviewer: "I'd shoot them. I carry a gun with me at all times, and if I found a kid who gave me a bad time, I'd just take out the gun and put one right between his eyes. You want to see my gun?"

Professor: "Not particularly."

Interviewer: "Well, here it is. It's a .38 revolver, and I don't mind telling you they'd better not mess with me."

Professor: "I thought we were going to discuss the population explosion."

Interviewer: "You eggheads give me a pain. I don't care about the population explosion, and I don't think anybody watching this show cares. I'm sorry we even asked you on the show."

Professor: "Well, I'll be happy to leave."

Interviewer (picking up the gun): "Not before the commercial break. What do you feel is the solution to the population explosion?"

Professor: "Strong birth-control measures."

Interviewer: "Don't you have any shame?"

Professor: "What do you mean by that?"

Interviewer: "You mentioned the words 'birth control' on a family show. I've got a good mind to pop you in the nose, but we have to pause for a commercial. Stay tuned, folks, to this informative, thought-provoking show that is not afraid to deal with controversial subjects and let the chips fall where they may."

ART BUCHWALD

THE FIRST SUPERSONIC FLIGHT

"Good day, ladies and gentlemen, this is your captain speaking, and I'm happy to announce that this is the first supersonic flight from New York to Paris. We will be flying at an altitude of sixty thousand feet and a speed of eighteen hundred miles an hour. Our flying time from New York to Paris will be two hours and forty-five minutes. Now please fasten your safety belts, and we will be ready to take off. . . .

"Ladies and gentlemen, I know you're wondering what the delay is, as we have been on the ground waiting to take off for the past two hours. Unfortunately, air traffic conditions are very heavy at this hour, and we have been asked to hold here on the runway. We are now the twentieth in line for takeoff. . . .

"Well, folks, we've been moving up, as you might have noticed, and we are now second in line. I'm sorry these last four hours have been so difficult, but the tower has assured us we will get clearance to take off in the next hour or so. . . .

"May I have your attention, please? It appears that there are more planes in the pattern than was expected, and we've been asked to hold further. Why don't you all relax? I've turned the No Smoking light off. . . .

"Ladies and gentlemen, we've finally been cleared for takeoff. Would you all please relax? I apologize for the six-hour delay at the runway, but this is something we have no control over. . . .

"Well, folks, we seem to have broken some sort of record. Our flying time to Paris was two hours and thirty-one minutes. Unfortunately, there are many planes circling the Orly Airport, and we've been asked to fly over to Copenhagen and hold there at fifty-five thousand feet. Paris assures us that as soon as it is feasibly possible, they will permit us to make an approach. . . .

"Ladies and gentlemen, this is your pilot speaking. Since I last spoke to you, ninety minutes ago, I regret we have not been

Have I Ever Lied to You, Putnam, 1968, pp. 142-143.

encouraged by Paris to come in, and they have asked us to maintain altitude and fly in a pattern over Sicily.

"The stewardess tells me there seems to be a shortage of drinks and water, so we are putting everyone on rations of one glass of water each.

"Also, I'm sorry to say we have run out of food.

"Some of you have complained about seeing the movie four times, so for the next two hours we'll play stereophonic music instead.

"You'll be kept informed about our progress. . . .

"Folks, this is the captain again. I know you're all very tired and hungry and thirsty, and so am I; but trying to knock down my door is not going to help anybody. We should be getting the green light from Paris any time now. . . .

"We've just heard from Paris, and we are now in the pattern and will be permitted to land within the next hour. Please fasten your safety belts. . . .

"This is your captain again. As you can gather, we are on the ground at Orly, France. Unfortunately, there doesn't seem to be any room at the ramp, and we've been asked to wait out here until someone leaves. It should not be more than forty or fifty minutes. . . .

"Well, here we are at the terminal, and I hope you've enjoyed your first supersonic flight. I'm happy to announce we beat the *Queen Mary*'s record by four hours and twelve minutes."

ART BUCHWALD

YES, WE HAVE BANANAS

It's very hard to be a parent of a teen-ager these days. You have to keep on your toes all the time. Just the other morning I walked into the kitchen and I caught my son taking a banana out of the fruit bowl.

"What are you doing with that banana?" I shouted.

"I'm going to cut it up and put it on my cereal," he replied.

"A likely story," I said. "You weren't going to smoke it, were you?"

"Smoke the cereal?"

"No, smoke the banana, smart aleck. I read all about you kids going around smoking bananas behind your parents' backs for kicks."

He became very interested. "How do you smoke a banana?" he wanted to know.

"You don't smoke the banana. You smoke the skin."

He looked at me in amazement. "What have you been smoking?"

"Now don't try to be smart with me," I said. "You know very well what I'm talking about. You take the skin and scrape it out, and then make a paste out of it, and then you bake it, and then you smoke it."

"What for?"

"So you'll have hallucinations, that's what for. First it was marijuana, then it was LSD, and now it's bananas. Don't you have any shame?"

"Look, all I want to do is have breakfast. I'll eat the fruit, and you can keep the skin if it bugs you that much."

Have I Ever Lied to You, Putnum, 1968, pp. 32-33.

"How do I know you didn't scrape off the skin before I came in?" I said.

"Search me," he yelled.

Just then my wife walked in to find out what the commotion was all about.

"I caught him eating a banana," I said.

"Well, what's wrong with that?" she demanded.

"Don't you read the newspapers? Kids all over the country are smoking bananas so they can take trips."

"Take trips where?"

"Wherever bananas will take them."

My wife looked scared. "Are you feeling all right?"

"Why does everyone think I'm crazy because I don't want my kids to smoke bananas?" I cried.

"Well, if you feel that strongly about it," she said, "I won't buy any bananas again."

"Sure, and then they'll sneak up to the fruit store and buy them behind our backs. At least this way we know they're getting good-quality bananas."

"Why don't we let him smoke a banana in front of us to get it out of his system?" my wife suggested.

"I don't want to smoke a banana," my son yelled. "In fact, I don't even want to eat my cornflakes."

"That's a good idea. We'll all smoke bananas together, and that way we'll know what the kids are experiencing. You're lucky you have modern parents."

I started scraping out the skins and making a paste. Then I baked it, and then I chopped it up and passed out three pipes.

The three of us sat around the floor of the living room and started to puff.

In about ten minutes I asked my son what he saw.

"I see Mom getting green."

"That's no hallucination," my wife said.

Five minutes later we all retired to our respective washrooms. This was the "trip" that everyone was talking about.

ART BUCHWALD

THE PROUD PARENTS

A lot of proud parents show up the month of June at university commencement exercises throughout the land. I was sitting next to a beaming couple, and during the ceremonies I struck up a conversation.

"You must be very happy today," I said to the father.

"Oh, I am. Martha and I have waited all our lives for this moment when Peter would graduate from college."

"Which one up there is Peter?"

"He's not there," the father replied. "He walked out when Secretary McNamara started to make the commencement speech."

"That's a shame," I said. "I guess you and your wife are pretty upset."

"Oh, no. He told us he originally planned to lie down across the podium, so we're very grateful he decided on a nonviolent protest."

"I'll bet you scrimped and saved to put Peter through college."

"Actually, the tuition wasn't too bad. We had set funds aside for that. But it was pretty hard to get up the bail money every time Peter got arrested. We managed though, except for the time he burned his draft card."

Have I Ever Lied to You, Putnam, 1968, pp. 23-24.

"He had to stay in jail for that one?"

"I'm afraid so. It wasn't just burning his draft card that got the administration angry—Peter accidentally burned down the gym with it."

"It must have played heck with the basketball schedule," I said.

"It did. But when Peter got out he started a freedom committee to burn down gymnasiums, and about a fourth of the school signed up."

"What did Peter major in while he was in college?"

"He started out majoring in modern anarchy, but he found it was too restrictive, so he took a straight liberal arts course with a minor in Nietzsche. Martha wanted him to study law, but Peter said, 'There are no laws.' And that was the end of it."

"Peter sounds as if he's got a mind of his own."

"I think you could say that. He's the only one in his class who stopped two troop trains going in opposite directions at the same time on the Atchison, Topeka, and the Santa Fe."

"You have to have convictions to do that," I said.

"You also have to have long legs," the father said. "Peter then walked from Anchorage to Nome, Alaska, because he claimed the Alaskans wouldn't let the Eskimos vote. And he also sat in Governor Romney's office for two nights as a protest against capital punishment."

"But Michigan doesn't have capital punishment."

"That's what Governor Romney kept telling him."

"It must have been an interesting four years for you."

"I guess you could say that, particularly during school vacations when Peter found it hard to get LSD."

"Now that Peter's finished college, what does he plan to do?" I asked.

"He's applied for training jobs with IBM, Time-Life Inc., and the Ford Motor Company. He figures there's a much better future with a large corporation than trying to start out on your own."

THE SELECTION AND EVALUATION OF TEXTUAL MATERIAL

by
Milton Kleg
University of South Florida

Students of education and teachers in the field are confronted with the selection and evaluation of textual material. The following discussion is one response to the question: How shall we evaluate texts? The response has two parts. Part One relates the guidelines for detailed evaluation. Part Two uses world history as an example of employing the design to further explain its utility.

PART ONE: THE DESIGN FOR EVALUATION

Section I. Lay-out design.

The criteria set forth in this section deals with the general physical format of the text. Depending upon the objectives of the course, cost allotment, use of the text, expected longevity of its use and level of students the text is to be used with, the value of these criteria will vary to some extent.

1. Is the text hardback or paperback?
2. Is the textbook part of a package program? (If so, what is included? Are workbooks adequate or mere parroting exercises? Is a package desirable in terms of your objectives?)
3. Date of first publication? This year...last year ...2 years...3-5 years...6years or longer.
4. Is the text revised and/or updated?
5. Is the reading level satisfactory for the students who are expected to use it?
6. Is the text written in such a manner that will most probably maintain interest?
7. Does the text contain <u>useful</u> illustrations to include maps, tables, photos, and drawings as opposed to a potpourri of miscellany?
8. Is there a table of contents?
9. Is there an index?
10. Is there a list of references for additional reading and for research?
11. Does the text indicate resources of information by use of footnotes?
12. Is there a bibliography given?

Original Manuscript.

13. Is the presentation of material in a chronological order, based upon regions or areas, problems, or a combination or these?
    a. Chronology
    b. Area study
    c. Problems
    d. Combination:_____

Section II. The author or authors.

The section deals briefly with the authority behind the textbook. Some knowledge about the author will assist the teacher in evaluating the text.
1. What is the academic background of the author? Is he a historian, educator, both, or other? Is he a social scientist?
2. What is the author's frame of reference?
    a. How does he view history?
       --Is this conducive to your objectives?
    b. How does he view social education?
       --Does he lean toward expository or discovery?
    c. Does he list objectives or state his purpose of the text? (rationale)
    d. Does he mention others with whom he has collaborated in preparing the text or does he lead you to assume he has relied upon his own research for the entire text? (Keep in mind the vast knowledge being covered.)
3. Does the author appear to maintain an ethnocentric philosophy?

Section III. Content and methodology.

This section deals with accuracy of content, presentation of concepts, generalizations and values.
1. Based upon a sampling of 5 or more statements of fact often misstated, does the text give an accurate factual account?
   Examples:
       a. Is Lincoln described as an abolitionist (F) or Free Soiler (T)?
       b. Does the text refer to Mohamadans (Misnomer) or Muslims (or Moslems) since 1400?
2. Does the textbook reinforce stereotyping?
3. Does the text present value statements in the form of authoritative facts?
4. Are concepts clearly stated and defined?--Are the concepts presented relevant to the objectives of the course?

5. Are generalizations and principles clearly stated and <u>explained</u>? (documented) --Does the text suggest an open-ended approach open to public inquiry regarding stated generalizations?
6. Does the text provide a method of inquiry to be employed by students beyond the use of the text?
7. Did the text employ a scientific or reflective method in establishing principles and generalizations or an authoritative method?
8. Does the text presentation present the student with and encourage the following opportunities?
    a. To question and analyze observations.
    b. To employ creativity and problem solving.
    c. To examine controversy (controversial issues).
    d. To examine values and value conflicts.
    e. To employ role playing, reconstructional situation analysis, role reversal, simulation.
9. Based upon a sampling of the questions presented, how are they classified based upon Bloom's <u>Taxonomy</u> ...or similar taxonomy?
    1. Knowledge____% ____#
    2. Comprehension____% ____#
    3. Application____% ____#
    4. Analysis____% ____#
    5. Synthesis____% ____#
    6. Evaluation____% ____#
    7. 1 and 2 ____% ____#
    8. 3 through 6____% ____#
    9. 1 through 3____% ____#
    10. 4 through 6____% ____#
10. Does the text (especially World History) reflect levels of ethnocentricity?
    a. Western Europe and "New World" focus.
    b. Equally balanced concentration.
    c. Eastern World focus.
    d. Are political systems objectively examined (pros and cons) without bias?
11. Is the vocabulary - use of terms - consistent?

Section IV. Teacher Text.
1. Is a teacher text provided?
2. Are teacher references for additional information cited?
3. Are springboards for inquiry recommended?
4. Is a critical analysis of the text given?

5. Are specific behavior objectives listed?
6. Are there recommendations for testing and measuring student behavior?
7. Are methods of evaluating student behavioral changes (learning) offered?
8. Are there actual tests given for use?--Is there sufficient data given concerning these tests (field test results, norms, item analysis, information, etc.)?--Are test questions broken down into various segments of the cognitive and/or affective domain?

PART TWO: WEIGHING THE ABOVE CRITERIA IN THE SELECTION OF A TEXT

First, it must be stated that valuing or ranking the importance of criteria depends to some degree on the following:

1. The objectives of the course.
2. The support material available.
3. The use the teacher intends to make of the text. That is, will the text be the main source of information or merely minor secondary import.

The criteria which I have set up may appear more detailed than one commonly expects. Nevertheless, such an analysis provides the teacher with an opportunity to become thoroughly acquainted with the text. Furthermore, quite often more than one teacher is involved in selecting a text. Committees are often set up. Furthermore, textbook evaluation should be a continuous process. The wise teacher does not select a text in a one-shot process. Textbook evaluation and selection is part of curriculum development. By keeping up to date on recent new and revised publications, the master teacher avoids a last minute rush to choose a text as well as other support material. Finally, additional supplements to these criteria can be added based upon the group of students to receive instruction. For example, in a ghetto school you might want to see if the text is presented in a manner which will obtain awareness and response of the children; or you may find it is better to not use a text because other materials, due to your objectives, may be more satisfactory.

Now, as to the selection or weighing of criteria, let us remember that regardless of the modifying factors mentioned, we can establish a FLEXIBLE heirachy of importance concerning the criteria. However, keep in mind that many of these criteria are INTERDEPENDENT and INTERRELATED. Since the question at hand asks to relate the more "important" criteria to text selection in an area of world history (my choice), I shall combine the two parts. First, a statement of the "important" criteria and secondly its relation to text selection in world history shall be given.

Section I, Question 4: Is the text revised and/or updated?

This criteria is very important. Texts written in different periods of history reflect the social, economic, political, and other cultural problems existing within the confines of the nation in which the text is published. The authors seem to be biased by the problems of the time. Furthermore, they often reflect the prevailing attitudes of major social forces. During the 1940-45 wartime, world history texts presented Germany as a war-mongering nation from its very inception. World history texts emphasized local nationalism-patriotism and smacked with ethnocentrism. By 1960 American world history texts passed into a period of anti-Soviet Union-ism and anti-Communism.

Another aspect conerns the role of world history in education and the impact of related social sciences such as sociology and anthropology. Emphasis of cultural case studies, social values, and cultural conflicts began to emerge in the mid and late 1960's. The previous treatment of world history, that of political changes and wars and its narrative and indoctrinating, came under attack. The use of "discovery" methods, open-ended, and inquiry approaches began to gain momentum.

Section I, Question 5: The reading level satisfactory...

Obviously, if the level is too difficult, the content and meaning risks being lost. This applies to world history as well as to other areas. If it is oversimplified, the lack of meaning and utility can occur. The reading level is an obvious major aspect, but it is not necessary to pursue it in specific terms of world history beyond the above point.

Section I, Question 6: ...written in...a manner that it will ...maintain interest?

This criteria closely relates to five. However, it should be pointed out that world history encompasses a wide variety of areas. The teacher may have to select pertinent areas of high concentration. This criteria is quite subjective, but sample testing on students might bring more valid conclusions.

ction I, Questions 7, 8, 9, and 10 are quite basic. #7 (useful illustrations) becomes important in situations where support material is limited as in some ghetto or poor rural schools. Since world history takes the student in distant past and present cultures, illustrations must be examined for tendencies to stereotype.

I am not highly concerned with 11 or 12 compared to other criteria since the teacher can supply references and bibliography. Footnoting is not essential but often very useful especially in terms of breakdown of the concept that the text author ergo textbook is omniscient.

Section I, Question 13: The method of presentation in terms of chronology, area study, problem...

This criteria is essential to world history. A chronological study is the simplest for most students due to past education. However, they often limit the text to specific areas, like Western Europe (starting in the Middle East) and reduce material on areas in Asia, Africa, and the Far East. Area studies are more holistic but difficult for perception. Both methods seem limited in bringing meaning and utility to the student.

The problems approach increases meaningfulness, involvement, and can be culturally balanced, but like the area approach it might be difficult unless a strong, clear frame of reference is set up. This problem is quite serious at the world history level. A combination might be the best criteria.

Section II, Question 2:   ...authors frame of reference...a...b...e

These criteria are quite essential in selecting a world history text. Knowledge of the authors frame of reference will reflect underlining values presented. It will reflect its goals. When the teacher is able to view the text through the eyes of the author, a whole new perspective of world history might come through and weigh heavily on discovering the text's limitations and assets. Also, it will sharpen the teacher's awareness of ethnocentrism on the part of the author and his tendency to stereotype.

Section III, Questions 1:   ...accuracy of statements of fact and 2:   ...stereotyping and 3:   ...values...statements...of...fact.

(1) World history, as has been noted, is a vast area of study. There is no one who is an expert in all facets of

"world history." Quite often, authors do a good job in some areas but often supply false information in areas they are not highly trained in or motivated in.

(2) Some texts may have false facts, false generalizations, and bland overgeneralizations. The conscientious teacher should examine this problem with care. Inaccurate or deceptive information can lead to a misinformed student. This often leads to stereotyping.

(3) Similarly, if the text presents value statements as authoritative facts, then you are on the way to indoctrinating the student in terms of the author's value system. Furthermore, this results in a distortion of history, expecially world history, to fit a closed-personal belief system. These three criteria are extremely important. One might be wise to determine these as very strong points for rejecting or accepting the text.

<u>Section III, Question 5: ...generalizations and principles clearly stated and explained? (documented)</u>

World history is so vast that authors are faced with setting down a mass of principles and generalizations. Nevertheless, this does not justify negligence in supporting generalizations and principles or providing counter-positions. A text full of unsupported generalizations and principles and without a balanced presentation of pros and cons is full of something else also and it "ain't HAY." Again this is a very major determining factor.

<u>Section III, Question 7: ...employ a scientific or reflective method and Question 8: ...opportunities.</u>

It should be obvious by this time that inquiry and openendedness are essential in learning. This is again especially important to world history. Without these methods, the content becomes meaningless if not useless. When world history becomes a dull narrative based upon intuition, introspection, and appeal to authority, so do the people, events, and cultures of the world. In reference to #7, when the author places himself in an authoritative position and embeds himself in the pretense of omniscient insight, students have no way of challenging his position since closed methods of knowing are not open to public inquiry! As for #8, besides the opening remark, we must keep in mind that education and involvement are bed partners.

Section III, Question 10:   ...level of ethnocentricity

We have already alluded to ethnocentrism, but a word of caution should be mentioned in regard to world history texts. Since America is steeped in Western Civilization and culture, the teacher often fails to realize that Asia, Africa, and the Far East have cultures and histories far greater in depth than western history. Yet, many world history texts extend only a flimsy lip service to these areas. It is important for a world history text to be well balanced. Furthermore, although this is extremely difficult, the teacher should be aware of the common tendency of authors to present problems in these areas in western terms. Seeing the East in terms of western standards has been a major problem in misunderstanding as well as miseducating!

Section IV, Question 4:   ...critical analysis

This is quite important to the teacher since it allows him to be aware of limitations. This applies to any area as does #5 list of objectives.

In a general sense, it has been stated that these criteria are interdependent and/or interrelated. Furthermore, various other criteria can be added depending upon objectives. For example, a teacher might want to examine the treatment of racial and ethnic minority groups. Another criteria can be the utilization of anthropological, sociological, and social-psychological concepts. But these involve a highly skilled individual. I recommend that the teacher using such criteria refer to studies (such as dissertations, ADL, NCA, Human Rights Commission, and American Federation of Teachers publications on the treatment of minority groups in texts.)

Finally, one might refer to Brown's outline of textbook evaluation in Social Education (Vol. 25, 1961). My initial list drops page numbers, appendices, and binding which Brown mentions. However, these are other criteria which can be considered if one wishes. In fact, when I recommended the use of appendices in Life Cycle, I considered this as a criteria of evaluation by educators in selecting the text.

Reading Skills in the Social Studies

by JOHN R. O'CONNOR

GENERALLY, one is considered to be skilled if he possesses a high degree of competence in a trade, profession, a sport, or, in school, in a subject area. The student with skills is the one who is bright, superior, able to grasp information and insights with little apparent effort. On the other hand, we label as a "slow learner" the student who has few skills—and often consider it impossible for him to achieve proficiency in the use of the skills in the subject area. If this is so, we may as well surrender our efforts to teach the "slow learner," for truthfully, without skills, no one can succeed in the social studies.

"Slow learner" has become that convenient term by which educators describe any child who seems yearly to fall further behind in his efforts to master conventional subject matter. Most often, however, when a pupil is categorized as a slow learner, what is really meant is that he is a *slow reader*. There is nothing startling about the fact that some children read less capably than others. This has always been so, and as long as we continue to establish a norm that purports to represent the "average" reader, we will always have pupils who surpass the norm or lag behind it. Although there is considerable hesitation in admitting that we will inevitably have slower readers, no matter what we do in our schools, the truth is that a "norm" decrees by its nature that some must be slower than others.

The task of the teacher, therefore, is one of *raising the norm*, so that the slower reader of today is the equal of the better reader of yesterday. And this is not an unlikely promise, for studies in both the reading and social studies abilities of present-day pupils reveal that slower readers of this age, in great part, achieve and surpass the norms established by standard measuring instruments of 30 years ago.[1]

In the social studies, the slow reader suffers because of the all-too-prevalent concept that a class must "cover" a certain amount of subject matter in an established number of weeks or months. The object of this article is not, however, to enter into a discussion of the nature of syllabi or the approaches to time allotments or emphasis upon the varied social studies disciplines. It is, rather, the censure of any orientation that provides lip service to social studies instruction without an emphasis upon social studies skills and the methods of instruction in those skills.

JOHN R. O'CONNOR *is Principal of the Francis Scott Key Junior High School in Brooklyn, New York.*

Let us admit, first, that the *basic social studies skills are reading skills*. Social studies teachers pride themselves on the fact that in their classes, if in few others, their pupils do read. After all, the textbook must be consumed and research must be carried out by means of a variety of reference materials. Assignments are made for out-of-class reading from library sources as well as the textbook. Often the daily homework assignment is, "Read pages 41 to 44 and answer these questions. . . ." Yes, the social studies student reads, or at least tries to read and to understand what is expected of him. But how does the slow learner—the slow reader—fare under this kind of reading program? Is he being taught to read within the framework of the social studies?

More often than not, the reading difficulty that plagues the majority of slow learners has caused them to fall behind in their social studies, and it has convinced them that they *cannot* read better than they do—and that failure awaits them again each time they renew the attempt. What is more, it probably does, unless there is a structure in social studies teaching that combines improvement in reading skills with the development of specific social studies skills, knowledges, and concepts. If there are certain skills whose development is an obligation shared by the social studies, we must *consciously* plan for their development. Students do not learn skills by chance. Inherent in any skills program is a fundamental concept: a skill must be taught, and it must be practiced, consciously and with effort.

In the 1963 NCSS Yearbook, *Skill Development in the Social Studies*, the skills in which the social studies at least share responsibility for development are listed: locating and gathering information; organizing and evaluating information; reading, speaking, and listening; interpreting pictures, graphs, charts, and tables. Going further, Eunice Johns and Dorothy Fraser emphasize that these skills must be taught *functionally* and in the *context of study*; there should be repeated opportunity to *practice* the

---

[1] J. R. O'Connor. "Social Studies Achievement, 1932-1962." *High Points* 46:46-50; March 1964.

Scores achieved by 207 seventh- and eighth-grade children on the Metropolitan Advanced Reading Test, Form A, administered in January 1964, were compared with scores attained by the same children on the Metropolitan Advanced Reading Test, Form A, 1932. Whereas 142 pupils were "below grade" in reading based on the 1962 norms, but 84 were below grade on the 1932 test. No children in either grade were more than one year below grade based on the 1932 standard.

Social Education, February, 1967, Vol.31, pp. 104-107.

skill; and that skills instruction must move from the simple to the complex.[2]

We can heartily subscribe to all these suggestions and recognize the service they render in the development of social studies skills.

But let us be specific. The basic skill that leads to most others in the "shared" skills category is the ability of the student to find the *main idea* of a paragraph or section (or even a sentence). Without this ability, we can forget about our students being able to outline, summarize, or take notes effectively. Going further, all the skills involving critical thinking, substantiating opinions with proof, and supporting generalizations are based upon the ability of the youngster to determine the main, the important, the central thought of the spoken and written word. The ability to recognize the main idea and its supporting details is related to the ability to separate the relevant from the irrelevant.

But how often have we asked pupils to utilize these skills without having taught them, given opportunity for practice and reinforced them continually? Normally, a social studies teacher expects that the skills have been taught—by someone else in some other class. Even if they have been, a skill is not just taught; it must be practiced. This practice is necessary even for the student with a high intellectual capacity if he is to acquire the competence of which he is capable. The skilled carpenter and surgeon have practiced their arts after first having been taught them.

Do not think that the recognition of the main idea of a selection is too difficult for the slower reader. The frequency of error of our slower readers of junior high school age on standardized reading tests has been analyzed and has revealed that questions requiring pupils to determine the main thought of a paragraph are answered correctly *most* often. There have been more correct responses for questions involving the selection of the main thought than for questions that test the ability to note significant details or the meaning of words in context. This is true whether the pupils were reading at a fifth- or tenth-grade level. The task of the social studies is to apply this skill as emphasized in the 1963 Yearbook, functionally and in the context of study.

I am not suggesting that the social studies teachers become teachers of reading exclusively. I am suggesting that in the social studies we should know the skills our students possess and ought to possess—reading skills, let's call them—and that the ability to use these skills is fundamental to their success in their studies. Let us examine a few practical applications of reading skills to the social studies.

The teacher begins by selecting a textbook passage about three paragraphs in length. He asks the students to read silently each paragraph in turn and to select the main thought of the paragraph. (What is the paragraph about?) Inquiry is then made as to the reason for the selection. Members of the class are encouraged to comment on the choices of their classmates. (This kind of discussion will prove invaluable as students progress in ability and become concerned with the author's purpose in writing.) As a result of this procedure, the class will have selected three main ideas—three headings for a basic outline. Now the *reasons* for the selections of these important ideas are recalled; these are the details that support each of the headings. Thus, a simple outline has been developed, while subject matter has been learned. This kind of developmental process can be used again and again until it becomes part of the student's equipment whenever he is called upon to outline and summarize. Furthermore, how much better he can study and digest a new lesson on his own with this aid to learning available to him!

In performing a basic research assignment, students will build upon the process of making an outline. The shopworn project that requires a student to look for information in the library from some nebulous source and make a report with pictures and charts (to be finished in two weeks) must go! This kind of project is best entitled, "Frustrating the Slow Reader."

Rather specific materials must be known to the teacher and the students must be directed to them and instructed in their use. For example, students may read a specific article from a magazine, preferably one that the teacher has read, and submit five important ideas from the article. Then, in conference with the teacher or in a class situation, the reasons for the selection of these ideas may be discussed. Logically, students will follow the lessons learned in class on the method of determining the important ideas. Now the article may be reread for supporting statements. The details are filled in and the outline for the report is made before the student moves on, in due time and with sufficient planning, to the more complex outline or summary.

What would you think when you observe such a scene as this in a classroom? The class secretary is at the chalkboard prepared to record the notes of the class discussion. After a few minutes in which the class suggests problems resulting from the introduction of machinery in the eighteenth century, the teacher asks the class to suggest the *main idea* of the discussion. The secretary dutifully writes the suggestion on the board. The teacher then asks, "What

---

[2] Eunice Johns and Dorothy McClure Fraser. "Social Studies Skills: A Guide to Analysis and Grade Placement," in Helen McCracken Carpenter, editor. *Skill Development in Social Studies*. Thirty-Third Yearbook, Washington, D.C. National Council for the Social Studies, 1963. p. 310 ff.

have we discussed that supports this idea?" As the class responds, the secretary writes the sub-topics in proper outline form. A glance at pupil notebooks reveals that on a series of successive lessons pupils have recorded notes with the labels of "main idea" and "sub-topic" next to the statements recorded. It does not require great wisdom to discern that this class is going to use this procedure in all their work.

In the process, content has not been forsaken. In fact, the important ideas of the passage have been made more memorable. It is not idle guessing to state that the student will probably retain such information for a greater length of time as well. For the student is not only practicing a skill, he is focusing on the important ideas—and the use of the skill makes it possible.

The same emphasis prevails during the viewing of a film or in listening to a speaker. Listening is one of the "shared" skills. During the presentation, notes are recorded. Instead of an immediate discussion of the film or speech, which can become rambling in nature, it is most effective to have the students present the ideas they have selected from the notes they have just recorded. When these ideas are seen on the chalkboard, it will be obvious that there is considerable overlapping in wording; some are then condensed into a single idea, and the important ideas evolve. The message of the presentation is spotlighted through the important ideas presented, and the skill is being practiced functionally.

Stress on this technique during a talk will help to overcome a common criticism that students do not listen. Do we *direct* their listening? Do we check their listening skills by reading in short bursts and calling for a brief statement of the important idea of the selection? Do we afford the opportunity for youngsters to judge the relative importance of the speaker's words? The answer to these questions must be an affirmative, for most of us secure much of our information from the spoken word. Practice in listening is as important as practice in reading in the social studies. And, the intensity of the concentration is even greater, for there is no chance for the listener to refer to material already spoken. Just as we expect youngsters to look for clues and inferences in the written word, we hold the same expectation for them in the spoken word. Too often we have assumed that listening has taken place. We must be assured that it *has* taken place.

Hopefully, the traditional homework assignment of "Read and answer these questions" is on its way out with the slow learner. Quite honestly, this type of assignment does have for its purpose the elicitation of the important ideas of the reading assignment. But if we wish our youngsters to concentrate on the location of important ideas and facts, why don't we specifically ask them to do so. The assignment may just as easily read (and with greater value in its statement of purpose and development of skill): "Read pages 61 and 62. Select the main idea of the first paragraph; select the main idea of paragraphs 2 through 5." The approach has been altered but not the emphasis, and the skills practice may result in better understanding than the search for specific and unrelated items.

Instead of "Identify these words or terms," we can ask: "What word in the second paragraph means the same as "growing in amount"? In the following paragraph as "route or road"? In the last paragraph as "journey to a holy place"? And the student might even be asked, after instruction in the skills of determining the meanings of words in context, to name the *clues that helped him* to tell the meaning of the word or expression.

Part of the task in improving skills, and perhaps the greatest part, is proving to the student that he can learn. He must succeed, and he will succeed as the instruction in skills becomes basic, specific, and continual. Even such an advanced skill as skimming for content can be taught to the slow reader, once he is convinced that he can do it. The fascinating instrument, the controlled reader, can be so manipulated as to convince the youngster that he can read faster than he believes he can by starting him at a faster rate and then slowing the rate until he is able to read with understanding. He will find that he is reading with comprehension at a rate that he believed was beyond his grasp.

The ability to skim social studies materials can be demonstrated by this simple process. Students are asked to open their books to a page selected by the teacher (preferably one without sub-headings) and simply read the first sentence of three or four paragraphs. Then, they close their books. After the sentences have been written or paraphrased on the chalkboard (or have been previously prepared for the overhead projector) a pattern appears in these sentences. The class is asked what this page is all about. You may be surprised how well they can determine the topic being discussed and even give a tentative title for the passage. Most often, the leading sentences become headings for an outline of the passage —and this understanding has accrued *before* the selection has been fully read. The reaction of students to this demonstration is evidence that here is a stimulus to intensive effort in the improvement of skills, for they have learned quickly and dramatically that they have the abilities that are useful, and that practice will sharpen them to a keen edge.

Students are expected to reason. This reasoning may involve the ability to make inferences from the spoken word or written material. Allied with the inferential ability are the skills of drawing conclusions, forming hypotheses, and making generalizations and judgments. All of these are skills of the social studies, and they are important components of instruments used to measure reading ability.

Our teachers have developed a group of questions that they have come to term "collateral questions." Their purpose is to develop in youngsters the ability to infer, predict, and characterize people and events. For example:

> What would be a good title for this selection?
> From what you have read, would you guess that . . . ?
> As a result of this action, would you say that . . . ?
> Reading between the lines, what do you think of the statement that . . . ?
> What will probably happen when . . . ?
> What do you think the result would have been if . . . ?
> What word would you use to describe . . . ?
> How would you characterize this person or event?

Of course, not all of these questions are posed in a single class session, nor are all of them adaptable for every lesson. But the possession by teachers of a fund of questions with specific purposes leads to the kind of thinking on the part of students that assists in the development of "thinking" skills. All of these are inherent in social studies instruction, and they would be used more often if there was an awareness of their purpose and their contribution toward the success we seek with our slow learners—and our rapid learners as well.

Unfortunately for our slower readers, new patterns in the social studies do not seem to take him into account. Emphasis on research materials has always required specific skills in the social studies. Now, there is an increasing emphasis on the ability to derive information from original documents. Curriculum planners have not faced squarely the problem of the slower reader in the "new emphasis." Quite honestly, new curricula will have little effect on any student who does not possess reading competence. There is little use in changing our areas of emphasis in the social studies without concerning ourselves with the most vital of means by which objectives are to be accomplished. It is certainly not in our interest to omit one-third of our students from the benefits of a new focus. There is an increasing need for the concern of *all* social studies teachers with the reading competence of *all* our students.

Herein lies a possible flaw in planning—unless adaptations are made individually by teachers everywhere. One can foresee the barriers placed before some of the youngsters when asked to read the Magna Carta. The Emancipation Proclamation, or a Supreme Court decision. For what good is familiarity with a document if it cannot be read with comprehension? Yet, the opportunities for reading growth are more readily available to us in the new curricula than even before. The opportunities cannot be lost. They will not be if social studies instructional practices are a reflection of the inherent importance of reading skills and their application within the framework of the social studies. There is no doubt that, if reading improvement is going to take place, social studies teachers are going to be the primary source of the improvement.

This is not an attempt to be either comprehensive or definitive on the subject of reading-social studies skills. I have tried to convey my deep concern at the assumption by some that what we should be doing in this field is not our proper function. *All* our students need instruction in fundamental skills. Of particular concern is the success of our slower readers, whose abilities can be harnessed within a structure that enables them to grow and succeed or who can be left to flounder and fail because they do not possess the necessary building tools. We are concerned with the need to "reach" the slow reader. Make no mistake—such pupils can succeed, and the development of basic skills in both social studies and reading is a primary step in the process.

HOW READABLE ARE OUR ELEMENTARY SOCIAL STUDIES TEXTBOOKS?

by
Roger E. Johnson
University of South Florida

How readable are social studies textbooks? That is a very relevant question; one that all teachers should ask themselves before saying something like, "Open your textbooks to page 123 and read to 146. Answer the questions on pages 147 and 148."

Textbooks are generally written with the assumption that teachers will carefully guide children through the text. The book is supposed to be a resource rather than the main instrument for learning. In an informal survey of 158 elementary teachers in the Tampa Bay area, only seventy-five stated that they regularly taught social studies and of these seventy-five, seventy-one reported that a textbook was their main teaching tool. The remaining eighty-three did not teach social studies regularly, even though they were the only teachers with whom their children might be studying it. The chief reason for omitting social studies, according to most of the eighty-three teachers, was that the textbooks were too difficult for the children to read. Most of the teachers who were using texts said that the texts were hard for some children but they felt that most could handle the material. The fact that many of the teachers gave textbook difficulty as reason for not teaching social studies, and moreover, that almost all who did teach the subject used the textbook as their chief teaching tool, led to an obvious question: Is the reading level of social studies textbooks too difficult for the children who use them?

In 1962, Gates (10) stated that children were then reading better than ever before, so one might assume that with continued progress the reading of social studies would be no problem today. However, Foley in 1951 found that student activities which involved reading were unpopular. Stewart in 1945 reported that drawing and constructing were the activities ranked highest by children, while those that involved reading and writing were ranked low.

Original Manuscript.

Other major investigations have concluded that children care little for social studies. Among the investigations were those by Holmes, 1937 (13), Jersild and Tasch, 1949 (14), Chase and Wilson, 1958 (3), Curry, 1963 (4), Herman, 1963 (12), and Rice, 1963 (15). All of these studies over the years have shown that children ranked social studies either "least likes," or close to it.

If this dislike does exist and if the textbook is an important cause for it, a closer look should be taken at the textbooks being used. An obvious approach was to assess the reading difficulty of textbooks.

Florida has State-adopted textbooks for all subjects in the elementary and secondary schools. In elementary social studies there are eighteen texts adopted for grades one, two, and three; and twenty-three texts for use in grades four, five, and six; a total of forty-one. Measures of readability were applied to each of the forty-one textbooks.

Two readability formulas were used at the primary grade level: The Spache Readability Formula for Grades I, II, and III (16), and the new Readability Graph by Edward Fry (8).

Four different readability scales were used for grades four, five, and six. They were the Dale-Chall Formula for Predicting Readability(5), the Direct Grade Equivalent Table for the Dale-Chall Formula by Charles Goltz (11), the Flesch Readability Formula (7), and the Fry Readability Graph (8).

Readability formulas use such factors as the number of unfamiliar words, the number of syllables, and/or the number of sentences in a specified sample, with several samplings per text. Usually several samples of 100 words are recommended. In this study the number of samples varied although all readability scales for each level were applied to the same samples. Some primary books were evaluated in their entirety because there was so little printed matter whereas in some upper grade texts a maximum of fiteen samples of 100 words each were used. Research has shown that these readability formulas usually correlate .90 or above with each other and with the reading levels of children (Fry, 9).

Dale and Chall (6) have defined readability as the total of all elements within a specific piece of printed material which affect the success a group of readers may have with it. This success is the extent to which the children understand it, can read it at an optimum speed, and find it interesting. Success also depends upon the reader: his skill in reading, his intelligence, his maturity, his interest, and his purpose in reading.

Obviously, formulas can not measure everything. Chall (2) cautioned that formulas should not be accepted as precise measures of reading difficulty, but rather as approximations; they consider only limited aspects of difficulty. Therefore, she stated, the reported level of difficulty may vary as much as one year in either direction from reality. Spache (17) states that his formula has a probable error of only 3.3 months.

Anderson (1) pointed out that by their very nature, readability formulas ignore such factors as the reading level of the student, (his maturity, experience, and motivation) or the interest level of the material.

Therefore, it must be noted that this study evaluated only the <u>reading levels</u> of the forty-one state-adopted social studies textbooks for grades one through six, and ignored the interest level of the material, any motivation provided by the teacher, and methods of instruction. It should also be remembered that the true reading level may vary as much as from 3.3 months to one year from the reported level depending upon which measuring instrument was used.

Table I reports the reading levels obtained for the eighteen social studies textbooks used in grades one, two, and three, as estimated by using the Spache and the Fry Readability Scales. The readability levels are rounded off to the closest grade level. The exact Spache reading level obtained is shown in parentheses by grade and month.

Table I

In Table I these results should be noted:

1. Not one of the eighteen books revealed a reading level below the grade for which the text was recommended.

2. Twenty of the thirty-eight readability levels obtained were above the grade level suggested by the publisher.

3. The readability levels obtained by using the Spache Formula were closer to the reading level suggested by the publisher than were those obtained with the Fry Formula.

Although the fact does not appear in Table I it should be noted that the readability levels of samples taken within a single text varied as much as three years. This is a very important factor because a text reported to have a reading level of fifth grade may have a great deal of material that will even be difficult for the better readers of a class.

Table II

Table II lists twenty-three state-adopted texts suggested for use in grades four through six with their reading levels as determined by the four readability formulas listed above. The readability levels are rounded off to the nearest grade level. The range of reading scores obtained in varying samples by the "Dale-Chall (Goltz)" contains reading levels obtained from the Goltz Table for the Dale-Chall Formula rounded off to the closest year. The actual scores obtained by this formula are in parentheses.

Analysis of Table II reveals the following information:

1. Only one measurement of one textbook of the twenty-three books evaluated had <u>any</u> readability rating below the teaching level suggested by the publisher. This was the Dale-Chall rating of <u>Old World Lands</u>, a grade six text, published by Silver Burdett Co. It revealed a reading level of fifth grade. The other three measures were all at the sixth grade.

2. Fifty-five of the ninety-two readability levels obtained by all four scales, (more than half), were at least one grade level above the publisher's suggested grade level.

3. The readability levels sampled within a single text ranged from one to five years. (This was especially noticeable where different people were responsible for writing separate parts or chapters within the same text).

4. The Dale-Chall formula ranked the texts closest to the grade levels specified by the publishing companies, while the Flesch method generally revealed a higher rating than the others.

The most important outcomes of this entire study were the findings that all of the forty-one textbooks adopted by the state had reading levels at or above the grade level for which they were intended and that 75 of the 128 readability levels obtained were above the designated grade level. If the readability levels are accurate, this indicates that only some of the textbooks used in this state (and possibly in other states as well) are appropriate to the average reader while most will require students to be above average readers. None are for the slow or low-achieving child.

What does this mean for the teacher? For one thing, he should realize that if he has an "Average" class, the chances are that at least half of the children may have some difficulty in reading the textbook. Therefore, it is not enough merely to say, "Open your books and read pages 123 through 146, then answer the questions on pages 147 and 148." **If he is going to use a textbook as his main teaching tool**, he should prepare a social studies lesson (plus other subjects such as science and language arts) as he would to teach a well-prepared reading lesson. He might introduce his lesson with something similar to the following: "Please open your books to page 123. Let's look at the title of the chapter. What does it tell us? Look at the map on pages 128 and 129. What is it a map of? This is similar to the map in the front of the room and if you prefer to use that one later on, go right ahead. You will find several new words in this chapter, and I have printed them in sentences on the board. Repeat them after me. What do each of them mean? You are to read this chapter just to get an idea of the geography of Western Europe and we will discuss it later. This will help us when we take our imaginary trip to Europe next week so we will know what the countries are like geographically and we can decide what clothes and equipment to take along. Remember that there are several other books on our library table that have stories about Western Europe. I want Mathew, Mark, Luke, John, and Mary to bring your books up to the chairs in the corner so that we can read the assignment together. Are there any questions? If you get stuck on a word, you may **ask** a neighbor for help. Now please read pages 123 to 146 for a general view of what the geography of Western Europe is like. If you forget the page numbers, they are written here on the board."

This teacher introduced the material, set a purpose for reading it, developed new vocabulary, provided materials for readers of defferent reading ability, made sure the assignment was understood, took care of possible discipline problems, and then would be concerned with all children during the entire lesson.

Remember that by law the children have to be there, but that poor teachers don't.

TABLE I
Readability Levels of the State Adopted Social Studies Textbooks Recommended For Use in Grades One, Two, and Three as Determined by The Spache and Fry Readability Formulas

	Spache	Fry Graph
THE WORLD CHILDREN LIVE IN SERIES (Silver Burdett)		
1. PETS AROUND THE WORLD, Grade 1	2 (2.4)	1
2. FUN AROUND THE WORLD, Grade 1	3 (2.9)	2
3. HOMES AROUND THE WORLD, Grade 2	3 (2.6)	2
4. SCHOOLS AROUND THE WORLD, Grade 2	4 (3.7)	3
GOING PLACES SERIES (Rand McNally)		
5. WHICH WAY?, Grade 2	3 (2.8)	2
6. HOW FAR?, Grade 2	3 (3.3)	3
7. WHERE?, Grade 2	3 (3.3)	4
HEATH SOCIAL STUDIES SERIES (D. C. Heath)		
8. A NEW HOMETOWN, primer	2 (1.6)	1
9. IN SCHOOL AND OUT, Grade 1	2 (1.7)	1
10. GREENFIELD, U.S.A., Grade 2	2 (2.2)	2
11. COMMUNITIES AT WORK, Grade 3	3 (3.1)	4
LEARNING FOR LIVING IN TODAY'S WORLD SERIES (Benefic Press)		
12. YOU ARE HERE, Grade 1	2 (1.9)	1
13. YOU AND THE NEIGHBORHOOD, Grade 2	3 (2.6)	3
14. YOU AND THE COMMUNITY, Grade 3	3 (3.4)	6
LIVING IN OUR TIMES SERIES (Allyn and Bacon)		
15. LEARNING ABOUT OUR FAMILIES, Grade 1, 1962	2 (2.2)	2
16. LEARNING ABOUT OUR NEIGHBORS, Grade 2, 1962	3 (2.6)	2
17. LEARNING ABOUT OUR COUNTRY, Grade 3, 1963	4 (3.5)	4
WAYS OF OUR LAND (Silver Burdett)		
18. WAYS OF OUR LAND, Grade 3	4 (3.7)	5

TABLE II

Readability Levels of the State-Adopted Social Studies Textbooks Recommended for Use in Grades Four, Five, and Six as Determined by Four Readability Scales

	Dale-Chall	Dale-Chall (Goltz)	Flesch	Fry
FLORIDA HISTORY--GRADES 4-6				
19. THE STORY OF FLORIDA, Grade 4 Steck Co., 1957	4 (4-6)*	5 (5.2)	7	6
20. OUR JOURNEY THROUGH FLORIDA, Grade 4 American Book Co., 1957	5 (4-8)	7 (6.6)	6	7
GEOGRAPHY--GRADES 4-6				
GEOGRAPHY FOR TODAY'S WORLD SERIES (Silver Burdett Co.)				
21. OUR BIG WORLD, Grade 4	4 (4-5)	5 (4.7)	6	5
22. THE AMERICAN CONTINENTS, Grade 5	5 (5-6)	6 (5.8)	7	5
23. OLD WORLD LANDS, Grade 6	5 (4-6)	6 (5.9)	6	6
LANDS AND PEOPLES OF THE WORLD SERIES (Ginn and Co.)				
24. AT HOME AROUND THE WORLD, SECOND EDITION Grade 4, 1965	4 (4-5)	5 (4.8)	6	4
25. THE UNITED STATES, CANADA AND LATIN AMERICA Grade 5, 1966	6 (5-7)	6 (6.2)	7	7
26. EURASIA, AFRICA AND AUSTRALIA Grade 6, 1966	9 (8-10)	9 (8.8)	8	7
PRENTICE-HALL SOCIAL STUDIES SERIES (Prentice-Hall, Inc)				
27. THE EARTH AND OUR STATES Grade 4, 1965	5 (4-6)	6 (5.5)	5	5
28. THE AMERICAS, Grade 5, 1964	5 (5-6)	6 (5.7)	7	6
29. NATIONS AROUND THE GLOBE Grade 6, 1965	6 (5-8)	7 (6.9)	7	6

186

	Dale-Chall	Dale-Chall (Goltz)	Flesch	Fry
SOCIAL STUDIES--GRADES 4-6				
MANKIND IN TIME AND PLACE				
(Silver Burdett Co.)				
30. LEARNING TO LOOK AT OUR WORLD, Grade 4	5 (4-6)	6 (5.5)	6	4
31. THE CHANGING NEW WORLD, Grade 5	6 (4-7)	6 (6.1)	7	7
32. THE CHANGING OLD WORLD, Grade 6	6 (4-8)	7 (7.0)	7	7
HISTORY--GRADES 4-6				
LAIDLAW HISTORY SERIES				
(Laidlaw Bros.)				
33. GREAT NAMES IN AMERICAN HISTORY, Grade 4	4 (4-5)	5 (4.8)	7	6
34. OUR COUNTRY, Grade 5	5 (5)	5 (5.3)	6	6
35. WORLD BACKGROUND FOR AMERICAN HISTORY Grade 6	6 (6-7)	6 (6.4)	7	6
THE ABC HISTORY SERIES				
(American Book Co.)				
36. UNDER FREEDOM'S BANNER, Grade 4, 1964	5 (5-6)	6 (5.5)	7	7
37. THE ADVENTURE OF AMERICAN, SECOND EDITION Grade 5, 1966	6 (4-7)	6 (6.1)	7	7
38. DISCOVERING OUR WORLD'S HISTORY Grade 6, 1964	6 (4-7)	7 (6.6)	7	7
(Harper and Row)				
39. THE STORY OF OUR COUNTRY, Grade 5, 1965	5 (5-6)	6 (5.9)	8	8
(Allyn and Bacon, Inc.)				
40. DISCOVERING AMERICAN HISTORY Grade 5, 1965	5 (4-6)	6 (5.5)	8	7
41. THE NEW WORLD'S FOUNDATIONS IN THE OLD Grade 6, 1964	7 (6-8)	7 (7.1)	7	7

* Range of scores on varied samples.

BIBLIOGRAPHY

1. Anderson, Jonathon, "Research in Readability for the Classroom Teacher," Journal of Reading, (May, 1965) 402-03, 05.

2. Chall, Jeanne, "This Business of Readability: A Second Look," Educational Research Bulletin, 35:93 (1956).

3. Chase, W. Linwood, and Gilbert M. Wilson. "Preference Studies in Elementary School Social Studies," Journal of Education, 140 (April, 1958), 1-28.

4. Curry, Robert L. "Subject Preferences of 1,111 Fifth Graders," Peabody Journal of Education 41 (July, 1963) 23-37.

5. Dale, Edgar and Jeanne Chall, "A Formula for Predicting Readability," Educational Research Bulletin, XXVII (January 21, 1948), 11-20.

6. Dale, Edgar and Jeanne Chall, "The Concept of Readability, Elementary English, 26:23 (January, 1949).

7. Flesch, R. F., "A New Readability Yardstick," Journal of Applied Psychology, 32, (1948), 221-233.

8. Fry, Edward B. "A Readability Formula That Saves Time," The Journal of Reading, 11, (1968), 513-516. (Formula).

9. Fry, Edward B. "The Readability Graph Validated at Primary Levels," The Reading Teacher, (March, 1969) 534-538.

10. Gates, Arthur I. "The Teaching of Reading - Objective Evidence Versus Opinion," Phi Delta Kappan, 43 (February, 1962), 197-205.

11. Goltz, Charles R., "A Table for the Quick Computation of Readability Scores Using the Dale-Chall Formula," Journal of Developmental Reading (Spring, 1964) 175-187.

12. Herman, Wayne L., Jr., "How Intermediate Children Rank the Subjects." Journal of Educational Research, 56 (April, 1963), 435-436.

13. Holmes, Ethel E. "School Subjects Preferred by Children, Appraising the Elementary-School Program," *Sixteenth Yearbook of the National Elementary Principal*. Washington, D.C.: National Educational Association, 1937, 336-344.

14. Jersild, Arthur T. and Ruth J. Tasch. *Children's Interests and What They Suggest for Education*. New York Bureau of Publications, Teachers College, Columbia University, 1949, 28, 146.

15. Rice, Joseph P. "A Comparative Study of Academic Interest Patterns Among Selected Groups of Exceptional and Normal Intermediate Children," *California Journal of Educational Research*, 14 (May, 1963), 131-137.

16. Spache, George D., *Good Reading for Poor Readers*, Garrad, (1962), 130-139.

17. Spache, George D., *Good Reading for Poor Readers*, Garrad, (1970), 211.

18. Stewart, Dorothy H. "Children's Preferences in Types of Assignment," unpublished master's thesis, Boston University, 1945.

Docility, or Giving Teacher What She Wants

Jules Henry

This essay deals with one aspect of American character, the process whereby urban middle-class children in elementary school acquire the habit of giving their teachers the answers expected of them. Though it could hardly be said that I deal exhaustively with this matter, what I do discuss, using suggestions largely from psychoanalysis and communications theory, is the signaling process whereby children and teacher come to understand each other or, better, to pseudo-understand each other, within the limited framework of certain schoolroom situations.

I think it will be readily understood that such a study has intercultural significance and interesting biosocial implications. The smooth operation of human interaction, or "transaction," if one prefers the Dewey and Bentley décor, requires that in any culture much of the give and take of life be reduced to a conventional, parsimonious system of quickly decipherable messages and appropriate responses. These messages, however, are different in different cultures, because the give and take of life is different in different cultures. At a simple level, for example, a Pilagá Indian paints his face red when he is looking for a sexual affair with a woman, whereas were an American man to paint his face red, the significance of this to other Americans would be quite different. Behaviors that have been variously called signal, cue, and sign are as characteristic of the animal world as they are of the human, and in both groups tend to be highly specific both with respect to themselves (signs, signals, cues) and with respect to the behavior they release in those for whom they are intended. Since, furthermore, each culture tends to standardize these, it would seem that any study of such behaviors, or rather behavior systems, in humans in any culture would throw light on two problems: (1) What the signal-response system is; and (2) How humans learn the system.

Since in humans the mastery of a signal-response system often involves the emotional life, and since in this paper on docility I am dealing with urban American middle-class children, it will readily be seen that a study of the manner in which they learn the signal-response system called docility carries us toward an understanding of the character of these children.

When we say a human being is docile we mean that, without the use of external force, he performs relatively few acts as a function of personal choice as compared with the number of acts he performs as a function of the will of others. In a very real sense, we mean that he behaves mostly as others wish him to. In our culture this is thought un-

Journal of Social Issues, 1955, Vol.11, pp. 33-41.

desirable, for nobody is supposed to like docile people. On the other hand, every culture must develop in its members forms of behavior that approximate docility; otherwise it could not conduct its business. Without obedience to traffic signals transportation in a large American city would be a mess. This is a dilemma of our culture: to be able to keep the streets uncluttered with automotive wrecks, and to fill our armies with fighting men who will obey orders, while at the same time we teach our citizens not to be docile.

It is to be supposed that, although the basic processes as outlined are universal, every culture has its own way of creating the mechanism of docility. It will be the purpose of the rest of this paper to examine the accomplishment of docility in some American middle-class schoolrooms. The study was carried out by several of my graduate students and me. Names of persons and places are withheld in order to give maximum protection to all concerned.

In the following examples I shall be concerned only with demonstrating that aspect of docility which has to do with the teacher's getting from the children the answers she wants; and I rely almost entirely on verbal behavior, for without cameras it is impossible to record non-verbal signals. The first example is from the second grade.

1

The children have been shown movies of birds. The first film ended with a picture of a baby bluebird.

Teacher: Did the last bird ever look like he would be blue?

The children did not seem to understand the slant of the question, and answered somewhat hesitantly: Yes.

Teacher: I think he looked more like a robin, didn't he?

Children, in chorus: Yes.

In this example one suspects that teacher's intonation on the word "ever" did not come through as a clear signal, for it did not create enough doubt in the children's minds to bring the right answer, "No." The teacher discovered that her signal had not been clear enough for these seven year-olds, so she made it crystal clear the second time, and got the "right" response. Its correctness is demonstrated by the unanimity of the children's response, and the teacher's acceptance of it. Here the desire of the teacher, that the children shall acknowledge that a bird looks like a robin, is simple, and the children, after one false try, find the correct response.

In the next example we see the relation of signal to cultural values and context:

2 a

A fourth grade art lesson. Teacher holds up a picture.

Teacher: Isn't Bobby getting a nice effect of moss and trees?

Ecstatic Ohs and Ahs from the children. . . .

2 b

The art lesson is now over.

Teacher: How many enjoyed this?

Many hands go up.

Teacher: How many learned something?

Quite a number of hands come down.

Teacher: How many will do better next time?

Many hands go up.

Here the shifts in response are interesting. The word "nice" triggers a vigorously docile response, as does the word "enjoy." "Learned something," however, for a reason that is not quite clear, fails to produce the desired unanimity. On the other hand, the shibboleth, "better next time" gets the same response as "enjoyed." We see then that the precise triggering signal is related to important cultural values; and that the value-signal must be released in proper context. One suspects that the children's resistance to saying they had learned something occurred because "learned something" appeared out of context. On the other hand, it would be incorrect to describe these children as perfectly docile.

The next example is from the same fourth grade classroom:

3

The children have just finished reading the story "The Sun, Moon, and Stars Clock."

Teacher: What was the highest point of interest—the climax?

The children tell what they think it is. Teacher is aiming to get from them what she thinks it is, but the children give everything else but. At last Bobby says: When they capture the thieves.

Teacher: How many agree with Bobby?

Hands, hands, hands.

In this example the observer was not able to record all the verbal signals, for they came too fast. However, it is clear that hunting occurred, while the children waited for the teacher to give the clear signal, which was "(I) agree with Bobby."

In all the examples given thus far, the desired answer could be indicated rather clearly by the teacher, for the required response was relatively unambiguous. Even so, there was some trouble in obtaining most of the answers. In the example that follows, however, the entire situation becomes exceedingly ambiguous because emotional factors in the children make proper interpretation of teacher's signals difficult. The central issue is that teacher and children are seen to have requirements that are complementary on one level, because teacher wants the children to accept her point of view, and they want to be accepted by her; but these requirements are not complementary on a different level, because the children's emotional organization is different from the teacher's. Hence exact complementarity is never achieved, but rather a pseudo-complementarity, which enables teacher and pupils to extricate themselves from a difficult situation. The example comes from a fifth grade schoolroom:

4

This is a lesson on "healthy thoughts" for which the children have a special book that depicts specific conflictful events among children. There are appropriate illustrations and text, and the teacher is supposed to discuss each incident with the children in order to help them understand how to handle their emotions.

One of the illustrations is of two boys, one of whom is griping because his brother has been given something he wants himself—a football, I think. The other is saying his brother couldn't help being given it—they'll both play with it.

(Observer is saying that this sibling pair is illustrated by three boys: (1) The one who has received the ball. (2) The one who is imagined to react with displeasure. (3) The one who is imagined to react benignly and philosophically, by saying: My brother couldn't help being given the football; we'll use it together.)

Teacher: Do you believe it's easier to deal with your thoughts if you own up to them, Betty?

Betty: Yes it is, if you're not cross and angry.

Teacher: Have you any experience like this in the book, Alice?

Alice tells how her brother was given a watch and she envied him and wanted one too, but her mother said she wasn't to have one until she was fifteen, but now she has one anyway.

Teacher: How could you have helped—could you have changed your thinking? How could you have handled it? What could you do with mean feelings?

Alice seems stymied; she hems and haws.

Teacher: What did Susie (a character in the book) do?

Alice: She talked to her mother.

Teacher: If you talk to someone you often feel that 'It was foolish of me to feel that way. . . .

Tommy: He says he had an experience like that. His cousin was given a bike, and he envied it. But he wasn't ugly about it. He asked if he might ride it, and his cousin let him, and then I got one myself; and I wasn't mean or ugly or jealous.

Here the process of signal development is intricate, and children and teacher do not quite manage to arrive at a mutually intelligible complex of signals and behavior. The stage is set by the presentation of a common, but culturally unacceptable situation: A child is pictured as envious of the good luck of his sibling. Since American culture cannot accept two of its commonest traits, sibling rivalry and envy, the children are asked by teacher to acknowledge that they are "bad," and to accept specific ways of dealing with these emotions. The children are thus asked to fly in the face of their own feelings, and, since this is impossible, the little pigeons never quite get home. This is because teacher and pupil wants are not complementary.

It will have been observed that at first Alice does well, for by docilely admitting that it is good to own up to evil, she correctly interprets the teacher's wish to hear her say that the ancient ritual of confession is still good for the soul; and she continues docile behavior by giving a story of her own envy. However, eventually she muffs the signal, for she says she was gratified anyway; she did get a watch. And the reason Alice muffs the signal is that her own impulses dominate over the signals coming in from the teacher. Teacher, however, does not reject Alice's *story* but tries, rather, to get Alice to say she could have "handled" her thoughts by "owning up" to them and talking them over with someone. Alice, however, stops dead because she *cannot* understand the teacher. Meanwhile Tommy has picked up the signal, only to be misled by it, just as Alice was. By this time, however, the matter has become more complex: Tommy thinks that because teacher did not reject Alice's story it is "correct." Teacher's apparent acceptance of Alice's story then becomes Tommy's signal; therefore he duplicates Alice's story almost exactly, except that a bike is substituted for a watch. Like Alice he is not "mean" or "ugly" or "jealous," not because he "dealt with" his thoughts in the culturally approved-but-impossible manner, but because he too got what he wanted. So far, the only part of the message that is getting through to the children from the teacher is that it is uncomfortable—not wrong—to be jealous, etcetera. Thus the emotions of the children filter out an important part of the message from the teacher.

We may summarize the hypotheses up to this point as follows: (1) By virtue of their visible goal-correcting behavior the pupils are trying hard to be docile with respect to the teacher. (2) They hunt for signals and try to direct their behavior accordingly. (3) The signals occur in a matrix of cultural value and immediate circumstance. (4) This fact at times makes interpretation and conversion into action difficult. (5) A basis in mutual understanding is sought, but not quite realized at times. (6) The children's internal signals sometimes conflict with external ones and thus "jam the receiver." (7) Both children and teacher want something. At present we may say that the children want acceptance by the teacher, and teacher wants acceptance by the children. (8) However it is clear, because of the mix-up that may occur in interpreting signals, as in the lesson on healthy thoughts, that the desires of teacher and pupil are sometimes not quite complementary. (9) Teacher must avoid too many frustrating (painful) failures like that of Alice, otherwise lessons will break down.

As we proceed with this lesson, we shall see how teacher and pupils strive to "get on the same wave length," a condition never quite reached because of the different levels of organization of teacher and pupil; and the unawareness of this fact on the part of the teacher.

> Two boys, the "dialogue team," now come to the front of the class and dramatize the football incident.
>
> Teacher, to the class: Which boy do you think handled the problem in a better way?
>
> Rupert: Billy did, because he didn't get angry. . . . It was better to play together than to do nothing with the football.
>
> Teacher: That's a good answer, Rupert. Has anything similar happened to you, Joan?
>
> Joan can think of nothing.
>
> (Observer notes: I do not approve of this business in action, though I have not yet thought it through. But I was intermittently uncomfortable, disapproving and rebellious at the time.)
>
> Sylvester: I had an experience. My brother got a hat with his initials on it because he belongs to a fraternity, and I wanted one like it and couldn't have one; and his was too big for me to wear, and it ended up that I asked him if he could get me some letters with my initials, and he did.
>
> Betty: My girl-friend got a bike that was 26-inch, and mine was only 24; and I asked my sister what I should do. Then my girl-friend came over and was real nice about it, and let me ride it.
>
> Teacher approves of this, and says: Didn't it end up that they both had fun without unhappiness? (Observer notes: Constant questioning of class, with expectation of affirmative answers: that wasn't this the right way, the best way, etc., to do it?)

Here we note that the teacher herself has gone astray, for on the one hand her aim is to get instances from the children in which they themselves have been yielding and capable of resolving their own jealousy, etc., while on the other hand, in the instance given by Betty, it was not Betty who yielded, but her friend. The child immediately following Betty imitated her since Betty had been praised by the teacher:

> Matilde: My girl-friend got a 26-inch bike and mine was only 24; but she only let me ride it once a month. But for my birthday my mother's getting me a new one, probably (proudly) a "28." (Many children rush in with the information that "28" doesn't exist). Matilde replies that she'll probably have to raise the seat then, for she's too big for a "26."

This instance suggests more clearly, perhaps, than the others, another possible factor in making the stories of the children end always with their getting what they want: the children may be afraid to lose face with their peers by acknowledging they did not get something they wanted.

As we go on with this lesson, we shall see how the children's need for substitute gratification and their inability to accept frustration prevent them from picking up the teacher's message. As we continue, we shall see how, in spite of the teacher's driving insistence on her point, the children continue to inject their conflicts into the lesson, while at the same time they gropingly try to find a way to gratify the teacher. *They cannot give the right answers because of their conflicts; teacher cannot handle their conflicts because she cannot perceive them.* The lesson goes on:

Teacher: I notice that some of you are only happy when you get your own way. (Observer noticed too, horrified.) You're not thinking this through, and I want you to. Think of an experience when you didn't get what you want. Think it through. (Observer wonders: Are the children volunteering because of expectations; making desperate efforts to meet the expectation, even though they do not quite understand it?)

Charlie: His ma was going to the movies and he wanted to go with her; and she wouldn't let him; and she went off to the movies; and he was mad; but then he went outside and there were some kids playing baseball, so he played baseball.

Teacher: But suppose you hadn't gotten to play baseball? You would have felt hurt because you didn't get what you wanted. We can't help feeling hurt when we are disappointed. What could you have done? How could you have handled it? (Observer notes: Teacher is not getting what she wants, but I am not sure the kids can understand. Is this a function of immaturity, or of spoiling by parents? Seems to me the continued effort to extract an idea they have not encompassed may be resulting in reinforcement of the one they *have* got—that you eventually get the watch, or the bicycle, or whatever.)

Charlie: So I can't go to the movies; so I can't play baseball; so I'll do something around the house.

Teacher: Now you're beginning to think! It takes courage to take disappointments. (Turning to the class) What did we learn? The helpful way. . . .

Class: is the healthy way!

Thus the lesson reaches this point on a note of triumphant docility, but of pseudo-complementarity. If the teacher had been able to perceive the underlying factors that made it impossible for these children to accept delayed gratification or total momentary frustration, and had handled *that* problem, instead of doggedly sticking to a text that required a stereotyped answer, she would have come closer to the children and would not have had to back out of the situation by extracting a parrot-like chorusing. The teacher had to get a "right" answer, and the children ended up giving her one, since that is what they are in school for. Thus on one level teacher and pupils were complementary, but on another they were widely divergent. This is the characteristic condition of the American middle-class schoolroom.

If we review all the verbal messages sent by the teacher, we will see how hard she has worked to get the answer she wants; how she has corrected and "improved" her signaling in response to the eager feed-back from the children:

1. Do you believe it's easier to deal with your thoughts if you own up to them, Betty?
2. Have you any experience like this in the book, Alice?
3. What could you do with mean feelings?
4. What did Susie (in the book) do?
5. (Rupert says that Billy, the character in the book, handled the problem in the better way because he did not get angry.) That's a good answer, Rupert.
6. (Betty tells how nice her girl-friend was, letting her ride her bike.) Teacher approves of this and says: Didn't it end up that they both had fun without unhappiness?
7. I notice that some of you are happy only when you get your own way.
8. What could you have done (when you did not get your own way)?
9. Now you're beginning to think. It takes courage to take disappointments. What did we learn? The helpful way. . . . and the class responds, is the healthy way.

Discussion and Conclusions

This paper has been an effort to describe the mental docility of middle-class American children *in their schoolrooms*. It says nothing about the home or the play group. The analysis shows how children are taught to find the answer the teacher wants, and to give it to her. That they sometimes fail is beside the point, because their trying so hard is itself evidence of docility; and an understanding of the reasons for failure helps us to see why communication breaks down and pseudo-understanding takes its place. When communication breaks down it is often because complementarity between sender (teacher) and receivers (pupils) is not exact; and it is not exact because teacher and pupils are at different levels of emotional organization.

We may now ask: Why are these children, whose phantasies our unpublished research has found to contain so many hostile and anxious elements, so docile in the classroom? Why do they struggle so hard to gratify the teacher and try in so many ways, as our protocols show, to bring themselves to the teacher's attention?

We might, of course, start with the idea of the teacher as a parent-figure, and the children as siblings competing for teacher's favor. We could refer to the unresolved dependency needs of children of this age, which make them seek support in the teacher, who then manipulates this seeking and the children's sibling rivalry in order, as our unpublished research suggests, to pit the children against each other. Other important factors, however, that appear in middle-class schoolrooms, ought to be taken into consideration. For example, our research shows the children's tendency to destructively criticize each other, and the teacher's repeated reinforcement of this tendency. We have taken note, in our research, of the anxiety in the children as illustrated in the stories they tell and observed that these very stories are subjected to carping criticism by other children, the consequence of which would be anything but an alleviation of that anxiety.[1] Hence the schoolroom is a place in which the child's underlying anxiety may be heightened. In an effort to alleviate this he seeks approval of the teacher, by giving right answers, and by doing what teacher wants him to do under most circumstances. Finally, we cannot omit the teacher's need to be gratified by the attention-hungry behavior of the children.

A word is necessary about these classrooms as middle class. The novel *Blackboard Jungle*, by Evan Hunt, describes schoolroom behavior of lower-class children. There we see them solidly against the teacher, as representative of the middle class. But in the classes we have observed we see the children against each other, with the teacher abetting the process. Thus, as the teacher in middle-class schools directs the hostility of the children toward one another (particularly in the form of criticism), and away from herself, she reinforces the competitive dynamics within the middle class itself. The teacher in the lower-class schools, on the other hand, appears to become the organizing stimulus for behavior that integrates the lower class, as the children unite in expressing their hostility to the teacher.

In conclusion, it should be pointed out that the mental docility (or near docility) achieved in these middle-class schoolrooms is a peculiar middle-class kind of docility. It is not based on authoritarian control backed by fear of corporal punishment, but rather on fear of loss of love. More precisely, it rests on the need to bask in the sun of the teacher's acceptance. It is not fear of scolding or of physical pain that makes these children docile, but rather fear of finding oneself outside the warmth of the inner circle of teacher's sheltering acceptance. This kind of docility can be more lethal than the other, for it does not breed rebellion and independence, as struggle against authoritarian controls may, but rather a kind of cloying paralysis; a sweet imprisonment without pain. Looking at the matter from another point of view, we might say that were these children not fearful of loss of love they would be indifferent to the teacher's messages. In a sense what the teacher's signals are really saying is: "This is the way to be loved by me; and this is the way I want you to love me."

---

[1] This and other references to research on these problems are documented in a forthcoming paper: "The Organization of Attitudes in the American Classroom."

THE TEACHING UNIT
What makes it tick?
By WALTER E. McPHIE

ANYONE WHO HAS COMPLETED a teacher preparation program at some university or teachers college has heard the word *unit*—and heard it often. It may be a teaching technique or method to some, a part of curriculum structure to others, or a combination of both to still others, but one thing is clear: the word itself is no stranger in the teaching profession.

Most of the literature on units in teaching is supportive. It is a rare methods text for either secondary or elementary school teachers that does not promote, either openly or by implication, teaching with units. It is championed as the *modern* way of teaching, the most effective method of curriculum arrangement.

Occasionally in the professional literature a questioning voice is heard which suggests that another look at the basic assumptions about unit teaching is needed. Criticism, however, is more often heard from practitioners in the field, new and experienced teachers who honestly and sincerely prefer to teach on a day-to-day basis.

EDITOR'S NOTE

The teaching unit—now here is an item that has been around! Some teachers regard this technique as sheer busy work, while others extol the teaching unit as the ultimate in classroom methodology. The gap in between is quite extensive and the author is intent upon closing this breach. He is an Associate Professor in the College of Education at Haile Selassie I University, Addis Ababa, Ethiopia, under a U.S. A.I.D. contract.

To some of the critics, developing units of study is "busy work," a nonsensical submission to the whimsical desires of people in ivory towers who are too far removed from reality. To others, unit teaching is still a hazy concept; these people are not really sure what a teaching unit is. In their eyes the literature seems to be contradictory, professors of education do not appear to be in full accord on the matter, and discussions with colleagues shed little additional light. For this group of teachers, unit teaching is not clearly enough defined to be seriously considered as an alternative to already established daily routine.

What is a "unit"? Perhaps the easiest way to define a unit of teaching is to draw back and look at the word in other contexts. For example, a busy mother, while shopping in a local department store, sees a skirt-blouse combination on sale which would just fit her daughter. She really likes the skirt but does not care for the blouse.

"How much would it cost if I just bought the skirt?" she inquires.

"I'm sorry," replies the clerk, "but we must sell this set as a *unit*."

Some people who become a little panic-stricken at the thought of being forced into using teaching units would not give a second thought to the explanation given by the clerk. They would immediately understand that for some reason the composite parts of the skirt-blouse set belong together as a whole entity and that to use them otherwise would be disadvantageous.

Other examples of the word *unit* could be given which would demonstrate the general use of the term (automobile mechanics

Clearing House, October, 1963, Vol.38, pp. 70-73.

speak of the various units in the complex make-up of their machines; refrigerator and radio repairmen often refer to units in their work; and so on). Certain common elements emerge from these examples, which should help to clarify the meaning of the term *unit* as it applies to teaching. First, there is a single mass or entity characteristic which is often composed of minor parts. Second, there appears to be some logical reason for the kind and/or size of the mass or entity and this reason most often is based on function or purpose. Therefore, a unit of teaching would be a single mass or quantity of subject matter (concepts, skills, symbols, and so forth) which for some logical reason appears to belong together or to form some reasonable single entity. Units of teaching involving *The American Revolutionary Period*, *Punctuation*, or *The Back-Stroke in Swimming* serve as good examples. In each case smaller bits and pieces of information are grouped together into a larger, meaningful mass of subject matter which can be identified easily as an entity and which can be referred to logically as a *unit*. Such a process is no more complex or confusing than seeing a skirt and blouse kept together for a given reason.

Why teach with units? Having established that the word *unit* is neither awesome nor difficult to understand in teaching or any other context, there still remains the task of demonstrating the advisability of using such an approach. Once again, it may prove helpful if activities in life other than teaching are examined first.

For example, consider the businessman who must drive from Salt Lake City to attend a conference in San Francisco. If asked where he is going he will respond unhesitatingly, "San Francisco." This response indicates an awareness of the *ultimate* goal—just as a teacher if asked what he is teaching might respond, "United States history," "home economics," or "algebra." If it were possible, however, for the questioner to look secretly inside the businessman's mind and just as secretly accompany him on his trip, he would discover that he does not *actually* drive from Salt Lake City to San Francisco but that he drives from Salt Lake City to *Grantsville*, from Grantsville to Wendover, from Wendover to Wells, from Wells to Elko, from Elko to Carlin, and so on *until he reaches his ultimate goal*, San Francisco. The 800-mile trip is too distant, too remote, and too time-consuming to represent a realistic, workable goal. Therefore, the traveler breaks the trip into smaller, identifiable goals which are more satisfying because progress is more easily seen and because achievement is in the immediate foreseeable future. It is significant to note, however, that he does not carry the breakdown of the ultimate goal to the extreme. For example, he does not attempt to drive from tar-strip to tar-strip on the highway, from telephone pole to telephone pole, or from mile to mile as indicated on his speedometer. Such short, unchallenging goals would be too small, too insignificant, and too unrelated to the ultimate goal for the traveler to find them useful.

Once home from his trip, the businessman notes that he has a backlog of unfinished tasks. As he starts to take care of the unattended chores, he once again demonstrates the natural tendency to approach major tasks in terms of *units*.

While mowing his lawn he finds himself cutting a swath across the middle of a particularly large section, dividing it into two or three smaller areas rather than working his way tediously toward the center of the apparently never-ending larger section. He does not, however, pluck the grass blade by blade, nor does he cut his lawn in square foot or square yard sections.

While other examples are plentiful, the foregoing clearly illustrate several obvious facts: (1) when man is faced with a large task, he naturally—almost automatically—divides the task into smaller segments which are more easily handled and are psychologically more motivating; (2) the smaller segments are not just selected at random, but represent logical, meaningful portions of the larger goal; (3) if the smaller segments of the large task become too small, they lose appeal, challenge, and identity with the larger task.

Teaching with the unit approach offers no exceptions to the generalizations given above. In teaching, the larger goal is represented by the basic knowledge which the students should acquire from a given course. Since this task of teaching is so large, it is unmanageable and too distant to be challenging. Therefore, the teacher divides the basic understandings of the course into smaller segments. These smaller segments (or units) are chosen on the basis of their logical cohesiveness and their ability to stand alone as subject matter entities. Teaching on a day-to-day basis rather than from within the framework of a unit is the equivalent of breaking the large goal into areas that are too small to be challenging and that are not easily related to the larger task.

How is a unit planned? Once a person has convinced himself that the unit approach to teaching is not mysterious and that it is the natural way to attack any large task, he is ready to start with actual unit planning. This will involve four basic steps: (1) selection of objectives, (2) determination of teaching procedures, (3) identification of teaching materials, and (4) justification of the three previous steps.

The teacher's first step, within the confines of the unit chosen, is to *select* the basic understandings (concepts), skills, or new vocabulary which need to be developed. This suggests that the teacher will analyze the subject matter contained within the unit very carefully and will decide on certain things to be emphasized, learned, and remembered. Some authorities disagree with such a suggestion; they maintain that such an authoritarian approach kills the incentive and initiative of the students. Such opposition is based on a misunderstanding of the proposal. The suggestion that the teacher should select the fundamental objectives to be achieved in advance *does not* imply a lack of flexibility. It simply suggests that it is necessary for the teacher to be prepared to give focus and direction in his teaching. It allows for deviation from the advance plan, *but offers something from which to deviate.*

The second consideration for the teacher is the procedures necessary to achieve the objectives. Most literature on unit planning speaks of multitudinous lists of activities which could conceivably fit within the framework of a given unit, but it seems advisable to seek out methods, techniques, and procedures which apply *specifically* to the individual objectives. Whether the teacher includes many or just a few procedures for teaching each objective depends upon whether the teacher wants the unit to be a resource unit or a unit plan from which to teach directly. In either case, however, there should be a specific relationship between the stated objective and the procedures proposed. Then nothing is left to chance; each objective has its corresponding procedures which have been planned to insure that the desired learning takes place. Again, this does not suggest rigidity. Rather, it insists on basic preparation with the clear understanding that the teacher has the right and obligation to deviate and make adjustments whenever the current situation demands.

Identifying materials which will aid in the achievement of the objectives is in reality part of the responsibility in determining procedures. It is given separate space here since many teachers feel that it is important to list the materials in a special place on the unit plan where the list can be quickly checked prior to commencing a lesson. This helps to prevent an often-heard statement: "I had meant to bring such-and-such today to demonstrate this point, but I seem to have forgotten." The advisability of using materials such as films, slides, realia, charts, graphs, pictures, the chalkboard, and other audio-visual aids is generally conceded by most teachers. The most important thing to be remembered is that these materials are only *means*—not ends.

The fourth task in unit planning is one which rightfully encompasses the other three. What is the justification for the objectives selected? For the procedures chosen? For the materials to be used? The teacher should ask: "Am I attempting to teach this basic concept because I have thought it over carefully and believe it is important for the students to understand *in the light of some purpose*—or am I attempting to teach something simply because it is today and I taught something yesterday which seemed to precede this? Am I going to show this film because it will really help to clarify a justifiable concept or skill —or is it because film-showing takes up most of the period and requires relatively little of me?" Unit planning which is scrutinized with such introspection cannot help but yield superior results.

In summary, the unit approach to teaching is a simple, natural one. It has been demonstrated that man uses this approach in nearly every large task. Unit planning involves the segmenting of large teaching goals into smaller, cohesive, and meaningful entities of subject matter. It also involves the selection of basic objectives within the smaller segments (units) which are important for the students to learn and retain. Once the latter has been done, it is then necessary for the teacher to determine the proper procedures to be employed in achieving the objectives, to identify appropriate materials to be used in the learning process, and to justify the objectives, procedures, and materials. With all of this clearly in mind, and with a determination to teach well, teachers should be able to look forward to the security and satisfaction which comes from knowing what needs to be done and how to do it.

SCHEDULING PROBLEMS:
How Many? How Long?

By SIDNEY L. BESVINICK

ONE OF THE MOST CONSTANT DESIRES of school personnel is to make allowance for individual differences. The variety of course offerings, materials, and multiple tracks attests to the earnestness of this desire. Yet, curiously, most schools have clung to two outmoded devices which place a gigantic roadblock in the way of tailoring programs to the needs of individuals. These two restricting concepts are the 30-student class and the one-hour period. If individualizing the program is truly a goal of modern schools, flexibility must be one of the governing principles, not some rigid method of organizing students and the school day.

Yet, if school personnel are freed from the number and time restraints, they must receive guidance and assistance in programming or they will quickly become lost. They will need to know how many they should teach at one time and for how long. To each the answer is, "It depends and should vary."

How Many?

While it may seem that saying "It depends" is an evasive answer, it is not. The clue to the number of students a teacher should have in a given learning situation is the intent and purpose of the meeting. Different purposes require different methods, arrangements, and numbers. The following descriptions indicate five class sizes which may be justified. The numbers which are shown in each case represent the author's best judgment based upon experience and research and indicate maximum class size which is desirable.

(1) *Unlimited size.* If the purpose of the meeting is the one-way transmission of knowledge and opinions by the teacher, a guest speaker, or a film, then the largest group that can be gathered to hear or see at one time is desirable. Efficiency should be the password. Neither teacher time nor student time should be wasted. One carefully prepared presentation should suffice to transmit the factual material. Many courses contain basic concepts which all students must grasp and which are necessary as background for further discussion. This size group should be used only for one-way transmission of such concepts, and no attempt should ever be made to conduct discussion or question-answer sessions at this time.

(2) *Moderate size.* Practice sessions in mathematics, grammar, physical education, and typing are examples of activities which deal with skill development. In these sessions teachers engage in little or no verbal contact with the class as a whole. After brief explanations or instructions, the teacher's time is spent in supervision of student seat-work or motor skill mastery. There is a dearth of research with respect to the

---

EDITOR'S NOTE

Admittedly, not all of the answers are furnished by the author, an associate professor of the University of Miami in Coral Gables, Florida. But he does make a conscientious effort to clarify two major issues in this scheduling business: How large should the classes be, and how long should they meet? If some light is shed on these items, fine! If not, we are sure you will let us know.

number of students a teacher can work with in this arrangement, but, with practice, teachers have been able to assist without difficulty 40 to 50 students in a skills laboratory setting.

(3) *Activity size.* In science laboratories, shops, art classes, language laboratories, and other activity programs, the number who can be supervised so that learning may progress effectively is still smaller, approximately 25. This does not mean the teacher would be unable to maintain order in larger groups, but his efforts would be spread so thin that explanations and supervision would be unavailable when most needed.

(4) *Small group size.* Group dynamics research has shown that the degree of participation and the number of cross-contacts in a discussion setting drops rapidly if the group includes more than ten to 12 people. Since the purpose of this setting is to permit interaction, the size of some classes should be kept within that limit. In a small group environment, with the guidance of the teacher, ideas from larger group sessions can be clarified and extended. Students may also challenge each other, explore new ideas, present findings, and familiarize themselves with group processes.

Some schools which have used this class size as a regular practice have found that students may pursue an idea in depth as a team and report to a discussion group of ten more readily than they will undertake such a task in a conventional class of 30. Students say the small class makes cooperative work almost mandatory, and the informality which is possible develops a sense of responsibility on the part of one learner towards the others in the class.

(5) *Independent study.* This concept of student self-responsibility for learning is only beginning to be explored, but no approach offers greater promise for individualizing learning. Most teachers and administrators recoil from the notion because they picture boys and girls "running around loose" or students simply working in a study hall. Neither concept is accurate.

Students are scheduled for a certain number of periods per week to central stations where they work on whatever material they wish, so long as it is in keeping with that station's subject emphasis. As a student shows, by achieving a certain level of proficiency, that he is capable in that area, he is released from reporting to the teacher and may concentrate his attention wherever he wishes. He may work in a science laboratory, do research in the resource center, confer with a teacher, or study. In short, in these sessions he has control of his education. This procedure permits teachers to gradually increase the degree of freedom of action a student may have, within the limits of the learner's ability to use the latitude which is given to him.

One other important point which should be stressed about class size is that no one size may fit all activities within a single subject. English classes, for example, may meet in large sections for introductory ideas and factual material about the novel and the specific information on the novel which is to be used as a center of emphasis. Students may meet in moderate size groups for practicing grammar skills and writing. Small groups may analyze the novel and discuss the author, other works, characters, and so on. Independently, the learner may develop a project on the novel, read more broadly in related areas, or, if he has a proficiency in English, work in any other subject area he wishes. Flexibility and individualization permeate the entire plan.

How Long?

For years the majority of public schools have acted as though all subjects could be effectively taught in equal blocks of time with equal frequency. Thus, a world history lecture course, a science laboratory, a physical education class, and a discussion group would all meet for one hour a day, five days a week. Obviously for some classes this would be fine, but for others it would be too short or too long.

The alternative is almost too simple—use a different unit of time in place of the hour or 50-minute period. Different schools are experimenting with a variety of time blocks (or modules, as they are called). Some use 20-minute modules; others, 30; still others, unusual but effective modules which fit their own situation.

The flexibility of modular scheduling can be easily demonstrated with 30-minute modules. Assume a school has a 6½-hour day, including a thirty-minute lunch period. There would then be 12 instructional modules and one for lunch. These may be subdivided in any number of ways. For instance, lecture periods could be two modules in length (large group); science laboratories, three or four modules once or twice a week; language laboratory, two modules; discussion groups, one module two or three times per week; independent study, one, two, or three modules, either in a row or spaced throughout the week.

Teacher schedules may be tailored to fit teacher specialties. Those who do large group instruction best may spend their time preparing and doing that, while those who enjoy the interplay of smaller groups may work with them. Loads are adjustable and conference time for independent study guidance may also be provided.

This article is too brief to prove the point, but schedules can be worked out which permit this flexibility. The master schedule must balance students, teachers, and learning stations for every module. The following information should also be known in advance:

(a) What objectives are to be sought?
(b) What subjects are to be offered?
(c) How many students are to take each subject?
(d) What is the time allotment for each subject?
(e) What size groups are to be used in each subject?
(f) Is the program to be graded or nongraded?

These ideas are suitable and useful in a school which is completely departmentalized, in one which uses a core program, or in any other. The challenge of school day and program organization demands innovation so that students in our growing schools can receive the personalized attention each deserves. Forward-looking administrators and teachers are meeting that challenge in ingenious ways.

ROLE-PLAYING AND SOCIAL STUDIES

by
Roger E. Johnson
University of South Florida

Social Studies has long been considered by many a subject where students just read from a textbook memorize such facts as the names of explorers, countries, states, capitals, rivers, mountains, products, and the fact that some people are different from "Us." But it is more than that!

Role-playing is often considered a time when a teacher will, because of a rainstorm, blizzard, or hurricane, have the students pretend to be someone or act out a story. This is done because children like to do such things and it's a good way to keep students entertained when the lesson plans for the day cannot be followed because of a change in schedule or weather.

Role-playing, creative dramatics, acting and many other terms are often used interchangeably by teachers and students. However, there are differences among these terms. Compared with the others, role-playing is more formalized, because it is concerned with specific settings, characters, and situations, whereas the others are less restrictive as to what the children do.

Role-playing can be loosely defined as a spontaneous dramatization by children of a situation involving human relationships which is meaningful to them. The role-playing then leads to group discussion and evaluation. The term, "Spontaneous" does not mean that all of a sudden a teacher will say, "Let's role play," and a group of young thespians will do their version of Macbeth. On the contrary, several specific steps are involved.

1. __Establishing the problem__. This is accomplished by the teacher reading from a book, telling a story, or making up a situation. This is so everyone knows the problem, the setting, and the characters.

2. __Selection of the players__. First of all, the teacher should review the different roles and describe the people.

Original Manuscript.

However, the characters should not be discussed too much for what the children do is to be spontaneous and an expression of their feelings according to the role they are playing. Volunteers should be called for and students should be selected according to their personalities and needs and the objectives of the lesson. Teachers should also occasionally play a role.

3. <u>Set the scene and brief the observers</u>. The scene should be established briefly and if any props are necessary classroom articles should be used although students can pretend to be trees, buildings, etc. The actors should be allowed a minute or so to get themselves ready while the teacher prepares the observers who are very important, for they evaluate the scene, and take the place of players in the re-enactment of the scene.

4. <u>Enactment</u>. The same procedure should be followed in all scenes. Begin with a word such as "Action," or "Act," and as soon as the point has been made, stop it with a word such as "Cut." If a scene is missing the point, it should be stopped and the observers should evaluate what is wrong. One word of caution is that criticism is never made of a student, but rather the person he is assuming to be. Such statements as, "I think William Tell would have been a little more sure of himself as he got ready to shoot the arrow," is fine, but students should not be allowed to make such comments as, "Boy, Roger sure is lousy!" This non criticism of the students will help them feel free to do what they want and not be frightened of doing something wrong. However, they should be reminded of the role they are playing.

5. <u>Evaluating the scene</u>. This step should follow immediately. Teachers must accept all ideas without favoring any of them. The teacher has a difficult role because they should not moralize, indicate any approval or disapproval, and not reveal conclusions. Instead they must ask, probe, and inquire until arriving at the objective. This does not mean teachers should not praise or reinforce students' efforts, however, they must not criticize the child. If things get out of hand, review the story, setting, and characters in order to get the students back to thinking of the situation and problem.

6. <u>Re-enact the scene</u>. New players should be selected and the scene should be re-enacted and re-evaluated. The scene should be re-enacted until the students have discovered the generalization, all students have had on opportunity to release their enthusiasm, all differences of opinion have been resolved, and/or the objectives have been achieved.

What is the relationship between Social Studies and role-playing? Role-playing provides opportunities for children to develop understanding. Through their role identity, they are not content in just seeing and hearing of various styles of life around the world; instead they must feel the past, and it is this ability to feel that makes it possible for children to understand. Through empathy they come to realize all aspects of a situation. This is a creative approach to the understanding of which breaks down emotional barriers and develops emotional barriers and develops emotional understanding.

Most children have an inherent desire to indulge in dramatic play. It provides an avenue whereby teachers can develop certain attitudes, values, and appreciations. It provides opportunities where students can experience creative thinking, working singly or in groups, ways of expressing ideas, opportunity to see and experience both sides of a problem, a place to release their emotions; and develop a sensitivity for people. It provides a situation where a teacher can observe students in the above mentioned situations as well as an opportunity to evaluate their comprehension of ideas, concepts, and generalizations. Role-playing is a conscientious attempt on the part of a teacher to use the natural tendencies of empathy for constructing natural group relations.

Let's take a look at how role-playing can be used in the Social Studies by investigating this relationship in topics which are geographically oriented even though this is only one aspect of the Social Studies curriculum.

There are three concerns of geographic study the teacher must stress. The first is a description which allows what occurs in the environment to be described with accuracy, whether these are within the immediate view or far over the horizon. Secondly, geography is concerned with the location of things, their direction, and their relation to other things. Last, is the concern of attaching significance or meaning to the things which may be described, located, and related to each other.

A teacher must remember that Geography, or any other discipline in the Social Studies, will be incomplete without relating it to the other disciplines and other subjects. From earliest times, man has kept a record of the area in which he lives. This must be stressed so students realize the significant importance of Geography in relation to the social and natural sciences. In the study of history, geography can be shown as it has helped or hindered man and how man has changed it for his use.

Many teachers evaluate geography by giving students a test on such things as the following: What city is the capital of Germany? On which continent is the country of Columbia located? Which ocean is the largest? Which country in Europe has the largest population of pigs? These are specific facts. Sometimes, the learning of facts are necessary as a basis for futher learning, but many times the learning stops with just this memorization of facts. Geography is much more than thememorization of facts, for students must know how these have affected man and a multiple-guess test is not the best method for finding out if children truly understand their significance. It is difficult to give such a test in the elementary school, especially in the primary grades, whereas role-playing can be used anywhere from Kindergarten to graduate school. Research has found out that children learn more and remember it longer when role-playing is involved than when inquiry is limited to the facts.

A few suggested role-playing activities that can take place in a classroom and which provide for evaluating what children know about geography, reinforcing proper comprehension, correction of any misunderstandings, and the teaching of geography are listed below. The only things needed are children and an idea.

>Obtain an aerial map of the community and demonstrate the understanding of direction and location of student's homes by guiding people around the community.

>A group of many kinds of people taking the same walk or riding a touring bus to see what they consider important.

Show the different ways community helpers help us at different times of the year as well as what community helpers in other countries do depending upon the location, climate, culture and season.

The role that climate and season have upon what we eat, what we wear, and where we live. You may also have the students react to what would happen and have to be done if a jungle hut was built in Alaska.

How people use the land and geographical features when they are doing such things as camping, traveling by automobile or building a house or city.

Describe how geography affects people who travel according to the method used and when they did so.

What geography had to do with Columbus' voyage, Daniel Boone's exploring the Wilderness Road, families moving West in a Conestoga Wagon and what these people did when they met a geographic obstacle.

Establish a site, possibly on a large island, describe the geographical features and have students determine where they would live, why they would do so, what they would use from the land, and how their living habits would be changed during the seasons depending upon their island location.

TAKE A REALISTIC LOOK AT PEOPLE AND CULTURES

by
Roger E. Johnson
University of South Florida

When students give reports about people they usually begin with a statement such as, "He was born on..." and end their report with "He died on...." These reports also usually include a few interesting facts which occurred between the person's birth and death, but rarely do they report about any of the person's ideas, concepts, or values with which the students can relate. These "Great Men and Women" are considered superhuman and above an honest and unbiased investigation.

Reports about countries often concentrate on the names of countries, their capitals, rivers, exports, imports, language, and religion. Very little is usually included which actually deals with the people, their likes or dislikes, what influences their way of living, and how their lives are similar to people in our country.

In today's Social Studies, educators try to help students realize that they, as human beings, are an important part of our society and that they live in a world which they have to understand and will eventually help to control. Therefore it is important for students to not only study about people and cultures which were influential in shaping the world, but students must also realize that these people being studied were humans who used their intelligence, senses, tools, and the available environment to make decisions.

It is therefore necessary that teachers have students investigate specific things, events, and/or periods in the lives of people in order to avoid the general birth to death type of report. Below are two lists of questions which teachers can use to help students better understand the people and cultures under investigation.

QUESTIONS ABOUT PEOPLE

1. Are there any things in your own life which are similar to his?
2. Are there things in the way he lived which would be good for people to follow today?

Original Manuscript.

3. For what things did you admire him most?
4. For what things do you feel you can not respect him?
5. Have you known any other adults who have these good or bad qualities?
6. What exactly did he achieve?
7. What influence does this achievement have on our world today?
8. Were his goals or aims at all like any you have dreamed up yourself?
9. What difficulties did he have to undergo to achieve his goals?
10. In what ways was he strong?
11. How did this help him?
12. In what ways was he weak?
13. How did this hurt him?
14. How would he have made out in our world of today?
15. Where did his life seem less satisfying?
16. Does he have large areas in his life which were not fulfilled?
17. What did his friends feel about him?
18. How important were their feelings to him?
19. In what ways were his friends' feelings influential upon him?
20. Did his enemies respect any of his qualities?
21. Where did he display his greatest courage?
22. Where did he display his greatest wisdom?
23. Where did he make his greatest contribution?
24. Who benefitted from this contribution?

QUESTIONS ABOUT OTHER CULTURES

1. What do the people want in the country you have chosen?
2. What things help or stand in their way of achieving their goal?
3. How do these people go about getting what they want?
4. What hopes do children have of bettering their lives?
5. What do the people know about their own country?
6. What do the people know about our country?
7. What do they think and know about politics or their government?
8. What do they think and know about politics and government in our country?

9. What is a day in their life like?
10. Where do they sleep and how many in a bed?
11. What do they fear?
12. When and who do they marry?
13. What do they do for recreation?
14. What part does religion play in their lives?
15. What is their idea of a good life and how does it compare with ours?
16. What influence has art and music had on these people?
17. Would your answers to any or all of these questions be the same for all classes of people?

SOCIAL ISSUES

ONE HUNDRED PER CENT AMERICAN

By Ralph Linton

There can be no question about the average American's Americanism or his desire to preserve this precious heritage at all costs. Nevertheless, some insidious foreign ideas have already wormed their way into his civilization without his realizing what was going on. Thus dawn finds the unsuspecting patriot garbed in pajamas, a garment of East Indian origin; and lying in a bed built on a pattern which originated in either Persia or Asia Minor. He is muffled to the ears in un-American materials: cotton, first domesticated in India; linen, domesticated in the Near East; wool from an animal native to Asia Minor; or silk whose uses were first discovered by the Chinese. All these substances have been transformed into cloth by methods invented in Southwestern Asia. If the weather is cold enough he may even be sleeping under an eiderdown quilt invented in Scandinavia.

On awakening he glances at the clock, a medieval European invention, uses one potent Latin word in abbreviated form, rises in haste, and goes to the bathroom. Here, if he stops to think about it, he must feel himself in the presence of a great American institution: he will have heard stories of both the quality and frequency of foreign plumbing and will know that in no other country does the average man perform his ablutions in the midst of such splendor. But the insidious foreign influence pursues him even here. Glass was invented by the ancient Egyptians, the use of glazed tiles for floors and walls in the Near East, porcelain in China, and the art of enameling on metal by Mediterranean artisans of the Bronze Age. Even his bathtub and toilet are but slightly modified copies of Roman originals. The only purely American contribution to the ensemble is the steam radiator, against which our patriot very briefly and unintentionally places his posterior.

In this bathroom the American washes with soap invented by the ancient Gauls. Next he cleans his teeth, a subversive European practice which did not invade America until the latter part of the eighteenth century. He then shaves, a masochistic rite first developed by the heathen priests of ancient Egypt and Sumer. The process is made less of a penance by the fact that his razor is of steel, an iron-carbon alloy discovered in either India or Turkestan. Lastly, he dries himself on a Turkish towel.

Returning to the bedroom, the unconscious victim of un-American practices removes his clothes from a chair, invented in the Near East, and proceeds to dress. He puts on close-fitting tailored garments whose form derives from the skin clothing of the ancient nomads of the Asiatic steppes and fastens them with buttons whose prototypes appeared in Europe at the close of the Stone Age. This costume is appropriate enough for outdoor exercise in a cold climate, but is quite unsuited to American Summers, steam-heated houses, and Pullmans. Nevertheless, foreign ideas and habits hold the unfortunate man in thrall even when common sense tells him that the authentically American costume of gee string and moccasins would be far more comfortable. He puts on his feet stiff coverings made from hide prepared by a process invented in ancient Egypt and cut to a pattern which can be traced back to ancient Greece, and makes sure they are properly polished, also a Greek idea. Lastly, he ties about his neck a strip of bright-colored cloth which is a vestigial survival of the shoulder shawls worn by seventeenth-century Croats. He gives himself a final appraisal in the mirror, an old Mediterranean invention, and goes downstairs to breakfast.

Here a whole new series of foreign things confronts him. His food and drink are placed before him in pottery vessels, the popular name of which — china — is sufficient evidence of their origin. His fork is a medieval Italian invention and his spoon a copy of a Roman original. He will usually begin the meal with coffee, an Abyssinian plant first discovered by the Arabs. The American is quite likely to need it to dispel the morning-after effects of over-indulgence in fermented drinks, invented in the Near East; or distilled ones, invented by the alchemists of medieval Europe. Whereas the Arabs took their coffee straight, he will probably sweeten it with sugar, discovered in India; and dilute it with cream, both the domestication of cattle and the technique of milking having originated in Asia Minor.

If our patriot is old-fashioned enough to adhere to the so-called American breakfast, his coffee will be accompanied by an orange, domesticated in the Mediterranean region, a cantaloupe domesticated in Persia, or grapes, domesticated in Asia Minor. He will follow this with a bowl of cereal made from grain domesticated in the Near East and prepared by methods also invented there. From this he will go on to waffles, a Scandinavian invention, with plenty of butter, originally a Near-Eastern cosmetic. As a side dish he may have the egg of a bird domesticated in Southeastern Asia or strips of the flesh of an animal domesticated in the same region, which have been salted and smoked by a process invented in Northern Europe.

Breakfast over, he places upon his head a molded piece of felt, invented by the nomads of Eastern Asia, and, if it looks like rain, puts on outer shoes of rubber, discovered by the ancient Mexicans, and takes an umbrella, invented in India. He then sprints for his train — the train, not the sprinting, being an English invention. At the station he pauses for a moment to buy a newspaper, paying for it with coins invented in ancient Lydia. Once on board he settles back to inhale the fumes of a cigarette invented in Mexico, or a cigar invented in Brazil. Meanwhile, he reads the news of the day, imprinted in characters invented by the ancient Semites by a process invented in Germany upon a material invented in China. As he scans the latest editorial pointing out the dire results to our institutions of accepting foreign ideas, he will not fail to thank a Hebrew God in an Indo-European language that he is a one hundred per cent (decimal system invented by the Greeks) American (from Americus Vespucci, Italian geographer).

GERTRUDE NOAR,* *New York City*
Anti-Defamation League of B'nai B'rith

The Nature of Human Relations Problems in the Classroom

IT IS SAFE to assume I believe that we are in agreement about that theory and those principles of human relations in education that stem from the basic philosophy of democracy and from the Judeo-Christian ethic to which we as teachers are expected to subscribe. For example, the significance of the individual and his innate worth and dignity and his right to an equal opportunity to develop his potentialities. I believe it is also safe to assume your agreement, that philosophy, theory, and principles remain generalities without substance unless and until the teacher behaves as a person and so conducts his classroom that those principles become realities for his pupils. Furthermore, it seems to me that I can assume that the youth of the land may not become committed to democracy and/or to education unless, in the classroom they have real, positive experiences with the democratic processes and that, in the democratic context, they experience warm positive relationships with significant adults, their teachers, and with the peer group which becomes increasingly significant to adolescents.

* Paper delivered at the Association's Annual Meeting, April 7, 1964. Miss Noar, who is National Director of Education for the Anti-Defamation League, has given invaluable consultative and editorial assistance to the North Central Association's studies on Human Relations in the Classroom. These three studies are reported in *Teacher Education for Human Relations in the Classroom: A Report from 1108 College Professors; Human Relations in the Classroom: A Study of Problems and Situations Reported by 1075 Second Year Secondary School Teachers;* and *Human Relations in the Classroom: A Challenge to Teacher Education.* Available from Office of the Secretary, North Central Association's 5454 South Shore Drive, Chicago, Illinois 60615. Price: single copies, 25¢; quantities of 50 or more, 20¢ each.

DIVERSITY: CHALLENGE OR FRUSTRATION?

Given those assumptions, let us examine the classrooms in which the teacher is expected to teach not only something but also somebody. In fact, the diversity of those somebodies presents him with his greatest challenge and possibly his greatest frustration. Many teachers groan with despair when confronted with the urgency of meeting the needs of pupils who differ from him and from each other. When we talk about human relations education to them they are likely to ask, "Must we teach and do all that, too?" Yet, unless the teacher is informed about, aware of, and sensitive to interpersonal and intergroup relations; unless he himself perceives human differences to be of positive value; unless he practices the art of living with difference and becomes skilled in creating good human relations, he will probably remain little more than a purveyor of information which some pupils will not learn and others will soon forget.

THE NEGRO SELF-IMAGE

Other race relations problems are of a quite different nature. They are caused by the absence of facts and pictures of Negroes in elementary school readers and storybooks, in secondary school literature books, in American history and social studies texts, and in biographies. Nowhere do Negro children find people like themselves with whom they can identify. They come to believe that their ancestors did not take part in settling, exploring and developing the nation. They find no discussion of the problems of living they and their families experienced and, therefore,

Pamphlet of the Anti-Defamation League, New York, 1964.

must come to believe they are unimportant to American writers, publishers, and teachers. They never get to read or hear about or see the great Negro authors, composers, artists, scientists, physicians, surgeons, inventors, and teachers who most certainly have lived and do live here, and who have contributed to our greatness. Inevitably, their feelings of inferiority bred by this unfair and untrue treatment are linked with those created by the still prevalent subordination and discrimination practiced by white America against Negroes in defiance of the Federal Constitution and the Bill of Rights. Only now and for the most part, with great dignity and patience are American Negroes saying, "We can wait no longer. We must have first class citizenship and our children must be given equality of educational opportunities."

MISUSE OF ABILITY GROUPING

Still other classroom problems for Negro children grow out of the widespread use of so-called ability groups and tracks. In many schools they are the devices which virtually create or maintain segregation. Moreover, when a group labeled low ability enters the classroom, many teachers slump into despair or suffer disgust. They expect nothing from the children and give little or nothing to them. The pace is slowed to the point of boredom and when pupils react badly to dullness and sterility, they are punished. Failure is heaped upon failure until all incentive is gone, all motivation is lost, all effort is destroyed.

Sometimes schools try to soften the effect of ability grouping by using group names. A friend of mine while attending an open house at his son's school asked a small boy a question. The child promptly answered, "I don't know." My friend tried to encourage him and finally asked, "Why don't you know?" The boy answered, "I don't have to. I am a turtle." The other half of the class were called hares. A little girl said to me, "In our school they call us Red, White, and Blues. I don't see why they don't call us flowers, vegetables, and nuts."

Segregation for any reason is undemocratic. Moreover, children soon develop self-images to correspond with the teacher's expectations and thereafter behave, like all of us do, as they perceive themselves to be. Nothing blocks learning more effectively than seeing oneself as a nonlearner.

There are other human relations problems caused by ability grouping. Among them are the intense anxieties caused by excessive demands upon the most able students for quantity production and high achievement. These may result in such anxiety illnesses as ulcers (increasing at the eleven year old level), neuroses, psychotic symptoms, and increasing attempts at suicide by teenagers. Moreover, their unwholesome attitude towards less highly endowed schoolmates means more experiences of rejection and exclusion for them.

Teachers seem often to equate high ability with high socio-economic class and low ability with poverty. This causes problems in relationships due to teachers' unrealistic expectations, demands, and the marks they give. The teacher's own feelings about a student also frequently affect his marking practices. For example, when a boy asked why the report on which he had worked so hard and which his well educated father had praised received only a passing mark, the teacher said, "You may as well know it now, I don't like you and nothing you turn in will ever get more than C." Some teachers have been heard to say about their eager Jewish students, "Who do they think they are?" or "I'll put them in their place."

Ability grouping does not serve to decrease and may even increase the dangers inherent in the excessive emphasis which many teachers give to competition. Gardner Murphy in his book "Human Potentialities," said, "Competition ... will frustrate and benumb most of those who fail and, for those who succeed, it can best give only the iterated satisfaction of winning again. This may destroy the ability to risk failures for the sake of attempting new and more interesting goals. In the direction of competition lies a convenient way of maintaining a status-minded society not their release of human potential."[1]

INSENSITIVITY TO RELIGIOUS BELIEFS

Differences in religious belief, for the very fact that to some people religion is so highly charged with emotions, cause classroom problems. Take for example the teachers who persistently schedule tests on Jewish holidays or the school which refuses to allow pupils who are absent on high holy days to make up the work they missed. Or, put yourself in the place of a child raised in an orthodox Jewish family, when, in home arts class she must cook bacon and the teacher scolds her for not eating it. Then try to imagine how Jewish children feel when most of the classroom activities for a period of two to four weeks are centered on Christmas. And, if you will permit me to go one step further, suppose a Jewish child is asked to play a role in the play which centers around the creche or to march in a candlelight procession. And how would you expect Jewish children to react when their textbook presents Jews only as an ancient homeless people always being persecuted or when the book and teacher brush off Germany's hideous crimes of genocide with a sentence like, "Many people were persecuted unjustly."

On the other hand, how must the sensibility of Catholic children be offended when the teacher angrily demands that they wash their faces when they come in after early Mass on Ash Wednesday? And how can they express their confusion and resentment when the history text presents Catholicism as the root of all evil and Protestantism as the source of all light in the period of the Reformation?

PROBLEMS OF SOCIO-ECONOMIC DIFFERENCES

The nature of the problem which, at the moment, gives teachers great concern is the lowest socio-economic class child's deprivation of those experiences which ready middle class children for schooling. Slum children lack the toys, the paper and pencils and crayons, the pictures and books which produce interest and readiness for reading and writing. They also lack language which in middle class families develops as children ask and receive answers to questions and engage in conversation with siblings and adults. They aren't ready for reading and so the teacher calls them dumb or even retarded. They are not used to following complex directions and so the teacher calls them disobedient. They are not trained to pay attention or to concentrate and so the teacher says she can't get them interested. They aren't future time oriented or used to hurrying so the teacher calls them slow and complains of their low aspiration levels. By fourth or fifth grade, these children develop strongly negative attitudes toward teacher, toward school and toward education. A disproportionate number of these children are non-white, Mexican-American Puerto Ricans, and Indians and so negative attitudes toward minority groups further complicate their human relations problems in the classroom.

To summarize, I think I have said that many of the human relations problems in classrooms grow out of differences in race, religion, socio-economic class and mental ability. Children who differ in those respects suffer damage to the self-image, exlusion, rejection, subordination, discrimination, and unequal educational opportunity. Such experiences create negative self-concepts and anxiety and emotional illness. Those children fail to develop their potentialities and often become cynical about democracy. In time they drop out of school to become the unemployed and dependent. The classroom teacher charged with responsibility for teaching democracy and for developing the unknown potentialities of every child, therefore, can no longer hide behind the statement, "We have subject matter to teach, there isn't time for human rela-

[1] Murphy, Gardner. "Human Potentialities" (New York, Basic Books, Inc., 1958) pp. 318–319.

tions." What the teacher teaches is often different from and even unimportant in comparison with what the child learns.

In conclusion, it seems to us, teachers must come to see that human relations in education is a way to help each individual to find what lies within him and thus to accept and make peace with himself. Writing in "The Fires of Spring" James Michener says, "For this is the journey that men make: to find themselves. If they fail in this, it doesn't matter much what else they find. Money, position, fame, many loves, revenge are all of little consequence, and when the tickets are collected at the end of the ride, they are tossed into the bin marked 'Failure.' But if a man happens to find himself—if he knows what he can be depended upon to do, the limits of his courage, the position from which he will no longer retreat—the secret reservoirs of his determinations, the extent of his dedications, the depth of his feeling for beauty, his honest and unpostured goals—then he has found a mansion which he can inhabit with dignity all the days of his life."[1]

[1] Michener, James. "The Fires of Spring" (New York: Random House, Inc. 1949).

THE IMPORTANCE OF ATTITUDES IN SOCIAL STUDIES

by
Milton Kleg
University of South Florida

At Chicago's 29th Street beach, a number of whites and blacks began pitching stones at one another. A Negro youth remained some yards out in Lake Michigan and observed the confrontation. As some stones began falling near him, he decided to swim further away. Suddenly he went under and drowned. Although a coroner's jury eventually determined that the youth had drowned out of fear of swimming inland, Negroes at the scene immediately accused a white man of hitting the boy with a stone thrown from the beach. A policeman was called to the scene and refused to arrest the white man. Instead, the officer arrested a Negro. The blacks attacked the officer, and within twenty-four hours a bloody race riot erupted in the midwest metropolis.[1]

In Los Angeles, two California Highway Patrolmen arrested Marquette Frye for allegedly driving under the influence of alcohol.[2] This incident percipitated a riot which resulted in the deaths of thirty-four persons and the wounding of 1,032. About 4,000 arrests were made, and over 600 buildings were destroyed or damaged by fire.[3]

These two riots occurred in 1919 and 1965 respectively. In 1967 more racial violence befell a number of cities throughout the United States. The worst wave of racial disorders erupted in the first two weeks of July. By the end of that month, President Johnson appointed a commission to investigate the causes of these latest riots.[4]

The National Advisory Commission on Civil Disorders concluded its study with a statement by Dr. Kenneth Clark. According to Clark, the report of the 1919 Chicago riot, the McCone Commission report on the Watts riot in Los Angeles, and the reports of riots in 1935 and 1943 make the same essential analysis, recommendations, and conclusions.[5]

Original Manuscript.

Likewise, the 1967 commission concluded that it had found nothing new. It is worth noting that the commission's conclusion failed to point out one essential difference between the violence of the sixties and the earlier riots. The sixties involved **blacks** acting out aggression toward whites. The disorders prior to the sixties constituted white anti-black aggression. The causes of the recent disorders involved the continuing polarization of American society into two hostile camps based upon racial identification.[6]

Many educators and especially those in the social studies are disturbed by the racial and ethnic tensions brewing throughout the United States and the world. Usually, when a societal problem emerges, the populace turns to education as the catholicon for social ills. However, educatiors, along with the remainder of the population, have generally ignored treating the critical questions of racial, ethnic, religious, and social class prejudices and conflict in terms of education. Nevertheless, as in the past, the role of social studies education remains concerned with developing the "right attitude" among the youth of the nation.

Social attitudes are a major element in social studies objectives and curriculum. Fenton states that the development of attitudes is the reponsibility of all members of the teaching profession and that attitudes are a vital element in a number of social studies projects.[7] Similarly, a number of pedagogues have expressed the view that education must consider the development of attitudes which are a necessary aspect of socializing the student in terms of the society.[8] Such views support Hunt and Metcalf's contention that most social studies teachers are concerned with enculturating students in terms of the national mores, myths, and heritage. Furthermore, they contend that teachers consider developing attitudes as a chief objective.[9]

Nevertheless, Michaelis argues that although attitudes are an integral part of teaching, minimum attention has been directed to the development and utilization of **affective** objectives.[10] Consequently, Michaelis presents a schema in which he lists several affective objectives, all of which are designed to develop attitudes.[11]

Regardless of the concern with the development of attitudes, relatively little research has been undertaken in the secondary school to determine the effect of cognitive knowledge on attitudes. Michaelis and others are quite willing to ignore the question and proceed on the assumption that if cognitive objectives result in cognitive knowledge, then affective objectives will result in attitudinal development. Frankel, for example, seems to accept this assumption when he discusses areas of needed research in the social studies. Although he acknowledges that research is needed regarding social attitudes, he does so without definition or direction. Such obscure recommendation leaves much to be answered.[12]

The assumption that attitudinal development and changes can be dealt with by affective objectives in the same manner as cognitive knowledge and cognitive objectives has become quite popular. Such assumptions tend to reduce the desire among educators to examine the interaction effects between the cognitive and affective domains.

Along with others, social studies pedagogues appear to treat the cognitive and affective as two distinct, separate areas without analyzing any overlap. Occasionally, however, they mention that one can not teach social studies without expressing attitudes or values. There is little research to support the contention that specific attitudes are developed when educational experiences are based upon affective objectives, just as cognitive learning stems from specific cognitive objectives.[13] Although Krathwohl and Bloom emphasize the need for further research concerning the relationship between the two domains, they proceed to treat the domains in a dichotomus manner.[14] The dichotomy which has been created by recent educators appears to cast aside the classical notion that emotion and knowledge are intertwining fibers of the same rope.[15]

In contrast to the cognitive-affective dichotomy which currently prevails, Rice suggests that cognitive-affective measures can be developed and employed in determining what kind of relationship exists between knowledge and attitudes.[16] Rice conceived this notion from Rokeach who intimated the relationship between attitudes and knowledge.[17] Rice contends that Rokeach's work suggests that curriculum builders may not only evaluate the knowledge content by means of achievement tests, but also the attitudinal contribution of the curriculum in which specific belief system and attitude scales may be structured with reference to critical cognitive elements.[18]

Until now, much of the treatment of content and attitudes has been based on incidental and premeditated interaction or bridge building. Others have suggested treating the cognitive and affective domains in a more independent manner.[19] The time has come for teachers and researchers to begin seriously examining the assumption that at some point knowledge and attitudes overlap. If this overlap does exist, then a change in knowledge may result in a change of attitudes.

Nevertheless, a change in knowledge may not result in a change of attitudes. If such is the case, a number of explanations could account for this occurrence. First of all, Fredrickson's study of adolescents' attitudes suggests that the school seems to be a major factor in determining educational attitudes, whereas the home and peer group seem to be most effective in determining attitudes which would deal with race, social class and caste, and religious and ethnic groups.[20] In the past, such areas of concern have not received heavy emphasis in the school curriculum. Even if ethnic and social class relations had received attention in the schools, attitudinal changes would not necessarily have been positive. After all, the educational institution of a given community generally represents a mirror image of the core values of the community. As Merton succinctly suggests, the teacher is a product of his community, and there is no reason to regard him as immune from cultural prejudices and ethnocentrism.[21] A more general statement concerning attitudinal change is expressed by Allport.

According to Allport, one must account for attitudinal changes, especially those concerned with prejudices, in terms of the subject's peer group and family as well as education.[22] Furthermore, since, according to Lewin's field theory, behavior is based on a variety of social forces, attitudes may remain unchanged due to variables other than knowledge.[23] Conformity to social norms often includes maintaining prejudiced attitudes. Allport's discussion of the conforming scapegoater illustrates what Lewin's theory suggests. Together they reaffirm the postulate that man is a product of his culture.

Another factor which might stifle attitudinal change involves the nature of the development of attitudes. In essence, one finds that whn knowledge is learned at an early age, beliefs become fixed. From this fixed knowledge base, attitudes are developed. As a consequence, the attitudes, in turn, become fixed, and attitudinal change at a later date is difficult.

Another explanation for the lack of influence of knowledge on attitudes may be due to compartmentalization. In this situation the individual does not allow basic beliefs to come into conflict with new knowledge. Thus, attitudes stemming from such beliefs remain separated and are expressed independently in terms of a given situation. This may explain the case of a teacher who at home or church reaffirms his belief that a supreme diety created the world in seven days but presents the scientific explanation of evolution in the classroom. Although these possibilities exist, they in no way limit the necessity of a study to determine whether or not the concept of a cognitive-affective domain is valid. Conversely, they seem to suggest even greater concern for such a study.

To determine the relationship of attitudes to knowledge in a cognitively based curriculum, one must first determine what effect cognitive knowledge has on attitudes. Furthermore, social science objectives in education typically emphasize the development of desirable attitudes. There is little research evidence to indicate the relationship of instruction to the formation of desirable attitudes. The research of a study dealing with attitudes would provide much needed data on the relationship of knowledge to attitudinal change.

Another important aspect of such a study concerns the subject matter of the treatment in the experimental groups. At present, there is no program extensively used in United States public schools which examines the nature of prejudice from a world view. In Fact, recent textbook surveys in Michigan[24] and Missouri[25] indicate that many social studies texts are inadequate in their handling of ethnic, religious, and racial groups.

The Missouri survey by Carpenter and Rank found only 7 of 50 secondary social studies texts adequate.[26] The following excerpt of their summary demonstrates textbooks may reinforce intergroup prejudices and hostilities.

1. ...the great majority of texts reviewed fail to depict adequately the multi-racial, multi-ethnic character of either the United States or the world.

2. ...many of the texts examined relegate material about minorities to separate chapters or sections of the work...World history texts usually ignore multi-racial societies...

3. The general criterion of democracy, requiring a frank acknowledgement that prejudice, discrimination and restrictive immigration policies are real, threatening 'social evils,' is violated: many textbooks play down the existence of these phenomena, and the conflict between them and the basic American value system.

4. ...Finally, many of the violations of inclusions and contributions stem from the failure to use the results of current research, and thus are violations of the criterion of factuality as well.[27]

SUMMARY

This presentation has attempted to review the importance of attitudes in social studies education. It has been noted that although a number of scholars in the area of social studies education have indicated that attitudes are important outcomes in education and although no one has argued that attitudes and knowledge are dichotomus domains, the treatment of attitudes and knowledge has, in practice, been to divide the cognitive and affective in a dichotomus manner. Furthermore, it has been suggested that teachers and educators seriously examine the assumption that knowledge and attitudes are inseparable, and that they initiate practices compatible with such an assumption. Finally, it has been noted that textbooks in social studies tend to reinforce innergroup prejudices and hostilities although many people regard textual material as purely cognitive in nature.

FOOTNOTES

[1]The Chicago Commission on Race Relations, *The Negro in Chicago: A study of Race Relations and a Race Riot* (Chicago: The University of Chicago Press, 1922), pp. 4-5.

[2]The Governor's Commission on the Los Angeles Riots, *Violence in the City--An End or a Beginning?* (Los Angeles: The State of California, 1965), pp. 10-11.

[3]*Ibid*, pp. 23-24.

[4]Otto Kerner and others, *Report of the National Advisory Commission on Civil Disorders* (New York: Bantam Books, Inc., 1968), p.1.

[5]*Ibid*, p. 483.

[6]*Ibid*, p. 1.

[7]Edwin Fenton, *The New Social Studies* (New York: Holt, Rinehart, and Winston, Inc., 1967), p. 17.

[8]H. H. Remmers and N. L. Gage, *Educational Measurement and Evaluation* (revised edition; New York: Harper and Brothers, 1955), p. 360.

[9]Maurice P. Hunt and Lawrence Metcalf, *Teaching High School Social Studies: Problems in Reflective Thinking and Social Understanding* (second edition; New York: Harper and Row, 1968), p. 23.

[10]John U. Michaelis, *Social Studies for Children in a Democracy: Recent Trends and Developments* (fourth edition; Englewood Cliffs, New Jersey: Prentice-Hall, Inc., 1968), p. 88.

[11]*Ibid.*, p. 9.

[12]Charles Frankel, "Needed Research on Social Attitudes, Beliefs, and Values in the Teaching of Social Studies," *Needed Research in the Teaching of the Social Studies*, Report of a Conference Held at Sagamore Conference Center of Syracuse University October 3-5, 1963, Roy A. Price, editor (Washington, D. C.: National Council for the Social Studies, 1964), pp. 27-43.

[13] David R Krathwohl, Benjamin S. Bloom, and Bertram B. Masia, *Taxonomy of Educational Objectives: The Classification of Educational Goals, Handbook II: Affective Domain* (New York: David McKay Company, Inc., 1967), p.20.

[14] *Ibid.*

[15] Anne Anastasi, *Psychological Testing* (New York: Macmillan Press, 1954), p. 577.

[16] Marion J. Rice, "Development of a Multi-Disciplinary Social Science Course: The Changing South for Grade 8" (unpublished curriculum improvement proposal, University of Georgia, Athens, Georgia, 1965), p. 6.

[17] Milton Rokeach, *The Opened and Closed Mind* (New York: Basic Books, Inc., 1960), p. 400.

[18] Rice, *loc. cit.*

[19] Michaelis, *op. cit.*, p.9.

[20] Lowry Fredrickson, "A Study of Adolescent Values" (unpublished Doctoral dissertation, The University of Iowa, Iowa City, 1967), cited in *Dissertation Abstracts*, Vol. XXVIII (January, 1968), p. 2773-A.

[21] Robert K. Merton, *Social Theory and Social Structure* (revised edition; New York: The Free Press, 1957), p.183.

[22] Gordon W Allport, *The Nature of Prejudice* (Reading, Massachusetts: Addison Wesley, 1955), p. 511.

[23] Kurt Lewin, *Field Theory in Social Science: Selected Theoretical Papers*, ed. Dorwin Cartwright (New York: Harper and Row, 1951), p. 77.

[24] Michigan Department of Education, *A Report on the Treatment of Minorities in American History Textbooks* (Lansing, Michigan: Michigan Department of Education, 1968).

[25] L. P. Carpenter and Dinah Rank, *The Treatment of Minorities: A Survey of Textbooks Used in Missouri High Schools* (Jefferson City, Missouri: Missouri Commission on Human Rights, 1968).

[26] Ibid., pp. 14-17.

[27] Ibid., pp. 27-28.

Contributions of History and Geography to Education
Designed to Combat Racial Prejudice

Louis Francois
(France)

1. I would propose the following definition of racism: any attitude--mental, verbal, social or economic--which tends to maintain that certain biological differences determine psychological differences and that these represent absolute qualitative differences which support the theory of "superior" and "inferior" races.

2. "The germ of racism exists in every one of us." Surprising though it may seem, this statement was received by an audience of young people not as an accusation, encouraging evasion or revolt, but as a truth deserving of reflection.

3. Little does it matter whether racism be innate or acquired, but the fact that, owing to the influence of the economic, social and cultural environment, it creeps into or develops within the human heart, which it contaminates, has unfortunately been proved by surveys carried out in France, a country so little prone to racism, as well as in allegedly enlightened circles.

4. This, however, is only individual racism. Racial infection is much more serious when it develops from a situation of oppression. Racism is then the systematic and permanent exploitation of real or imaginary differences for the benefit of the accuser and to the detriment of his victim, in order to justify his privileges or his aggression. The desire to assert oneself, resulting from a situation of oppression, engenders a feeling of superiority. This superiority, which is felt intuitively, requires, if it is to be viable, justifications which individuals, fatally caught up in the process, have no difficulty in finding. The oppressors become alive to the fact that there is a danger of opposition and seek for a justification for their oppression. Racism then becomes the racism of a whole class of society, of a whole nation. We have been subjected to and are still witnesses of the utter horror of this racism.

5. We can therefore measure the importance of education designed to inculcate a spirit of peace in the minds and hearts of young people and to give them the necessary strength to overcome prejudice, especially racial prejudice.

6. What contribution can be made in this connection by history and geography teachers?

The role of history teaching

7. This is an extremely delicate subject.

8. History has been too often made to serve all kinds of causes, the most poisonous of all being Nazism. Even in the so-called free countries, history has been tampered with and used as a tool in civic and social education. It has been compromised by propaganda.

Unesco Report ED/MD/4, October 24, 1968, pp. 31-34.

"Good" propaganda--even propaganda for peace or for the eradication of racial prejudice--would not rehabilitate it, would not give it back its respectability. History is like a lady who has lost her reputation. To enlist it in the service of peace and the eradication of racial prejudice would be a sure means of turning the best historians away from the cause of peace, whether international or interracial.

9. Some people maintain that history, by its very nature, is incompatible with any cause, however noble it may be. History has no other aim than to satisfy man's deep urge to find out how things were in the past. History is concerned with truth and exact knowledge.

10. Consequently:

   i. History is a disinterested science that cannot be used for any propaganda purposes.

   ii. Knowledge of the past cannot be used in the service of present-day action. Conditions never repeat themselves in exactly the same form. All comparisons are misleading owing to the complexity of the factors involved. "Semper eadem, sed aliter." "Always the same things, but in a different form"--this is the best definition of history, and we owe it to Cicero.

   iii. History does not show us that mankind follows an ascending path, but rather one with ups and downs. There are too many events in recent history that indicate a return to barbarous times. History is rather a school of skepticism.

11. It might be retorted that:

   i. An accurate picture of the past does not show only horror and darkness, but also beauty and great rays of light.

   ii. If the study of the past does not provide us with any ready-made answers, it does offer useful experience of the problems concerning the life of men in society.

   iii. While the guiding rule for the historian is "the truth, the whole truth and nothing but the truth," the fact remains that this ideal is difficult to achieve. According to the country or social group to which he belongs, every historian establishes his truth, which may conflict with the truth of another historian. We should not expect too much from history, for it represents an effort to introduce order into disorder, and the manner of doing so may vary considerably.

   iv. Moreover, the historian remains a man of his time. In the Seventeenth and Eighteenth centuries, he wrote histories of dynasties; in the Nineteenth century, histories of nations, and now he is undertaking economic, social and universal histories.

12. That is why another school maintains that the aim of history should be to make it easier to understand the present through a study of the past. History thus contributes to civic and social education. Against this, it is said that history can be made to prove anything, that it teaches us absolutely nothing, for it embraces everything and offers disturbing and convincing examples of everything.

13. The question is whether there is any way out of all these contradictions other than by abstention.

14. A history teacher is not the historian who writes history. He transforms the science of history into an instrument of culture. He cannot recount the whole of history to young people or make them learn it. From the vast dead past he selects those facts that are still living and of current interest. He uses history in order to teach his pupils to discover and understand the world about them and to play a part in it, intelligently and generously, as men and as citizens.

15. Within the limits of his power and professional competence, he has still much to do in order to combat racial prejudice.

   i. We still see sections of the population separated by racial prejudice, resentment and hatred. Memories are strong enough to prevent them from coming together again.
   a. It has been recommended that all derogatory references and errors due to ignorance or passion should be eliminated from textbooks and oral teaching. This is essential but insufficient.
   b. The crux of the problem is not to be found in the facts --the ancient hostility between Egyptians and Hebrews, the conflict between Greeks and Barbarians, the destruction of Israel by the Romans and the Diaspora, the Christian anti-Semitism which sprang up in the Middle Ages, the Dreyfus case, colonialism and the new form of enslavement, etc. It is to be found in the interpretation of these facts. Everything depends on how they are presented and on how they are explained. Accurately placed in the context which gave rise to them, historical facts, which seem to justify racist theories, will lose some of their virulence and certainly some of their topical interest. They will cease to be absolutes which are bandied as propaganda between conflicting groups and will become what they actually are: facts relating to a particular historical situation that is generally no longer relevant.

   ii. However, a cold and impersonal explanation will no longer suffice when racism leads to the enslavement of nations, to the genocide of millions of human beings. The anti-Semitism of the Nazis should certainly be analysed lucidly, but it is also necessary not only to show what is effects were, so as to provoke a feeling of horror and disgust in young people, but also to denounce the abomination of racism, which treats "the Other" as no more than an object and which led the SS to perpetrate so many crimes without feeling the slightest remorse. The teacher must, above all, remain human.

   iii. History teaching, less national and more open to the whole world and to the different systems represented by the major civilizations, helps to break down mental attitudes or, at any rate, to make more flexible an outlook which each of us owes to his national and social environment and of which he is often an unwitting prisoner. There are two prerequisites: the peoples of Asia and Africa should be accorded in history teaching a place corresponding to the role they have played and now play in the world; civilizations should be placed in their chronological and geographical context, as this is essential for an understanding of them. This does not rule out "themes," which makes it possible to span history and to combine it with national and foreign literature, drawing etc., but it relegates them to the rank of auxiliaries or special subjects of study.

16. Can anything more be expected of history? It provides a fund of information and experience; it helps to clarify judgement; it shows how any ideal must correspond to a particular historical situation if it is to be effective; but it is not its task to provide this ideal or to dictate a decision.

The role of geography teaching

17. While teaching in general may be regarded as the discovery of man, of men and of the world, this discovery is the whole purpose of geography, and thinking in geographical terms means thinking in universal terms. The state of man on the earth's surface is one of the basic concerns of the geographer.

18. Every human group has its own characteristics and sometimes even exceptional ones, owing to some particular factor. It is the geographer's duty to stress them, for the singularity of man's destiny argues in favour of his greatness and accounts for the birth of civilizations. However, like any science, geography tends to generalize, to reduce the facts to a common measure by means of satisfactory explanations and comparisons. The geographer finishes by assigning men their place in mankind as a whole, by uniting them in a vast common undertaking.

19. The question is whether we should pass rapidly over these differences and stress the resemblances which can be found, without great difficulty, between human groups. In our view, it is more useful to recognize this diversity and to explain it to pupils by relating it to the variety of geographical environments and historical developments, so that the pupils may be led to regard it as a fact that does not necessarily create inferiority and superiority between men or prevent them from pursuing together the same aims.

20. Consequently, in this varied, divided and often antagonistic world of ours, the first stage towards interracial understanding would be to understand the existing differences. The civilizations farthest removed from one's own would be studied and regarded as systems of values based on social structures, on particular mental outlooks. If peoples' minds were penetrated with the relativity of institutions, manners and customs, we could reasonably hope that nations would be less inclined to come into conflict and more disposed to tolerate, understand and respect each other.

21. The progress of science, technology and mass communication and increasing exchanges are making the world a smaller place and bringing into contact with one another different races and peoples, which have neither the same standard of economic development nor the same social structures nor the same collective outlook. It is essential to establish harmony and co-operation between peoples which had previously developed along very different lines and which have not reached the same stage of development, but which can now become part of a civilization that is tending towards uniformity.

22. Geography does not need to be given a particular slant in order to contribute to better interracial understanding. This can be achieved naturally if geography is taught intelligently and honestly; if the teacher establishes true relationships between facts, endeavours to be objective and to seek after truth, distrusts the sensational and rejects propaganda of all kinds.

Conclusion

23. For eradication of racial prejudice, we can always place our trust in the teacher who is convinced that respect for human rights (as proclaimed in the Declarations of 1789 and 1948) is a perennial cause; who is fully convinced of the validity of the Moscow Declaration on the biological aspects of the race question (1964); who believes in active teaching methods which accustom young people to discuss things with other people, help them to get to know, understand and respect others, and integrate them in a school community in which segregation and the lack of understanding between the two different "races" (teachers and pupils) are gradually disappearing.

Recommendations Concerning Terminology in
Education on Race Questions

A. Babs Fafunwa
(Nigeria)

1. Prior to the Fifteenth century and before the commencement of intensive proselytization and colonization, there was little reference to racial discrimination in text materials. The three most important factors that contributed to the development of racial prejudice between the Sixteenth and Twentieth centuries were:

    a. trade and commerce;
    b. religion; and
    c. colonialism.

The early Christian missionaries in their naivete believed that theirs was a "civilizing" mission; that the "noble savages" or the "warring tribesmen" of Africa and Asia needed Christ if they were to be uplifted from their "primitiveness." The colonial powers on the other hand had to justify their action by claiming that the "natives" were too "primitive" to rule themselves and they had to be "brought up" gradually and systematically before they could reach a stage of self-government and perhaps self-determination.

2. As mentioned above, the three major factors that contributed to the perpetuation of prejudice are trade, religion and colonialism:

    a. Trade and Commerce

3. Prior to the Fifteenth century, hardly 400 years ago, there was little difference between Africa and Europe in terms of social and economic development. Europe gained advantage over the rest of the world first through the slave trade, followed by extensive trading in other commodities after the abolition of the human traffic, backed by religion and force of arms. The industrial revolution, which, again, started first in Europe, gave the West an additional advantage over the rest of the world.

4. The European slave dealers believed that the African was naturally suited for menial and plantation work in the new world, as the Indians in the Americas were either too hostile or not physically able to cope with strenuous work. The new settlers in the new world were either too few to work the enormous plantations which they carved out for themselves and/or preferred to play the role of supervisors and masters. The early Greeks, Romans and Egyptians employed slave labour in the construction of their palatial mansions, roads, dams and other public and private amenities. Dark skinned slaves were preferred to fair skinned ones--the same preference was shown in domestic work. It is not surprising, therefore, that the European slave dealers of the Sixteenth and Seventeenth centuries as well as the new world settlers laboured under the same misconception and perpetuated the same stereotype. Millions of Africans were taken by the shipload to the new world and Africa was drained of its able-bodied men and women for over two centuries. By the time slavery was declared illegal early in the Nineteenth century, the harm had already been done; although peace-

Unesco Report ED/MD/4, October 24, 1968, pp. 23-27.

ful trade in goods and commodities replaced the ignominious human traffic, the racial prejudice which the latter engendered was to continue for another century or more.

b. Religion

5. Religious intolerance is another contributory factor to racial prejudice in Africa. The early Christian missionaries genuinely but naively believed that their mission was to convert the "African pagans and muslims" to Christianity and thus bring light to the "benighted" Africans. The early Christian attitude presumed that the Africans' own religions were inferior and should be ruthlessly eliminated. The missionaries, in collaboration with local colonial administrators, joined forces together in imposing their own religion and culture on the African populace. Indeed the "good" citizen in most parts of Africa until very recently was one who was only African in blood, Christian by religion and British or French in culture and intellect. He must shun things African such as images artefacts, local attire, African mores and customs--all in the name of Christianity and civilization. School textbooks, church sermons and other built-in educational devices were employed to drive the message home. The physical and the psychological assault on African culture through religion and politics combined to produce in the African what is now commonly known as "colonial mentality," or a sense of rejection of things African. The lesson has been so well learnt by the generality of the African population that even today the erroneous definition of the "good" citizen still prevails in some degree in many independent African countries. Worse still, the continuation of mission-run schools or church-related institutions tends to perpetuate this stereotype idea and in most cases, at the local tax-payers' expense. Without belabouring this point, the most effective solution would be for schools to become secular and citizenship-orientated. The mission schools over a period of hundred years or more succeeded in producing Baptists, Anglican, Catholics and Muslims, but have not succeeded in producing Nigerians, Ghanaians, Kenyans, Togolese, etc. Instead they have helped intensify endless rivalry and sometimes outright hostility among the various religious sects while the larger and more important issue of citizenship was related to the background.

c. Colonialism

6. The colonization of most parts of Africa was ostensibly explained away by the colonial powers as a means of enforcing the abolition of the slave trade and of establishing peaceful administration among the warring local groups and chiefs; and finally to insure the flow of trade and commerce on land and sea; that is to say; to make Africa, or Asia for that matter, safe for European businessmen. In many instances force had to be used by the representatives of the metropolitan countries to compel the local chiefs to pledge allegiance to the metropolitan government. Thus the colonial powers at various times compelled the local people by force of arms to accept the Christian missionaries. Force was also employed to protect and further the interests of European merchants and traders. In employment, most of the colonial powers until recently assigned minor roles to the African worker, irrespective of his educational attainment, while higher responsibilities were reserved for expatriate staff recruited from the cosmopolitan country.

7. The aforegoing was a very brief historical background to what led to prejudice and discrimination against the Africans between the Fifteenth and Twentieth centuries. As a result of this historical accident, coupled with similar developments in other parts of

the world during the same period, the following derogatory words found their way into textbooks and other written materials and became part of the permanent vocabularies of the English-speaking world:

> tribe
> native
> savage
> primitive
> jungle
> pagan
> kaffir
> bushmen
> backward
> underdeveloped
> uncivilized
> vernacular
> Negro
> coloured
> race

These words are commonly found in school textbooks, particularly in history, literature, geography, novels and readers. They also abound in learned journals, magazines, newspapers, radio and television. In archaeological, sociological and anthropological studies, many of these emotive words are employed on the pretext that they are used purely as objective, scholarly and scientific terms.

8. It is the thesis of this paper that whatever may be the scholar's justification for their use, the people to whom these labels are given reject the appellation, for they contend that the usage stereotypes and damns them. It is our contention, therefore, that if there is no other ulterior motive behind the usage, sincere scholars must strive to work for an acceptable substitute instead of resolutely fighting to maintain the status quo. At the First Congress of Africanists held in Accra in December 1962, and attended by over 600 delegates from all continents, the writer tabled a resolution calling on all Africanists to expunge from their writings henceforth the use of these emotionally charged words. The matter was debated briefly and postponed for further discussion at another conference.

9. To underscore the extent to which the usage of these words has damaged human relations and promoted racial prejudice, we shall explain briefly how some of these words are defined in the Shorter Oxford English Dictionary, which was first published in 1933 and revised in 1959. Being a standard work, the Oxford Dictionary has greater circulation and use than any work in sociology, anthropology, geography or history and is often used as a final arbiter in disputes concerning meaning and use of words and phrases in the English-speaking world.

Tribe

10. The word "tribe" is defined as "A group of persons forming a community and claiming descent from a common ancestor;" it is also defined as "A race of people; now applied especially to a primary aggregate of people in a primitive or barvarious condition under a headman or chief." It is interesting to note that the word tribe is principally used nowadays to describe African ethnic groups. It is used to cover groups in Asia and other non-European communities but since most of the Asian countries became independent between 1947 and 1954, the word gradually disappeared from the textbooks and journals, thanks to the Unesco effort in this direction.[1] How

an ethnic group with two or ten million people in East or West Africa, with a parliamentary government, can be described as a trive and not the Irish, the Scot, the Welsh, the French or the English, still baffles the non-European.

11. To promote better understanding among all nations, it is absolutely essential that the word be eliminated from textbooks, journals and scholarly abstracts.

Native
12. The word "native" is defined as "One born in a place; left in a natural state, untouched by art, unadorned, simple; In modern usage, especially with connotation of non-European origin." In Western journals, magazines and textbooks for primary school children, authors out-do themselves in making the label stick. The word "native" in terms of current usage is synonymous with the African. If no harm is meant by the users of this word, then conscious effort must be made to avoid the use of it by writers and publishers. The writer had a lengthy correspondence with a world-wide magazine editor on this issue but sadly enough the editor insisted that if the writer was familiar with the English language, he should realize that it was perfectly in order to say "a native of New York, London or Lagos." But the learned editor refused to accept the distinction between "New York native" and a "a native of New York," which was in fact the issue that generated the exchange of correspondence in the first place!

Savage
13. The word "savage" is defined as wild, uncultivated with implication of ferocity; uncivilized, existing in the lowest stage of culture. One is tempted to ask; "Whose culture and whose civilization" are we employing as a yard-stick/ It is our contention that only some animals will fit into this catefory and perhaps when animals learn to speak, they too may object to this description.

Primitive
14. The Oxford Dictionary defined the word as "simple, rude or rough like that of early times: old-fashioned." Again, this word is often used to stereotype some African art, culture, mores, religion or stage of development. By setting ourselves up as the sole arbiter of who is "primitive" and who is "civilized," and what is "good" and what is "bad," it means that we are playing God and that role can only lead to greater misunderstanding and intolerance among the peoples and nations of the world.

Vernacular
15. The word "vernacular" means, inter alia: Language of "a home born slave." It is currently in use in Africa today and seldom used in most of Asia and Europe. Yet the Luo, the Yoruba, the Luganda, the Ga, the Tiv, the Kikuyu or any other African language is no mor a vernacular than the Irish, Welsh, Greek or the German languages.

Race
16. The word "race" needs to be re-examined in the light of the present-day development. Classification of peoples into watertight compartments tends to perpetuate prejudice and racial discrimination Numerous studies have been conducted an a number of materials have been produced to show that nationality and race bear no necessary relationship to one another. The writer had been confronted a number of times with immigration and admissions forms calling for racial classification and description in terms of colour of skin, eyes, and hair. To get out of the embarrassment, the writer always filled the Race portion, thus: Race--HUMAN. Of course, this would

annoy the immigration officers no end and the action often resulted in considerable argument and delay in clearance procedure. Other words that are used in conjunction with race are "Negro" and "coloured," but Africans preferred to be "African," no "Negro" or coloured."

Pagan
17. The word "Pagan" is defined as "one of a nation or community which does not worship the true God." How any human being can arrogate to himself the power to determine who and who does not worship the true God is still one of the mysteries of life and living.

18. Other words that need reconsideration in terms of textbook writing, journals, magazines, movies and television, are:

> Jungle - "Land overgrown with underwood" is jungle in Africa Asia, Latin America, but "everglad" in Florida and other places.
> Uncivilized
> Backward
> Underdeveloped
> Kaffir
> Bushmen, etc.

19. Article 26 of the Universal Declaration of Human Rights states:
> "Education shall promote understanding, tolerance and friendship among all nations, racial or religious groups, and shall further the activities of the United Nations for the maintenance of peace."

To achieve this noble objective, the following steps should be taken by Unesco to combat prejudice and racial discrimination in text materials designed for education and information:

1. Hold regional or international conferences, of authors and publishers for the improvement of textbooks, journals, magazines and other teaching and informational materials.

2. Encourage learned societies in history, geography, civics, anthropology and sociology to devote a portion of their conference programmes to discussion on "Bias in text materials" and "How to promote international understanding through the written word."

3. Sponsor a conference of religious leaders--Christians, Muslims, Buddhists, Bahais, etc., to discuss the religious aspect of prejudice.

4. Unesco should assume full leadership in ensuring that words such as tribe, native, savage, primitive, jungle, pagan, kaffir, bushmen, backward, underdeveloped, uncivilized, vernacular, Negro, coloured, and race are eliminated from text-materials and learned journals.

20. We, the people of the world, cannot afford to ignore the epithets that tend to divide us into dangerous warring factions. The greatest lie of all is the lie of silence in the face of truth.

A PROFESSION WITHOUT PROFESSIONALS?

by
Milton Kleg
Assistant Professor of Education
University of South Florida

During the past ten years teachers have witnessed major changes in education. They appear to have received a slight dose of such concepts as non-graded, scientific method, inquiry, cognitive and affective domains among others. These concepts do not appear detrimental to the educational process. Yet, there is a sneaking suspicion that a cursory treatment of such concepts can lead to a lower grade of education. The following presentation attempts to relate some of the misconceptions and misuses of limited understandings of the aforementioned concepts.

The concept non-graded refers to grouping children based upon their individual needs in achieving educational objectives. A number of schools throughout the nation have instituted non-grading and some school systems appear to be employing the concept in its proper perspective. Nevertheless, in a number of cases non-grading has been misconceived and misused at the expense of children.

One common pitfall in misusing non-grading is the practice of keeping a child in a particular level or group for an entire quarter or even year regardless of the child's individual progress. In other words, children are placed in groups at the beginning of a year and tend to remain there until the following year. In a truly non-graded school, children are moved the moment they are ready to perform at another level and distinct from other members of the group in which the child is currently working.

Another pitfall in employing a non-graded structure without sufficient understanding is the stigma which generates from teacher to child. Since children are grouped by achievement levels, some teachers receive homogenous groups which consist of students who are viewed as "poor achievers" when compared to other students of the same age who are more skilled and knowledgeable in achievement. It does not take long for teachers to begin comparing groups and labeling them. Terms such as "slow," "dummies," "retarded," "poor," and "bad" begin to creep into the teachers' vocabulary when referring to specific groups.

Original Manuscript.

As a result, the teacher limits his expectations of what these students are capable of achieving and both teacher and student tolerate a rather intolerable situation. For nothing is more intolerable than to be under the charge of an adult who cannot help to cast aspersions of stupidity upon you. Nor do many teachers appreciate having the "bottom of the barrel." It is unfortunate that many teachers in so-called non-graded situations do not realize that no group of children in a non-graded school are below or above another group as to be classified in derogative terms. It might be helpful if teachers remember that when adults immigrated to the United States and attended schools to learn English, they were not compared to the national norms or the grade levels suggested by textbooks. Instead, they were viewed merely as individuals learning a language.

The scientific method and inquiry are also misused and not very well understood within the context of social studies education. A number of teachers believe that teaching a student how to gain knowledge through inquiry is the end goal of education. Unfortunately, this leads to the assumption that it is not important for students to obtain basic information. Indeed, this is a contradiction of the premise that students gain knowledge through inquiry. Such a contradiction, in turn, leads teachers to the misconception that they can teach process without a sufficient understanding of content on their part. In other words, content and process are intertwining fibers of the same rope, but this is seldom realized.

Recently, for example, a student-teacher approached me concerning a unit she was assigned to prepare and teach. All she had was the textbook. Following a brief discussion of her unit topic which was on U.S. Westward Movement including the Louisiana Purchase and the Lewis and Clark Explorations, I suggested that she gather more data through library research. The following day she returned. According to her notes (synthesized) Lewis and Clark set out from Independence, Missouri, which is about 250 miles west from Woodriver or St. Charles from whence they actually set out. It was apparent that the student-teacher had not learned that discovery, inquiry, or the scientific or reflective method is not a substitute for basic information. If this example seems difficult to comprehend, try the following on for size. According to some university juniors and seniors who had completed most or all of their course work and were preparing to teach elementary social studies, the following reasons were given in a questionnaire:

1. Florida was acquired from Spain during the Spanish-American War (1898). (That is 53 years after Florida had already been a State.)

2. The United States neither won nor lost the War of 1812 because the U.S. was not involved-- England fought Spain. (How interesting for the United States to accept Francis Scott Key's song as referring to the United States when he was describing Spain.)

3. Columbus was English (tell that to the Italian community in New York on October 12.)

4. The Blacks were happy and better off in the South until Lincoln caused all the trouble. (Frederick Douglass should have been so well informed.)

Unfortunately, a number of well meaning educators will hang out Bloom's Taxonomy of Educational Objectives and argue that students must learn to analyze and synthesize and that cognitive levels of recalled recognition are not important. This argument is not in the tradition of Bloom or any major scholar. It is, on the other hand, quite clear that in order for analysis and synthesis to occur the student must have accurate information which is in part recognized and recalled. Emphasis on process is not a cover up for lack of knowledge.

Finally, there is another misconception stemming from Bloom and Krathwohl's works on cognitive and affective educational objectives and goals. Many teachers are receiving the notion that cognitive and affective domains are dichotomus. Neither Bloom nor Krathwohl admit to such buffoonery. Notwithstanding their claim that the domains are not dichotomus, they appear to treat them as such to the glancing eye. As a result, we have youthful teachers entering education with the notion that they can teach "knowledge and method" without influencing attitudes. In reality, attitudes and knowledge are constantly interacting at various dynamic degrees and directions. It would be wise for teachers to recognize that beliefs, knowledge, feelings and behavior are components of attitude in the theoretic structure of attitude set forth by social psychologists.

In concluding this presentation, I believe that if today's education is to be of worth, it must consider the competency of teachers. This position assumes that good teachers do make a difference. It, therefore, calls upon educators to be professionals -- by which we mean receiving intensive educational training, retention of knowledge, and utilization of such knowledge in teaching. Superficial training and acquisition of information can produce devastating outcomes. The time is long overdue for teachers to become professionals in the teaching profession.